Children and their Environments

This fascinating book examines theories of children's perceptions of space and place and explores how these theories are applied to the world of children. The focus is on children in large real world spaces; places that children live in, explore and learn from. These include classrooms, playgrounds, homes and yards, towns, communities, countryside, natural environments, and the wider world. An international team of authors compare the experiences of children from different cultures and backgrounds. Often excluded from discussions of place-design on the presumption of lack of awareness, young children have many environmental competencies which should lead to their inclusion. They can read maps and study photographs, respond to the natural and man-made world with great sensitivity, and contribute considerably to the community. This book will appeal to environmental and developmental psychologists and geographers, and also to planners by linking research on children's understandings and on their daily lives to recommendations for practice.

CHRISTOPHER SPENCER is Professor of Environmental Psychology at the University of Sheffield. His books include *The Child in the Physical Environment: The Development of Spatial Knowledge and Cognition* (with M. Blades and K. Morsley, 1989), *Readings in Environmental Psychology: The Child's Environment* (1995), *and Psychology: A Contemporary Introduction (1998)*.

MARK BLADES is a Senior Lecturer in Developmental Psychology at the University of Sheffield. He has jointly authored several books including *The Child in the Physical Environment* (1989), *The Cognition of Geographic Space* (2002), and *Understanding Children's Development, fourth edition* (2003).

Children and their Environments

Learning, Using and Designing Spaces

Christopher Spencer and Mark Blades

University of Sheffield

CAMBRIDGE UNIVERSITY PRESS

CAMBRIDGE UNIVERSITY PRESS
Cambridge, New York, Melbourne, Madrid, Cape Town, Singapore, São Paulo, Delhi

Cambridge University Press
The Edinburgh Building, Cambridge CB2 8RU, UK

Published in the United States of America by Cambridge University Press, New York

www.cambridge.org
Information on this title: www.cambridge.org/9780521837781

First published 2006

A catalogue record for this publication is available from the British Library

ISBN 978-0-521-83778-1 hardback
ISBN 978-0-521-54682-9 paperback

Transferred to digital printing 2008

Contents

Notes on contributors   *page* vii

An introduction   1
CHRISTOPHER SPENCER AND MARK BLADES

Part I   Children's understanding of places

1   Scale in children's experience with the environment   13
    SCOTT BELL

2   The problem of lost children   26
    EDWARD H. CORNELL AND KENNETH A. HILL

3   Children's understanding of environmental representations:
    aerial photographs and model towns   42
    BEVERLY PLESTER, MARK BLADES AND
    CHRISTOPHER SPENCER

4   Children's knowledge of countries   57
    MARTYN BARRETT, EVANTHIA LYONS AND
    ALISON BOURCHIER-SUTTON

Part II   Children's experience of places

5   Learning neighbourhood environments: the loss of
    experience in a modern world   75
    ANTONELLA RISSOTTO AND M. VITTORIA GIULIANI

6   The classroom environment and children's performance –
    is there a relationship?   91
    SANDRA HORNE MARTIN

7 'Sometimes birds sound like fish': Perspectives on children's
   place experiences   108
   TORI DERR

8 Is contact with nature important for healthy child
   development? State of the evidence   124
   ANDREA FABER TAYLOR AND FRANCES E. KUO

9 Environmental child-friendliness in the light of the
   Bullerby Model   141
   MARKETTA KYTTÄ

Part III   Adolescents' worlds?

10 On the other side of the tracks: the psychogeographies
   and everyday lives of rural teenagers in the UK   161
   HUGH MATTHEWS AND FAITH TUCKER

11 The socio-environmental affordances of adolescents'
   environments   176
   CHARLOTTE CLARK AND DAVID L. UZZELL

Part IV   Children and the design process

12 Children as agents in sustainable development: the ecology
   of competence   199
   HARRY HEFT AND LOUISE CHAWLA

13 Children and city design: proactive process and the
   'renewal' of childhood   217
   MARK FRANCIS AND RAY LORENZO

14 A learning-based network approach to urban planning with
   young people   238
   LIISA HORELLI

15 Young people's participation in constructing a socially just
   public sphere   256
   SHARON EGRETTA SUTTON AND SUSAN P. KEMP

Index   277

Notes on contributors

MARTYN BARRETT is professor of psychology at the University of Surrey. He received his degrees from the Universities of Cambridge and Sussex, and worked at Royal Holloway University of London before taking up his present post. His research focuses on the development of national and ethnic identities in childhood and adolescence; the development of prejudice and stereotyping; children's understanding of societal institutions, structures and social groups; children's representations of large-scale geographical places and territories; the development of language; and children's drawings. He has led two multinational research networks funded by the EU, and has published numerous papers and several books including *The Development of Language* (1999) and *Children's Understanding of Society* (2004). He is currently Editor of the *British Journal of Developmental Psychology*.

SCOTT BELL is an associate professor of geography at the University of Saskatchewan. He received his PhD in geography, with an emphasis in cognitive science, from the University of California at Santa Barbara. His primary research interests are in spatial cognition and behavioural geography, with particular emphasis on geographic information science and geographic education. He has published several papers on each of these topics and currently holds, with collaborators, two Social Science and Humanities Research Council of Canada research grants. Additional interests include cartographic communication, geographic information systems, ethics in research, and playing with and reading to his two sons, McKinley (Mac) and Finbar.

MARK BLADES is a senior lecturer in developmental psychology at the University of Sheffield, UK. He has degrees from the Universities of Cambridge and Sheffield, and a PhD in developmental psychology (Sheffield). His research has considered several aspects of children's environmental cognition, including their way-finding abilities; their understanding of environmental representations; and the mobility skills of children with disabilities. He has jointly authored several books including: *The Child in the Physical Environment* (1989), *The Cognition of Geographic Space* (2002) and *Understanding Children's Development: Fourth edition* (2003). He is currently an associate editor of the *British Journal of Developmental Psychology* and on the editorial boards of several journals including *Journal of Environmental Psychology*, and *Children, Youth and Environments*.

ALISON BOURCHIER-SUTTON is a lecturer in psychology at Brunel University. She received her PhD from the University of Surrey. Her research focuses on children's cognitive development, theory of mind, and children's understanding of pretence and reality. She has published several papers on these topics, including a major review article accompanied by peer commentary in the journal *Developmental Science* on children's understanding of the pretence-reality distinction. She is currently the Review Editor of the *British Journal of Developmental Psychology*.

LOUISE CHAWLA is a professor in the Whitney Young School of Honors and Liberal Studies at Kentucky State University and an associate faculty member in the Doctoral Program in Environmental Studies at Antioch, New England Graduate School. She holds an MA in education and child development from Bryn Mawr College and a PhD in environmental psychology from the City University of New York. She has published widely on topics related to children's participation in community development, children's environmental experience, the development of environmental concern and responsibility, and cultural interpretations of nature, including the book *In the First Country of Places: Nature, Poetry and Childhood Memory* (State University of New York, 1994). She is editor and co-author of *Growing Up in an Urbanising World* (UNESCO/Earthscan Publications, 2002), which is based on her work as International Coordinator of the Growing Up in Cities project for UNESCO.

CHARLOTTE CLARK is a post doctoral research fellow in the Department of Psychiatry, Queen Mary's School of Medicine & Dentistry, University of London. She received her PhD in environmental psychology from the University of Surrey. Her research focuses on how the environment can affect mental health, well-being and quality of life and how individuals can utilize the environment to support their needs and development. Her current research includes the RANCH project, which is examining the effect of chronic aircraft and road traffic noise exposure on children's health and cognition and the RELACHS project, a longitudinal study of adolescents' mental and physical health.

EDWARD CORNELL is professor of psychology at the University of Alberta. His research focuses on way finding by children and adults in natural environments. In collaboration with Professor C. Donald Heth, Cornell is currently developing expert systems software for the management of search for lost persons.

TORI DERR is currently a consultant in community forestry and development, and works on several projects that focus on youth involvement in Southwest US forest restoration. She obtained her PhD in forestry and environmental studies from Yale University, where she conducted research with northern New Mexico children and families. Tori has designed educational garden spaces for children in New Mexico, involved children in community planning, and developed participatory research projects in medicinal plants, traditional ecological knowledge, and forest restoration with communities and youth throughout the Southwest United States. Other professional experiences include designing and leading experiential environmental education programs for children, coordinating youth conservation corps teams in natural resources, and community development and education in West Africa.

MARK FRANCIS, FASLA, is professor of landscape architecture at the University of California, Davis. Trained in landscape architecture and urban design at Berkeley and Harvard, his research and design work has focused on the meanings that children and youth attach to built and natural places. He is Associate Editor of the *Journal of Architectural and Planning Research* and past President of the Environmental Design Research Association. His books include *Community Open Spaces* (Island Press, 1984), *Public Space* (Cambridge, 1992), *The Meaning of Gardens* (MIT, 1990), *The California Landscape Garden* (California, 1999) and most recently *Village Homes* (Island Press, 2003) and *Urban Open* Space (Island Press, 2003).

VITTORIA GIULIANI is senior researcher at the Institute of Cognitive Sciences and Technologies (ISTC) of the National Research Council in Rome. She has been involved in environmental psychology for the last twenty years, with responsibility for many research projects and as affiliated lecturer at the University of Rome "La Sapienza". Her research topics include residential preferences and satisfaction, home related behaviour, urban renewal and residential quality, and the role of attachment in people-environment relationships. She has participated in many national and international conferences, and has published numerous papers on these topics. Recent works include papers on 'Theory of attachment and place attachment' in M. Bonnes, T. Lee, and M. Bonaiuto (eds.) (2003), and 'Residential preferences and attachment across the lifespan', Ch. Spielberg (ed.) *Encyclopedia of Applied Psychology*.

HARRY HEFT is professor of psychology at Denison University, Granville, Ohio, USA. He received a PhD in environment-behavior studies from The Pennsylvania State University. He is author of *Ecological Psychology in Context: James Gibson, Roger Barker, and the Legacy of William James's Radical Empiricism* (Erlbaum, 2001). Other publications concern the relationship between environmental conditions and the development of perceptual and cognitive competencies; way finding and environmental cognition; and affordances and action. He is a member of the board of directors of the International Society for Ecological Psychology, serves on the editorial board of *Environment & Behavior*, and is Book Review Editor for the *Journal of Environmental Psychology*.

KENNETH HILL is professor of psychology at Saint Mary's University in Halifax, Nova Scotia, Canada. He received a PhD in psychology at the University of Alberta. He teaches courses in cognition and environmental perception, and conducts research in way finding and lost person behaviour. He has published numerous articles pertaining to search and rescue operations. He is the author of two books, *Managing the Lost Person Incident* (1997), and *Lost Person Behaviour* (1999).

LIISA HORELLI is associate professor of environmental psychology at the Helsinki University of Technology, Centre of Urban and Regional Studies. She received her PhD in housing research at the Helsinki University of Technology, Department of Architecture. Her dissertation dealt with the dwelling as a psychological environment. Her research focuses on the methodology of participatory planning with children, young people and women as well as on the theory of human friendly environments. She has published numerous papers on these topics. Her most recent book is co-edited with Miretta Prezza, *In Search of Child-Friendly Environments* (2004).

SUSAN KEMP is associate professor at the University of Washington School of Social Work. Born in New Zealand, she was educated at the University of Auckland and at Columbia University, New York, where she completed her PhD. Her research focuses on environmental and community-based interventions, low-income children and families, and social work history and theory. She is co-author of

Person-Environment Practice: The Social Ecology of Interpersonal Helping
(Aldine de Gruyter, 1997) and is currently at work on a book on the
history of environmental intervention in direct social work practice
(forthcoming with Columbia University Press). She pursues her interest in the spatial as a faculty affiliate of CEEDS, the University of
Washington's interdisciplinary Center for Education, Environment,
and Design Studies.

FRANCES KUO is assistant professor of environment and human health
at the University of Illinois at Urbana-Champaign. She received her
MA and PhD in psychology at the University of California, Berkeley,
and the University of Michigan, respectively. She examines the role of
urban nature in creating a healthy human habitat. One line of work
documents the ways in which neighbourhood green space contributes
to stronger, safer neighbourhoods. Another documents the links between day-to-day exposure to nature and psychological health, including better cognitive functioning, reduced aggression, better impulse
control, more effective management of major life issues, and reduced
AD/HD symptoms.

MARKETTA KYTTÄ is an environmental psychologist, who works as a
researcher in the Centre for Urban and Regional Studies at Helsinki
University of Technology. Her research covers issues concerning
human-friendly environments, for example the aesthetical experiences, perceived density and perceived environmental quality of lay
people, participation in urban planning, social impact analysis, and
the qualities of child-friendly environment. Her doctoral thesis is
called *Children in Outdoor Contexts* (2003). She has lectured and taught
in several universities in Finland and elsewhere.

RAY LORENZO is a planner trained at Harvard, currently working in
Italy. He is a consultant to numerous city and national government
agencies on children and cities and participatory planning including
the Italian Ministry of Environment's Program for Sustainable Cities
For and With Children, Local Agenda 21 and UNICEF's Child
Friendly Cities Initiative. He was formerly assistant professor in the
Environmental Psychology Program, Gradate Centre of the City Uni-
versity of New York. He is author of *Italy: Too Little Time and Space for
Childhood*, (UNICEF, 1992) and *La Ciita sostenibile: participazione,
luogo, comunita* (Eleuthera, 1998).

EVANTHIA LYONS is a senior lecturer in the Department of Psychology,
University of Surrey. She received her degrees at Bedford College
and the Institute of Education, University of London. Her doctoral

research was concerned with social psychological processes in adolescent everyday decision making. Since then she has carried out research into the development of national identities in children, the role of social memories in maintaining inter-group conflicts and processes involved in the construction of European identities and citizenship. She currently co-ordinates a cross-national project on constructions of political trust amongst young people in ethnic minority groups in eight EU and post-communist countries.

SANDRA HORNE MARTIN is research fellow at the University of Central England. She received her PhD in design at Goldsmiths University of London in 1999 with her thesis titled *The Classroom Environment and its Effects on the Practice of Teachers*. She has been working as a post doctoral research fellow for the past three years. Her current research focuses on training teachers about the effects of environmental awareness and competence in the use of the classroom setting and its consequences on the behaviour of children. She is also involved in research in design risk management. She has published numerous papers on these topics.

HUGH MATTHEWS is professor of geography and Dean of the Graduate School at University College Northampton. He received his PhD in geography at the University of Wales, Swansea and held posts at Coventry University before taking up his present appointment. His research focuses on children's and young people's use of place and space and their participation in local communities. He has published over 100 papers and monographs on these topics and several books, most recently *Children and Community Regeneration* (2002). He is currently inaugural editor of *Children's Geographies* and Director of the Centre for Children and Youth at UCN.

BEVERLY PLESTER is a senior lecturer in psychology at Coventry University. She received her MSc in psychology from Brigham Young University, and PhD in developmental psychology at the University of Sheffield. She held posts at Solihull College, Daemen College, and Northern State University before taking up her present post. Her research focuses on children's understanding of spatial representations and their use in problem solving in the naturalistic environment. She has published papers on these topics, and chapters in books including *Human Spatial Memory: Remembering Where* (G. L. Allen, ed.) and *Researching Primary Geography* (S. Catling and F. Martin, eds.).

ANTONELLA RISSOTTO is researcher at the Institute of Cognitive Sciences and Technologies (ISTC) of the National Research Council in Rome. Her degree is in biological sciences at the University of Rome. She participated in several programmes on children's environmental education and, with Francesco Tonucci, in the international Project on 'The children city'. She is currently responsible for joint research by the City Council of Rome and ISTC on the evaluation of the initiatives and services for children's well-being promoted by the Municipality of Rome. Her research focuses on children's participation in urban planning.

CHRISTOPHER SPENCER is professor of environmental psychology at the University of Sheffield, UK. His DPhil from Oxford University was in social psychology, but he soon discovered that there was also a physical environment to behaviour whilst he was working as a field primatologist in Malaysia (where he was on the staff of Universiti Sains Malaysia). With David Canter, he was in at the beginning of the *Journal of Environmental Psychology*. Much of his research has been on environments for children: their cognitive maps; their understanding of aerial photographs; and (with young blind children) their ability to use tactile maps at an early age. And in another life, he wrote *Drug Abuse in East Asia* for Oxford University Press. Other books include *The Child in the Physical Environment*, *Readings on the Child's Environment*, and *Psychology: A Contemporary Introduction* for Blackwells.

SHARON EGRETTA SUTTON is professor of architecture and urban design, and Director of CEEDS (Center for Environment Education and Design Studies) at the University of Washington. She has held positions at Pratt Institute, Columbia University, the University of Cincinnati, and the University of Michigan where she became the first African American woman in the United States to be promoted to full professor of architecture. She has degrees in music, architecture, psychology, and philosophy, all earned in New York City, is a Fellow in the American Institute of Architects, a Distinguished Professor of the Association of Collegiate Schools of Architecture, and an inductee in the Michigan Women's Hall of Fame. She previously practised architecture in New York City and, as a professional musician, performed with the Bolshoi and other ballet companies, and in such Broadway hits as *Man of La Mancha*, *Fiddler on the Roof*, and *A Funny Thing Happened on the Way to the Forum*.

ANDREA FABER TAYLOR is a researcher of children's environments and behavior at the University of Illinois at Urbana-Champaign. She received her MSc and PhD in natural resources and environmental sciences at the University of Illinois, Urbana-Champaign. Her research has focused on the connection between greenspace and various aspects of children's healthy functioning and development, and has included children living in poverty and children with Attention-Deficit Hyperactivity Disorder (ADHD). She has also been a lecturer at the University of Illinois for the course, 'Residential Landscape Design'.

FAITH TUCKER is lecturer in geography at University College Northampton. Her research interests are in the area of children's geographies, and in particular young people's use of outdoor space in rural areas. Her recently completed PhD research, carried out at the Centre for Children and Youth, University College Northampton, focused on the lifestyles of teenage girls growing up in rural south Northamptonshire.

DAVID UZZELL is professor of environmental psychology at the University of Surrey, and leads the Environmental Psychology Research Group. He is president of the International Association of People-Environment Studies (IAPS), and joint co-ordinator of EPUK (Environmental Psychology in the UK). He is also European editor of the *Journal of Architectural and Planning Research* and on the editorial board of the *Journal of Environmental Psychology*. Current research includes the psychology of sustainable development (especially in relation to climate change, waste, and transport); architectural appraisal and urban design; heritage and environmental interpretation, and education; and diversity, social exclusion, and the countryside.

An introduction

Christopher Spencer and Mark Blades

In this book, you are about to meet people who are passionate about environments *for* children. The environments *of* children are not always environments *for* children: in many cases, the places where children grow up, play, and learn are, at best, designed for them by adults, at worst they are the spaces left over from the 'adult world'. So it is not surprising that many researchers in this area do not remain neutral, but instead take an involved, action-orientated stance in their work.

Environmental psychology has indeed become one of the least neutral areas of the discipline of psychology, striving to work for better environments, working to discover the correlates of well-being, arming designers with the information that they need about people's needs and perceptions, and providing the tools for evaluating places and buildings as they affect behaviour and well-being.

Theories and applications

We have asked the author of each chapter to review theories of children's perceptions of space and place, and to show applications to the world of children. So, for example, Edward Cornell and Kenneth Hill apply the literature about children's developing ideas of themselves in geographical space to predict what children are most likely to do if they find themselves lost in the outdoors. This is research that has immediate practical importance for advising police search teams on how far a child is likely to have wandered.

Another example: basic research in environmental psychology is confirming people's intuition that *places* are fundamental to the child's developing self-concept and identity. Environmental psychology has investigated how we can discern what are the most important features of familiar places, and how varied they can be. In this book, for example, comparisons of rural and urban children show just how different these features can be, and we have chapters about children in New Mexico (Tori Derr), in Finland and Belarus (Marketta Kyttä), and in different

1

parts of the UK (Charlotte Clarke and David Uzzell; Hugh Matthews and Faith Tucker).

In a closely related field, Andrea Faber Taylor and Frances Kuo ask whether contact with nature and with animals is important for healthy child development. Such a relationship is popularly assumed to be the case: but does the evidence support such an assumption? Taylor and Kuo provide a review of the steadily accumulating evidence for a positive link.

Several chapters in the book discuss theory relating to children's concepts of small and large scale spaces. Scott Bell reviews theory on scale and describes differences in the way that children behave in differently sized spaces. Beverly Plester gives young children an aerial photograph of their school playgrounds as a way to finding out about the children's spatial abilities, and Sandra Martin's chapter focuses on the world of teachers and pupils in a school classroom. On a larger scale Martyn Barrett, Evanthia Lyons and Alison Bourchier-Sutton investigate what children know about their own and other countries in Europe.

Several chapters consider the ecological psychologists' concept of 'affordances'. In other words, the properties and possibilities that places can provide for those users, whether or not those possibilities were originally envisioned by the designers and planners. Harry Heft and Louise Chawla discuss the concept of affordances, and other chapters show how such a concept can be of use to those designing child-friendly places (Mark Francis and Ray Lorenzo; Marketta Kyttä).

Indeed, one of the major practical issues in our field is how to work with children on the design of these child-friendly places. What would engage them and facilitate their creativity? How to go beyond a mere tokenism? Sharon Sutton and Susan Kemp show us how to use the 'charette' to engage children as full members of their community in the physical renewal of their neighbourhood; and Liisa Horelli proposes a community-based 'learning network' as another technique.

Themes running through the book

All topics in this book relate to the world as perceived and lived by children. The environmental psychology tradition is to work 'in the real world' as much as possible, rather than working with reduced laboratory based stimuli. For this reason all the chapters in this book focus on children in large real world spaces; the type of places that children live in, explore, and learn from. These include classrooms,

Figure 0.1. The affordances and challenges of the built environment: a place for children?

playgrounds, homes and yards, towns, communities, countryside, natural environments and the wider world.

As one of the pioneers of real world work with children, Roger Hart (1997) has said, children's daily lives are complex, unique, and inherently spatial. Learning about the whereabouts of things such as resources, support, and dangers is obviously a vital survival skill for any species, even for one with a relatively long dependency phase such as humans have. So too is the capacity for realizing the potential of places and objects, and the affordances that they offer.

Given the complexity of the world children inhabit, and the range of aspirations and objectives that they have in using the world, one of the first issues is to see how this complexity can be structured in a way that makes information about the world easier to handle. Developmental psychology has already given us good accounts of how such structuring takes place: from the early integrative templates formed in infancy, before the child has the opportunity for self-locomotion, through the phases of early exploration of limited spaces of house and

Figure 0.2. The natural environment can have deep resonances and importance for all humans.

garden, through to the older child's expanding knowledge of locality, neighbourhood, town and region; and increasing awareness of places beyond direct acquaintance.

Some devices can support understanding of spatial relationships beyond that which is immediately viewable. Scott Bell discusses the way that geographical space can be made clear by *representations* like maps, models; and how children can make decisions using such representations. Beverley Plester uses aerial photographs to show that even young children are capable of developing search strategies using a representation that is in many ways transformed from the child's ground-level experience. The evidence is strong that the use of symbolic representations of space is developed early in childhood.

Another theme that pervades many chapters is that of the *competence* of the child in handling the complexities of space and place: it is generally an underestimated competence as far as the adult world is concerned. This is highlighted in the chapters on children's participation in planning. Several authors show that children, including young ones, can be effectively involved in designing and planning environments, especially ones that are most relevant to them.

Even in cases showing children's apparent incompetence (for example, in the chapter on lost children), what is noticeable is the early emergence of strategic thinking about space. What leads to 'becoming lost' and disorientated is often an episode where way finders encounter an unexpected scene or path, or when they cannot find a particular landmark. Case studies of children who have realized that they have become lost indicate that many children can then adopt a goal-oriented problem solving strategy.

The *variation* in children's experiences is another of this book's themes: it is highlighted by Tori Derr in her chapter, and elaborated on by many of the other contributors. Mainstream psychology has a tendency to underplay variety, and to look for generalities; but, happily, environmental psychology is aware of (and in some cases, celebrates) diversity. Recent studies of children's environments have increasingly recognized that this variety in children's experiences shapes their learning, social development, and play. Not surprisingly, different childhood settings have different affordances; but less obvious is the finding that in the same setting, children's experiences may differ significantly. Family circumstances and all the usual social factors will impact; but a central factor is the child's own pattern of activities. Active exploration characterizes some children much more than it does others, and such exploration not only increases place knowledge but also develops the child's strategies for acquiring and integrating that knowledge.

Children also differ in the extent that they, to borrow Tori Derr's phrase, *place-makers*, use this 'as a means of looking inward, of establishing something of their own and developing a sense of self'. Individuals may also be more or less sensitive to places. Little (1987) has suggested place/person specialism as an important dimension in adults, and we should add it to the research agenda for those working with children. There is also clear evidence that children differ in their environmental sensitivities, which may perhaps relate to their experience of caring for animals, gardens, etc.(see the chapters by Derr, and by Taylor and Kuo). This links to the chapter by Heft and Chawla, who ask directly what experiences prepare children to value and care for their local environment, and to join in with community decision making. Local residents' expert knowledge, they argue, should guide environmental planning and decision making; and children have a share in this expertise.

What the child's environment affords

Children may then differ in what they bring to their environments: and equally, places differ in the extent to which they are *child friendly*, offering opportunities for independent mobility and for actualizing the affordances. Kyttä offers us an analytic typology for thinking about places in terms of these two dimensions, with 'Bullerby' (author Astrid Lindgren's noisy village) as the ideal type. Several of the chapters offer anthropological-detail studies of what such different environments are like in practice, whether for younger children in rural and urban New Mexico (Derr), prosperous urban south of England (Clarke and Uzzell) or less prosperous rural areas in the English Midlands (Matthews and Tucker). Lessons learned in each setting often tie the child into the local way of life and the cultural convergence of narratives, histories, and social identities.

What places afford we argue is not just important for the child's here-and-now ('This place is exciting' . . . through to. . . 'I'm bored!'), but also for their long-term personal cognitive and emotional development. There is now a growing body of literature that evidences what children gain from their experiences of places: ranging from those 'special places' which allow for the imagination, and a sense of personal control and freedom, to those social venues where one can learn about one's community, and be recognized by others for one's part in it. Designing and supporting places which maximize the chances for a child's cognitive and social development are therefore another campaigning issue where environmental psychology can offer convincing evidence, in support of those arguing for the rights of the child.

Mindful of this are those who raise alarms at the increasingly inactive, computer screen-focused lives of many contemporary children, and it is not just sunshine and fresh air that children are missing out on as over-anxious parents restrict their children's exploratory travel. Antonella Rissotto and Vitttoria Guiliani write about the loss of children's experiences of their local environments in this modern world. Francis and Lorenzo write with alarm that in many parts of the developed world, children are increasingly disappearing from the urban scene: they are not using public space, or only doing so under much greater adult surveillance than would have occurred in earlier generations. As a result, children have lost street-sense and city-knowledge. Francis and Lorenzo's chapter offers us a checklist of qualities of city design for children. These include easy accessibility of resources from home; mixed use rather than strictly zoned; with a density and a patterning that allows for more opportunities for encounters, not only with known friends but also with a wider community. These authors share with Hart (1997) the vision of children not as a separate society, but as making decisions with the adolescents and adults of their community in a proactive process.

To take another example: rural areas are often idealized as places to grow up in, but they too have become less satisfying. In their interviews, Matthews and Tucker heard many British adults describing the perceived benefits of a rural upbringing, saying that children can grow up and develop in settings that enable a close association with nature. But this was a view that rural teenagers rarely shared: they instead talked of the restrictions on their movements, and the lack of things to do. Many of the visible natural spaces have been 'fenced-off' by adults as private land, which is often fiercely defended by the adults of the community.

As described above, children can benefit from or feel restricted by their experience of their local environment. Children can also learn from experience of more distant environments, as when they travel abroad to another country (as discussed in Barrett *et al.*'s chapter). Such travel might be thought to have positive effects upon children's knowledge and attitudes, but the evidence so far is mixed. One cannot conclude that travel inevitably broadens a child's mind, but this may depend on the quality of the child's experience when abroad.

Similarly the evidence for the impact of formal education on attitudes and beliefs about distant lands is mixed. There is no straight-line relationship between knowledge and tolerance. Indeed, as many studies of teaching materials and textbooks have shown, the selectivity of environmental images that a child sees as 'representative' of a country may actually emphasize the strangeness and difference of that country compared to the child's own familiar world (see, for example, Blaut's 1993 polemic about the images used in geography textbooks).

From childhood into adolescence

Without conducting a rigorous survey, it is clear to us that the number of studies on environments for children outweighs the number of studies focusing on adolescents. Indeed, Clarke and Uzzell believe that their chapter is the first-ever review of adolescents' use and evaluation of their environments. They, like other contributors, find the concept of affordances (see above) a useful one for assessing the adolescent experience of urban areas. Not surprisingly, the needs and experiences here are in some ways similar to those of younger children; but in other ways, given expanding horizons and aspirations, importantly different. And as such, given limitations in social access to urban resources, adolescents may well find themselves less satisfied by the town's affordances than they had been when they were younger.

In general, Western cities do not seem as aware of adolescents' needs as they are of children's, nor is there as much advocacy for adolescents. As Chawla's (2002) UNESCO study showed, this is true for other areas of the world as well. Are there, Clarke and Uzzell ask, sufficient urban niches for adolescents to select compatible ones for themselves; or does the town have sufficient flexibility to allow them to shape a place to their own needs? Some of the niches may be the casual ones of childhood, adapted; some may be the commercially provided ones of cafes and sports areas, not ignoring schools (where much of the week is likely to be spent) and the home (which remains important as a place of retreat and restoration).

How can adolescents *communicate* their ideas to the planners and decision makers? Horelli's chapter includes a description of her learning-based network approach – one in which young people and adults took part in what Horelli described as interdependent actor networks. Complainers became agents of change, and local changes in resources for young people did indeed result.

So many themes cross the fifteen chapters of the book that we have only attempted a loose organization into four sections. First, we consider children's understanding of places: environmental perception and cognition. Next, we look at children's experience of places, all the way from the classroom to the natural world; and reflect on recent changes in the child's world. Similarly, the two chapters on the adolescent experience, in country and in town, ask what quality of experience is available to them. Then in the final section, we move from current affordances to the future worlds and children's part in their planning and design.

Not all our chapters 'join up' yet. This is because the 'environmental psychology' of childhood and adolescence is still a new and developing field, and researchers come from diverse backgrounds including education, sociology, geography, and planning, as well as psychology. (We have for simplicity's sake referred to the field as environmental psychology, and apologise to anyone who feels colonized by this). Nonetheless, despite the diversity of authors in this book there is already a remarkable level of consensus between them, and the variety of methods and approaches that these different researchers bring to the study of children in the real world is a strength of the field. And what links our authors most of all, as we said at the outset, is a passionate commitment to children and their environments.

References

Blaut, J. M. (1993). *The Colonizer's Model of the World: Geographical Diffusionism and Eurocentric History*. New York: Guilford Press.

Chawla, L. (ed.) (2002). *Growing Up in an Urbanising World*. Paris: UNESCO, and London: Earthscan.

Hart, R. (1997). *Children's Participation: The Theory and Practice of Involving Young Citizens in Community Development and Environmental Care*. Paris: UNESCO, and London: Earthscan.

Little, B. (1987). Personality and the environment. In D. Stokols and I. Altman (eds.), *Handbook of Environmental Psychology*. New York: Wiley.

Part I

Children's understanding of places

1 Scale in children's experience with the environment

Scott Bell

Children's daily lives are complex, unique, and inherently spatial (Hart, 1979). Children explore the space around them even before they are mobile. Before they can locomote, or move from place to place (crawl, walk, run, etc.) independently, infants are interested in many of the things that fall within their reach. As will be discussed later, and as Piaget and others have suggested, these early explorations play an important role in how children come to know the world around them. One way we can understand the role that space plays in the lives of children is through scale. Scale provides a context within which spaces, places, and environments of different types can be integrated and better understood.

Definitions of scale and space

As valuable as scale is for understanding the relationships among different environments it is also a complex construct that has been extended to disparate classes of spaces, places, and geographies. For example, geographers study phenomena at various scales and often use the term scale to help define their research interests. Scale is also employed in many other disciplines to help define phenomena, concepts, interactions, and relationships. Lay definitions of scale, both related and unrelated to the stricter definitions employed in academic endeavours, also exist. For these reasons the use of the term scale varies in different contexts and can lead to confusion.

There have been a few attempts to categorize the nature of these different classes of definitions and provide a systematic understanding of scale across disciplines. The initial section of this chapter will examine the diverse ways in which scale is used by geographers and other researchers. This will be followed by an examination of spatial extent as scale, the scale most relevant to children's environmental experiences.

Cartographic scale

When the term scale is employed in a spatial, environmental, or geographic context it is contingent on the existence of an internally related set of spaces. This internal relation provides the basis for which any single 'scale' can be embedded within other related scales. If something is said to be scale-dependent or scale-specific we can assume that there are different spaces in which that phenomenon would act differently or might not exist (in the case of scale specificity). While this is true, these types of statements (scale dependency or specificity) do not suggest anything about the spatial nature of scale for the phenomenon or process in question. Taking cartographic scale as an example one can see the range of scales that become possible within this single definition.

Cartographic, or representational, scale is based on the mathematical relationship (ratio) between the extent of the representation and that part of reality which it represents (representation size: represented size, usually reduced to 1: represented size). The *representative fraction* exists within the continuum of ratios of any two rational numbers. Some might suggest that an extension of this broad definition be that the ratio must be less than 1, resulting in a representation that is smaller than that which it represents. It is for this reason that I included the term *representational* after *cartographic* above, to allow for representations, or models, that are larger than that which they represent. Therefore, this application of scale results in an infinite number of scales, some of which are used as standards for certain applications (1:25,000 or 1:50,000 respectively for standard US and Canadian topographic sheets, for instance). Representational scale can be applied to two-dimensional representations (often associated with cartography, or map making) or three-dimensional models.

Cartographic scale is convenient for many reasons, not the least of which is that it provides an immediate understanding of the quantitative spatial relationship between any two scales. As cartographic scale changes, a direct relationship between the representation and the referent space is explicit and known; space and scale are dependent on each other. In the case of cartographic scale, the ratio of the representation to reality is purely quantitative, and has no necessary relationship with the content or meaning held by the representation. The relationship between the real world and its representation is explicit and absolute, providing an opportunity to examine how representations of reality can be used to solve real world problems. An important component of *cartographic scale* that relates to children's spatial cognition is when and how very young children can use models and representations to solve real world problems.

From developmental research we know quite a bit about when children first become able to make judgments based on scale models of decision spaces. DeLoache (1989 and 1990) has shown that young children are capable of finding a play object hidden in a referent space (large space) after viewing the object being hidden in a smaller model of the same space. When children are very young, and incapable of this task, and are told that the model in which the object is originally hidden is being placed in a machine that is making it larger they are subsequently able to find the hidden object in the larger space (DeLoache, Miller, and Rosengren, 1997). Keep in mind that these are very young children (twenty-nine to thirty-three months), but that the evidence suggests that the use of symbolic representations of space is developed quite early and can be used to solve goal-directed problems (see also Plester, Blades and Spencer, this volume). What this research does not tell us is whether children solve problems in smaller spaces differently than problems in larger spaces, or if their ability to solve spatial problems is more advanced in certain spaces at a given age.

Problem scale

Problem scale refers to the relative *size* of the space covered by a process or phenomenon. Large scale problems cover relatively large spaces while small scale problems cover relatively small spaces. For example, climate change and variability are large scale problems because their impact is global, while developing a kerbside recycling program in Saskatoon, Saskatchewan is a small scale problem because it is an issue affecting only the city of Saskatoon. These differences are relative because there are no finite boundaries between a large space and a small space, or among other spaces of a designated size (medium, vast, etc.). Stratospheric ozone depletion might be considered a large scale environmental concern because its impact will be felt by a large proportion of the southern hemisphere, but it is a relatively smaller problem than climate variability, a concern that has the potential to affect the entire planet. *Problem scale* is limited to individual situations, and should be modified if a process or phenomenon varies with scale or physical extent. This application of scale will be expanded on in the following section on *functional scale*.

Many researchers would suggest this use of the term scale could, and perhaps should, be replaced by the word 'size'. As will be made evident below, *problem scale* is a more pervasive, or commonly used, conception of scale than *cartographic*. *Problem scale* is used to describe differences in spatial extent as they extend to functional relationships that exist in both physical and cognitive reality. This is better left to the following discussion of *functional scale* as another use of the term scale. *Problem scale*, not unlike *cartographic scale*, takes advantage of common terms of reference for changes in scale; these include, but are not limited to, small, medium, large, etc. While problem scale is also based on a relative relationship between the sizes of the space in which problems exist, the nature of this size (physical extent) scale relationship is quite different than that between varying *cartographic scale* and the referent space. Unlike *cartographic scale*, changes in *problem scale*, or comparisons between two scales, are not quantifiable, and between-scale comparisons are not commensurable. While a local problem is obviously a smaller scale problem (as defined by *problem scale*) than a regional or global problem, it is difficult to calculate a ratio between the two because discrete boundaries are more than likely unavailable. In addition, the range of problems that can be described is so broad that a large scale space for one problem might be a small scale space for another problem.

Functional scale

Functional scale refers to those situations where the general concept of *problem scale* (large scale refers to large spaces) can be used to describe a relationship between changing scale and the function of some phenomenon or process. *Problem scale* is relevant when comparing across types of phenomena or processes; *functional scale* should be applied in situations in which spatial extent is used to define a classification scheme for a process or related phenomenon. In situations where a process or function varies as spatial extent (or scale) varies, and scale is used to define that variability, *functional scale* is a relevant concept for describing the spatial component of that relationship. While spatial extent may be the determining factor in the variability of some process or phenomenon the nature of this relationship with space is determined by characteristics internal to the process or phenomena. It is for these relationships that the hierarchical nature of scale is most relevant. For a given phenomenon or process it is important to define its existence, or how it functions, across difference scales, and whether an optimal scale (or range of scales) exists. For example, in a hierarchical political administration, provincial or regional decisions affect a smaller space than state or national decisions for a single embedded political system (one country). The hierarchical nature of the size of each level of the political system is only true internally for a single country (many provinces or sub-national regions are larger than some countries), but can be applied to any political system with a hierarchical system of governance. These internally structured scaled relationships result in what can be called an *internal functional scale*. Later the concept of an *external functional scale* will be introduced.

Classification of scale and the effects of scale

Psychologists, cognitive scientists, geographers, and many others have examined the cognitive dimensions of space and scale (Egenhofer and Golledge, 1998; Freundschuh and Egenhofer, 1997; Gärling and Golledge, 1987; Mandler, 1983; Montello, 1993). Each of these classifications has subdivided space based on human interactions (physical, cognitive, and perceptual) with spaces of different size. Relatively larger spaces require different mechanisms than smaller spaces. An example would be the search for a hidden object. If that object is hidden on a desk the individual performing the search would likely move objects around on the (cluttered) desk in order to reveal hidden objects. In a larger space, perhaps a university campus, one would be compelled to walk around the space in order to place oneself in a position to see hidden objects that are obscured by other (likely immovable) objects such as buildings. Thus, a common objective results in quite different behaviors in these two different size spaces.

Children interact with spaces of different size in a variety of situations. What will become evident later is the degree to which we can start to understand some of the mechanisms that play an important role in how children solve problems and come to know these different spaces. The notion that children think about their environment based on its spatial extent or the type of interactions one can have in different size spaces is not new. Piaget and Inhelder (1956) outlined cognitive spatial development based on the relationship between a child and the space in question. That some of Piaget's conclusions, such as the sequence of skill attainment (or emergence) with respect to spatial tasks, have held up under more rigorous experimental scrutiny is noteworthy, particularly in light of the less than thorough understanding we still have about how the size of a space affects spatial cognition among children. Furthermore, size has been shown to be critical at very early stages of spatial interaction between children and their surroundings. Newman *et al.* (2001) have shown that larger objects draw infants' visual attention over smaller objects as early as five months, while older children (eight and a half to twelve months) show a preference for grasping smaller objects. Although this research is related to objects it is clear that perceptual and relative size does play a role in behaviour among even very young children. It should therefore come as little surprise that differences in behaviour based on scale and spatial extent should also exist for older children and in different contexts.

The 'size is equivalent to scale' relationship works nicely for internal classification schemes, or when a common process or feature can be used to determine how size and phenomena interact, such as the different strategies that might be used to solve a similar problem in two different size spaces. There are many situations in which the relationship between scale and the terms to which it is appended do not have easily described relationships with changes in spatial extent. These situations often arise when the term scale is used to differentiate between spaces based on characteristics that are primarily non-spatial. For instance, certain problems that are endemic to built environments with high population densities are often described as occurring at the urban scale, or being urban scale issues. In order for this definition to exist (*urban scale*) non-urban scales must also exist, but these are not necessarily tied to changes in spatial extent or spatial properties of any kind (location, distance, area, etc.). In individual situations the urban scale may extend over larger or smaller spaces than the rural scale. The nature of the difference between the two scales (urban and rural) is based on non-spatial properties such as demographic character, organizational structure, culture, cultural landscape, transportation features, etc. These types of scales are often said to be socially constructed, and while they have important spatial characteristics they are not defined by their spatial nature.

The use of the term *external* in the latter scale is not based on the relative importance of space to the variations in scale but rather on the fact that for each scale employing this definition (rural, urban, exurban, homeless, education, etc.) the critical processes or phenomena have important non-spatial bases. It is these non-spatial characteristics that form the basis of a definition for *external scale* (in the case of rural and urban it is the essential *rural* or *urban* nature of the environment) and are uniquely important to that scale. What is also critical is that within any *external scale* a hierarchy of component scales must exist, or at least there must exist entities that can be identified and declared (Brenner, 2001; Purcell, 2003). The urban scale is made up of individuals, households, neighbourhoods, precincts, etc.; the rural scale is made up of individuals, households, community groups, municipalities, etc. that are unique to the respective rural or urban setting.

Scale as a spatial and psychological construct

Children need to process information from spaces of different sizes, but as yet there has been little research into the effects of scale on children's spatial cognition. Therefore, one objective for researchers is to understand the effect that varying scale may have on children's spatial behaviour and decision making.

Until a few years ago there was relatively little research in this area. Since the mid-1990s there have been several attempts to define a scale-based classification scheme for spatial cognition (Freundschuh and Egenhofer, 1997; Ittelson, 1973; Lockman and Pick, 1984; Montello, 1993; Tversky, Morrison, Franklin, and Bryant, 1999). Changes in relative size impact on our interactions with space, although our understanding of the specific nature of the impact is not well known (Larsen and Abravanel, 1972; Lockman and Pick, 1984; Roskos-Ewoldsen, McNamara, Shelton, and Carr, 1998; Weatherford, 1982). The majority of these schemes have relied on existing results from experiments conducted in spaces of varying size. Unfortunately, very little of the work tying into the relationship between cognition and scale has been developmental.

Lockman and Pick (1984) discussed research and theory pertaining to the importance of size in spatial cognition, behavior, and development. They argued that not only are problems faced in spaces of different size, but that children and adults react directly and indirectly to changes in size. Direct responses to size change provide evidence for quantitative differences in perception and cognition of size information, while indirect behavioral responses in different size spaces is evidence for qualitative differences resulting from changes in spatial extent, or size (Lockman and Pick, 1984). Bell (2002) found that seven- and nine-year-old children provided richer and more complex verbal descriptions of larger, environmental spaces than they did of similarly laid-out desktop spaces. The complexity and richness related to both spatial components, including location references, boundaries, and frames of reference along with non-spatial components, including number of words, names of features, colour, etc.

Researchers have traditionally been interested in a variety of spaces, particularly with respect to spatial extent and the functional nature of the activities that take place in them. Gärling and Golledge (1987) characterized small, medium, and large-scale spaces. This classification does not make distinct the method of integration (single perspective versus navigation or locomotion dependent), although it does imply a need for extended and necessarily piecemeal knowledge integration, particularly with respect to large-scale spaces. In Mandler's (1983) and Gärling and Golledge's (1987), medium-scale spaces, the spatial relations can be viewed from a single perspective, although Mandler (1983) does explicitly indicate that complete viewing is only possible via locomotion through the space. The addition of extended knowledge integration implies a more meaningful relationship between the space of our everyday activities and traditional spatial cognition research and theory (Gärling and Golledge, 1987; Mandler, 1983).

More recently there have been a number of reviews of scale along with systems for defining the full spectrum of spaces with which humans interact. Montello (1993) presented a thorough classification of spatial scale that provided a qualitative scheme by which spaces of varying size and format could be differentiated. Freundschuh (1997) and Freundschuh and Egenhofer (1997) have repackaged the Montello classification as an argument for applications in geographic information systems and naïve geography. Two of Montello's spaces in particular are central to this research, and although his entire classification is based on '. . .*projective* size of the space relative to the human body, not its actual or apparent absolute size' (Montello, 1993: 315), it has influenced not only the selection of experimental spaces but the presentation of those spaces as well. The smallest space indicated in the classification is *figural* space; figural space is protectively smaller than the body and can be perceived from a single vantage point. *Figural* spaces can be further subdivided into *pictorial* and *object* spaces, *object* spaces being small three-dimensional spaces, *pictorial spaces* being small flat spaces. The *object* class of spaces is most descriptive of the small space used in much research, while another larger space, termed *vista* by Montello, acts as the second comparison space. A *vista* space is larger than the human body but can be visually perceived in its totality from a single perspective. Other names for figural spaces have included *object* (Ittelson, 1973), *small-scale* (Mandler, 1983), and *manipulable object space*, while alternate names for Montello's *vista* space have included *pictorial* and *panoramic* (Mark, 1993). Bell (2002) found that when specific frames of reference were unavailable children (nine years of age) were able to solve a spatial location recall task in a large environmental space (a *vista* space) more accurately than in a smaller desktop space (an *object* space). Children two years younger were unable to perform this task accurately in either space (Bell, 2002).

Although Montello does not allude to the potential interaction an individual might have with these two spaces (*vista* and *object*) the evidence he calls upon to support his classification scheme does. Huttenlocher and Presson (1979) conducted experiments that included having participants respond to questions about location in *object* and *vista* spaces. The pattern of responses indicated that participants were moving objects in the smaller space (mentally) while they moved their own body in the larger space, even though interaction with both spaces was similar

(Huttenlocher and Presson, 1979). Unfortunately, even in the case of the *object* space in this experiment the entire experimental object could not be viewed from a single perspective without manipulating the object or the individual participant's position.

To provide additional weight to some of the preceding schemes for organizing spaces of different size, Tversky, Morrison, Franklin and Bryant (1999) present empirical evidence distinguishing between three spaces, each of which can be related to categories in both the Montello and Freundschuh et al. schemes. Their three categories are navigational space, the space immediately around the body, and the space of the body (Tversky et al., 1999). They use reaction time data and alignment tendencies to support their classification scheme.

There are a number of physical and information processing differences between different size spaces that might contribute to differing performance or strategies. This is consistent with differences in spatial performance that are related to other spatial and non-spatial variables such as spatial relationships (Quinn, Adams, Kennedy, Shettler, and Wasnik, 2003), type of environment or activity level (Herman, Kolker, and Shaw, 1982; Herman, Roth, Miranda, and Getz, 1982), spatial arrangement (Uttal, Schreiber, and DeLoache, 1995), object identity (Hund and Plumert, 2003), whether the object is a spatial prototype (Plumert and Hund, 2001), and the type of representation that is used for testing (Uttal, 1990). The manner in which knowledge is acquired and integrated is a general concern that is multivariate and which requires numerous analytical perspectives.

The type of direct interaction afforded by a space will play an important role in how children (and adults) build mental representations of space (cognitive maps). That these interactions vary with the size of the space is intuitive. More importantly, however, it seems that the potential for interaction of different types is critical, rather than the interaction itself (Ittelson, 1973). Ittleson (1973) and others have used interaction, or the potential for it, to differentiate between categories of space (Montello, 1993; Tversky et al., 1999). Can the space be entered? Or is potential interaction limited by its size (if interaction is limited by something other than size the possibility of interaction might still be enough)?

With respect to determining how different size spaces are mentally represented it is important that the differences be limited to size. Once this is accomplished it is then necessary to enumerate the differences that remain between the spaces in question. As an object's size is increased, given a constant distance from a static viewing position, the relative size of that object's representation on the retina also changes. This can be compensated for by increasing the distance from the observer to the object at a rate consistent with the scale change in the size of the object. Although the physical characteristics of spaces can be controlled in such a way to produce qualitative differences limited to size, there are other indirect differences that cannot be controlled (Lockman and Pick, 1984).

Large environments offer the viewer many different perspectives from which to learn about the objects present in those spaces and the relationships among those occurrences (Ittleson, 1973). Montello's *vista* space provides the viewer with the potential for physically navigating through the space, even if the current viewing perspective provides a complete view of the environment. These types of environments can be viewed from outside or from within, they can be explored actively as in goal-directed navigation or they can be viewed from a stationary perspective. A space offering this rich array of opportunities for acquiring and integrating spatial knowledge will influence the internal representation that will be developed as a result of interacting with and acting in the large space. This is the case even if the interaction is static and from a perspective outside the space, as happens when interacting with smaller manipulable space. This relates directly to the manner in which different spaces are mentally represented. Different spaces provide and rely on different frames of reference, spatial relations, and structure for internal representation that are dependent on characteristics of the space, one of which is size (Tversky *et al.*, 1999).

This was confirmed in a study requiring two groups of children (seven- and nine-year-olds) to learn and recall the locations of a set of five unique geometric objects in two different spaces. The spaces differed only in size. One was a *vista* space – a layout of (large) geometric shapes in a playground, and the other was an *object* space – a layout of (small) geometric shapes on a desktop (Bell, 2002). Children were not allowed to enter either space during the learning phase of the experiment. When asked to replace one of the objects from memory, the 9-year-olds tested in the larger space were able to locate this object more accurately than children tested in the smaller space. A follow-up task required children to describe verbally the locations of objects in the experimental space in which they were tested. When describing the larger space both the seven- and nine-year-olds included more spatial terms, and based locations on a wider range of frames of reference. In particular they used environmental features other than the experimental objects in the space. Even though the boundaries of the spaces and surrounding features were identical and in similar relationships with the experimental space and objects these items were not included in the descriptions of the small space. This suggests that when trying to recall and place the first object in the larger space children could draw upon more spatial information and knowledge than those children trying to complete the same task in the smaller space.

In other words, children used different strategies to explore, interact with, and solve problems in spaces of different size. Results of quantitative (errors associated with returning objects to correct locations) and qualitative (descriptions of arrangements and locations of objects) tasks performed in desktop and environmental spaces indicate that specific spatial primitives underlie how children perform spatial tasks in these spaces. Our knowledge of children's experiences with their environment indicates that extensive and varied opportunities are explored on a daily basis (Hart, 1979). Understanding the relationship between small space cognition and large space cognition can help to bridge the gap between our knowledge of children's environmental cognition derived from experimental studies, usually in small spaces, and what we know of children's cognition from studies of their real life experience in large scale spaces. In particular we need to know much more about the ways in which skills and strategies learnt or used in one space transfer to other spaces. Scale is a critical variable to consider in spatial research on cognition, development, and decision making. Scale matters.

References

Bell, S. (2002). Spatial cognition and scale: A child's perspective. *Journal of Environmental Psychology*, 22(1–2), 9–27.

Brenner, N. (2001). The limits to scale? Methodological reflections on scalar structuration. *Progress in Human Geography*, 25(4), 591–614.

DeLoache, J. S. (1989). Young children's understanding of the correspondence between a scale model and a larger space. *Cognitive Development*, 4(2), 121–39.

DeLoache, J. S. (1990). Young children's understanding of models. In R. Fivush and J. A. Hudson (eds.), *Knowing and Remembering in Young Children. Emory Symposia in Cognition, vol. III* (pp. 94–126). New York: Cambridge University Press.

DeLoache, J. S., Miller, K. F. and Rosengren, K. S. (1997). The credible shrinking room: Very young children's performance with symbolic and nonsymbolic relations. *Psychological Science*, 8(4), 308–13.

Egenhofer, M. J. and Golledge, R. G. (1998). *Spatial and Temporal Reasoning in Geographic Information Systems*. New York: Oxford University Press.

Freundschuh, S. and Egenhofer, M. (1997). Human conceptions of spaces: Implications for Geographic Information Systems. *Transactions in GIS*, 2(4), 361–75.

Freundschuh, S. M. (1997). Research in geography, space, and development: How can it inform geographic education? In R. G. Boehm and J. F. Petersen (eds.), *The First Assessment: Research in Geographic Education* (pp. 68–81). San Marcos: The Gilbert M. Grosvenor Center for Geographic Education.

Gärling, T. and Golledge, R. G. (1987). Environmental perception and cognition. In E. H. Zube and G. T. Moore (eds.), *Advances in Environment, Behavior, and Design* (vol. II, pp. 203–36). New York: Plenum Press.

Hart, R. (1979). *Children's Experience of Place.* New York: Irvington Publishers, distributed by Halsted Press.

Herman, J. F., Kolker, R. G. and Shaw, M. L. (1982). Effects of motor activity on children's intentional and incidental memory for spatial locations. *Child Development,* 53(1), 239–44.

Herman, J. F., Roth, S. F., Miranda, C. and Getz, M. (1982). Children's memory for spatial locations: The influence of recall perspective and type of environment. *Journal of Experimental Child Psychology,* 34(2), 257–73.

Hund, A. M. and Plumert, J. M. (2003). Does information about what things are influence children's memory for where things are? *Developmental Psychology,* 39(6), 939–48.

Huttenlocher, J. and Presson, C. C. (1979). The coding and transformation of spatial information. *Cognitive Psychology,* 11(3), 375–94.

Ittelson, W. H. (1973). Environmental perception and contemporary perceptual theory. In W. H. Ittelson (ed.), *Environmental and Cognition* (pp. 1–19). New York: Seminar.

Larsen, G. Y. and Abravanel, E. (1972). An examination of the developmental relations between certain spatial tasks. *Merrill-Palmer Quarterly,* 18(1), 39–52.

Lockman, J. J. and Pick, H. L. (1984). Problems of scale in spatial development. In C. Sophian (ed.), *Origins of Cognitive Skills.* Hillsdale, NJ: Lawrence Erlbaum Associates.

Mandler, J. M. (1983). Representation. In P. Messen (ed.), *Handbook of Child Psychology* (4th edn, vol. III, pp. 420–94). New York: John Wiley and Sons.

Mark, D. M. (1993). Toward a theoretical framework for geographical entity types. In A. U. Frank and I. Campari (eds.), *Spatial Information Theory: A Theoretical Basis for GIS* (pp. 270–83). Berlin: Springer-Verlag.

Montello, D. R. (1993). Scale and multiple psychologies of space. In A. U. Frank and I. Campari (eds.), *Spatial Information Theory: A Theoretical Basis for GIS* (pp. 312–21). Berlin: Springer-Verlag.

Newman, C., Atkinson, J. and Braddick, O. (2001). The development of reaching and looking preferences in infants to objects of different sizes. *Developmental Psychology,* 37(4), 561–72.

Piaget, J. and Inhelder, B. (1956). *The Child's Conception of Space.* London: Routledge and Kegan Paul.

Plumert, J. M. and Hund, A. M. (2001). The development of memory for location: What role do spatial-prototypes play? *Child Development,* 72(2), 370–84.

Purcell, M. (2003). Islands of practice and the Marston/Brenner debate: toward a more synthetic critical human geography. *Progress in Physical Geography,* 27(3), 317–32.

Quinn, P. C., Adams, A., Kennedy, E., Shettler, L. and Wasnik, A. (2003). Development of an abstract category representation for the spatial relation between in 6- to 10-month-old infants. *Developmental Psychology*, *39*(1), 151–63.

Roskos-Ewoldsen, B., McNamara, T. P., Shelton, A. L. and Carr, W. (1998). Mental representations of large and small spatial layouts are orientation dependent. *Journal of Experimental Psychology: Learning, Memory, and Cognition*, *24*(1), 215–26.

Tversky, B., Morrison, J. B., Franklin, N. and Bryant, D. J. (1999). Three spaces of spatial cognition. *Professional Geographer*, *51*(4), 516–24.

Uttal, D., Schreiber, J. C. and DeLoache, J. S. (1995). Waiting to use a symbol: The effects of delay on children's use of models. *Child Development*, *66*(6), 1875–89.

Uttal, D. H. (1990). *Young Children's Mental Representation of Spatial Information Acquired From Maps*. Unpublished PhD thesis, University of Michigan.

Weatherford, D. L. (1982). Spatial cognition as a function of size and scale of the environment. *New Directions for Child Development* (15), 5–18.

2 The problem of lost children

Edward H. Cornell and Kenneth A. Hill

Ken Hill has been living with the ghost of a nine-year-old Nova Scotia boy for over eighteen years. Hill can picture Andrew Warburton as he was on a sunny day in July 1986 when he was enjoying activities near his aunt's rural home. Dressed in swimming trunks, a tank top, and sneakers, he independently set off to meet his older brother at a lake several hundred meters from the house. Although he had previously walked the path with playmates, Andrew disappeared in the forest on his way to the lake. A massive search effort resulted, ultimately involving over 5,000 community volunteers, fire fighters, and military personnel. The police search manager called the nearby university and asked for a psychologist who knew anything about children's spatial behaviour. Professor Ken Hill agreed to meet the search manager at the incident command post. Hill was asked to indicate on a map of the surrounding environment where search efforts should be focused. Hill remembers that he could think of nothing in the sizable literature on the development of children's spatial representation that applied to this problem. It was obvious that Hill had little to offer, and as the coordinators of the search continued to converse among themselves, Hill slipped away from the post to join one of the ground search teams. After eight days of the search effort, Andrew Warburton was found dead from hypothermia, approximately 3.2 km from the place where he had last been seen.

Ken Hill never knew Andrew Warburton, but the impact of the youngster's disappearance and the helplessness that Hill experienced changed his career. Hill joined the local search and rescue team and as a field researcher began conducting interviews with lost persons who had recently been rescued. As a start, Hill segmented their descriptions into their initial experience of disorientation, their efforts to find safety and the eventual outcome of the incident. Hill discovered the statistical summaries of lost person behaviour self-published by Syrotuck (1977) and began keeping similar records of the distance travelled by persons lost in Nova Scotia's environs. In 1996, Hill was asked by the

United States National Association for Search and Rescue to write their handbook *Managing the Lost Person Incident*. In 1999, Hill edited *Lost Person Behavior* for the Search and Rescue Secretariat of Canada. Now he believes that he can provide a good estimate of where to search for children like Andrew Warburton.

Definition and incidence

As are most interesting psychological states, being lost is difficult to define. People are considered to be oriented – to know where they are – if they label or otherwise state their location accurately within some frame of reference. Yet, recently, wilderness wardens and rangers have reported incidents of lost adults with portable global positioning systems who knew exactly where they were according to the geographic co-ordinates used to map our planet. Nevertheless, these adults could not translate their co-ordinates into routes or procedures for getting to where they wanted to be. Montello (1998) also points out that in most day-to-day activities people efficiently travel to disparate locations yet are biased or surprisingly inaccurate when asked to estimate distances or indicate their bearings by pointing to landmarks. Evidently, people do not feel lost unless they are uncertain about how to get to their intended destination.

This more procedural or route-based geographic disorientation is not unusual; it includes episodes when way finders encounter an unexpected scene or path or when they cannot find a particular person, road or landmark. People usually tolerate these events but may begin to feel lost as the time or distance of travel increases beyond what was expected. People also report that they may not feel truly lost as long as they can see other people. Children wandering in urban environments may feel lost because they are shy, afraid or instructed not to approach strangers. In sum, lay descriptions of being lost include cognitive components such as failure of way finding procedures as well as emotional components such as anxiety and fear (Montello, 1998; Hill, 1999).

Police and search and rescue agencies operationally define a lost person as the subject of a search. As we shall see, this definition has a statistical application and overlaps with the more common and inconsequential forms of being lost. For example, in the Canadian Police Information Centre, a *missing* child incident is categorized as a case of a child becoming *lost* when the police report indicates that a person under the age of eighteen is presumed disoriented or confused, has wandered from supervision, has departed from a care facility or institution without wayfinding competence, has not returned when expected when walking, camping or participating in other wilderness activities, is overdue or in unfamiliar territory after leaving home or other family location, or has not returned when expected from school, a friend's house, or a meeting (Dalley, 2002). This lost category was assigned to 594 incidents, accounting for 1 per cent of 66,532 missing children reports in Canada in 2002. Seventy-nine per cent of these missing children reports involved the *runaway* category, youngsters who are usually adolescents. The yearly number of lost children incidents in this registry ranged from 496 to 822 within the decade 1993 to 2002.

Although most lost children incidents end with the child returned to safety within two to four hours of police or other search and rescue agencies becoming involved, search is dictated as an immediate response when one of the following conditions occurs: the child is twelve or younger, is alone, is mentally or medically challenged, is in a hazardous environment, is in inclement weather, is judged to be incapable of way finding and in unfamiliar territory, or is unprepared, without adequate clothing or other necessary resources (Hill, 1997; ERI, 2001). In some Canadian locales, such as Nova Scotia or Ontario suburbs bordering on forests and watersheds, police call outs to search for lost children may occur one to six times a year. Between 7 and 19 per cent of searches for people lost in rural or wilderness environments involve searches for lost children (Hill, 1997; Syrotuck, 1977).

Despite the low proportion of missing children who are lost, diligent police and search and rescue agencies begin investigation and analyze the urgency of each probable incident upon receipt of the call. The area for search expands quadratically as time passes. Professional agencies have trained search managers who may call out considerable resources, including command post pathers, specialized terrain vehicles and snow-mobiles, helicopters and fixed wing aircraft, watercraft, and certified diver, canine, equestrian, mountain bike, cross country ski and ground search teams. An emergency response by professionals is justifiable because the lost child may be vulnerable to criminal predation or environmental hazards, may be experiencing traumatic fear, or may die alone and exposed. During search operations, it is not unusual that a lost child's parents, friends or community leaders undergo anguish that impairs judgment. The situation may be incomprehensible to the family of victims, especially when the child has become lost while innocently indulging in outdoor play. For example, in 1993, nine-year-old Ashley Krestianson took up her sister's challenge to race to their mother's car in a remote area of rural Saskatchewan. Ashley apparently intended to win the race by taking a short cut. When she did not appear for hours, a massive search effort ensued, continuing unsuccessfully for several weeks. Months later, her body was found by a hunter. Ashley had died of hypothermia.

Events such as these haunt most experienced search managers. The argument that it is rare that children become seriously lost or that urban incidents typically end without consequence is no help when search managers have to decide where to deploy their resources.

Approaches to research

Several lines of research may help with the problem of lost children. The most applicable is analyses of actuarial data, or case histories from police and wilderness ranger's files (Syrotuck, 1978; Hill, 1997; Heth and Cornell, 1998). Data such as the typical distance traveled have been aggregated to provide useful generalizations about lost person behavior. In addition, search and rescue organizations are increasingly maintaining records of local incidents; indigenous data reflect environmental features and outdoor user profiles that are unique to the area. For example, regional search and rescue veterans will know that a bike path has a tricky turn that, if missed, leads a cyclist into a different network of paths.

Another line of research is process oriented, examining what leads children astray and how they navigate on their own. This research studies the attention, memory and problem solving abilities of children of different ages during exploration and way finding. The results provide clues about typical behaviour, such as forecasting where a six-year-old might step off a path when returning along a new route. We provide representative examples of these lines of research in the sections that follow.

Distance travelled as the crow flies

The basic index of travel of lost children is the distance as the crow flies between the point last seen and the point found. The *crow's-flight distance* is measured as a straight line drawn on a scaled map. The line does not intend to represent the actual path that a child took to arrive at the point found, a path that is usually longer and includes turns. There are two reasons why the crow's-flight distance is an important summary.

First, actuarial records of lost child incidents typically only specify the point last seen and the point found. Sometimes the investigation conducted during the search will reveal the intended destination of the child, which is also a point. It is rare that records include a map of the actual paths taken by the child during his or her wandering. These maps may be included when there is a path of evidence or footprints, but the paths usually have large gaps.

Actuarial records seldom include a reconstruction of the incident by the lost person. Lost persons typically have difficulty retrieving memories of their wandering, and their reported activities are poorly anchored in space and time. When found, a lost person may be mobile and able to converse in a normal manner, but 'Only upon close questioning does it become evident that they are unable to remember where they spent the first night, whether they had any water to drink, or whether they crossed the river yesterday or the day before' (Syrotuck, 1977: 8). Such memory deficits are associated with systemic response to fear. For example, Ledoux (1996) summarizes how the hormones produced under stress disrupt perception, problem solving and the formation and retrieval of memories. He describes a 'hostile takeover of consciousness by emotion' as the amygdala, in concert with numerous other structures in the brain and body, comes to dominate the processing of information when people are afraid.

Because memories may have been inadequately encoded during their wanderings, the subsequent reconstructions of incidents by lost persons often become schematic, resembling a heroic struggle in which the lost person began with a reasoned plan but encountered natural obstacles which in turn required sub plans and resolution (Hill, 1997). However, evidence of lost persons running in panic or wandering past people while in shock is not consistent with these reconstructions. Experienced search managers believe that there is a short window between when a found child is calm enough to provide good recall and when the child has reconstructed events several times, assimilating the nature of questions and stereotypical attributions of searchers, investigators, parents, media and peers. The study of children's eyewitness memory and testimony suggests procedures that may lead to valid interviews of found children (e.g., Milne and Bull, 1999).

The second important characteristic of the crow's-flight distance measure is that it can be mapped as a radius for a circle that defines an area for search operations. Examining cases from wilderness parks, Syrotuck (1977) organized forty-six records of children's crow's-flight distance travelled. He plotted distributions that search managers could use to prioritize circular areas around the point last seen. Syrotuck suggested that the median crow's-flight distance travelled was a good probabilistic estimate of the distance walked by a subject of a wilderness search; his distributions, as subsequent summaries, are skewed by one or two case histories of subjects who were found at unusually long distances from the point last seen (Heth and Cornell, 1998; Hill, 1999). Syrotuck recognized that forecasting children's behaviour would be more accurate if distributions reflected variables such as the age and behavioural tendencies of the lost child as well as characteristics of the environment. For example, he noted that in bad weather some small children (between one and six years of age) were difficult to detect as they had burrowed or covered themselves in an effort to keep warm. His comparison of the elevations of the point last seen and the point found was consistent with reports that the majority of small children used game paths or followed a drainage channel that afforded a downward path of least resistance.

The circular area defined by the crow's-flight distance radius serves to contain more detailed analysis of environmental variables. In rural and wilderness areas, evaluation of the features of the terrain such as paths, barriers, watersheds, topography and vegetation usually suggests two to five probable routes that should be searched initially. In contrast, urban and suburban environments are designed to afford ease of pedestrian travel and frequent intersections allow many choices with different headings. Urban police must initiate containment procedures to prevent lost children from encountering traffic, construction, or unsafe neighbourhoods. Containment means early posting of personnel near busy intersections, bridges or environmental hazards to watch for the lost child.

Home range

Studies of children's *home range* indicate how the crow's flight distance measure can be useful for locating children lost in urban and suburban environments. A child's home range refers to the outdoor territory that surrounds his or her home and provides a context for independent travel, play and exploration (Anderson and Tindal, 1972). When children are reported lost or missing in cities, police typically ask parents about their child's favourite activities and, 'Where is the farthest place from home your child has ever gone to alone?' The crow's-flight distance from the home to this location can serve as a radius for a circle to delimit some initial search operations.

The area that a child typically traverses on their way to a distant destination can be represented as a section of this circle. Cornell and Heth (1996) observed the actual paths taken by groups of three- to twelve-year-old children when they walked from their suburban homes to their farthest neighbourhood destinations. The section was drawn to include any paths on both sides of the crow's-flight line that were part of the child's established route and observed wandering to the distant destination (see Figure 2.1). If the child did not show

Figure 2.1. The crow's flight distance is measured along a straight line between the child's home (H) and intended destination (ID). The child's actual path is depicted as an irregular dashed line and the dispersion of travel can be indexed as the angle of the section that minimally includes the actual path. Here, the child's path is on both sides of the crow's-flight line, so the total angle of dispersion consists of a small and large angle. Cornell and Heth (1996) listed distributions for different age groups when the size of each child's large angle was doubled. The researchers suggested that search managers could centre a median result on either side of the crow's-flight line between the point last seen and the intended destination of a lost child. This would provide a section to delimit search when it was not known whether the child would travel farther to one side or the other.

extensive travel lateral to the crow's-flight line, the section resembled a wedge. The research provides an estimate of the dispersion of children's travel in suburbia, so a search manager can prioritize areas for search when a child's intended destination or favourite sites are revealed by investigation.

Interestingly, the median size of the section increases from 79° to 150° between seven and ten years of age, indicating that older children show more dispersion in their distant travel. More than 10 per cent of children between the ages of seven and twelve select routes that are contained within a section with an angle greater than 180°, indicating that they have gone outside of the half-plane between their home and their intended destination. Travel as disperse as this challenges the argument that development in middle childhood is associated with efficient route choices, or least distance solutions. The expansion of home range is at least partially motivated by the quest for autonomy, exploration, and adventure. During these activities, inattention or miscalculation often leads to errant travel, leading children to realize the value of landmarks (Cornell, Hadley, Sterling, Chan and Boechler, 2001; Hart, 1979).

Some parameters of home range have been derived from interviews and sketch maps by children who live in urban centres and rural towns (Tindal, 1971; Hart, 1979). However, when summarizing travel reported by urban school children, Matthews (1992) discovered that free recall sketching and verbal reporting yielded smaller estimates of home range when compared to the distant locations that children recounted visiting in response to aerial photos and large-scale plan maps. The discrepancy may reflect the well-known observation that, owing to the amount or structure of information presented to facilitate retrieval, measures involving recall underestimate knowledge relative to measures of recognition. It is risky to underestimate the travel of a lost child. Useful data for search managers may require behavioral observations and unitary indices of distance and dispersion of travel in different environments.

Processes of way finding

In many communities, parents initially show their children a route and then permit brief unsupervised travel on that route for visits to neighbouring friends or play sites within calling range. As early as three years of age, young children enjoy this independence and begin exploring close to home. Their excursions typically involve stepping off an established route without losing sight of familiar territory (Cornell *et al.*, 2001). By ages five to seven, many children have accompanied peers or older playmates to sites that are beyond the views from their home. Children may first experience the problem of *way finding* when repeating a familiar route and a portion is forgotten. Way finding encompasses a set of perceptual and cognitive skills for orientation and directing travel.

Recognition processes. For example, visual recognition processes can inform children that they are off route in two ways. One is that there is an accumulating absence of familiar or expected cues. The other is noticing something en route that the child is sure that he or she has never seen before. These types of information are correlated, because environments are patchy and features near paths are more likely to be different as the child travels farther from a known area. Novelty can be ambient if a child has established *place schemas*, or has expectancies of the typical environmental features within his or her home range (Cornell, Heth and Skoczylas, 1999). For example, playmates may realize that they have misinterpreted the directions to a friend's suburban house if they find themselves amongst high rises.

When unexpectedly lost, young children often seek familiarity. This involves directing scanning, accuracy of recognition memory and judgments of whether a landmark, path or scene has been experienced before (Cornell, Heth and Alberts, 1994; Heth and Cornell, 1997). Children develop these skills so that by twelve years of age their place recognition abilities are not reliably different from those of adults. Nevertheless, when returning from an off-route excursion, children may correctly recognize a junction as familiar but not be able to judge the way to turn. Features of all of the intersecting paths would have been seen before from different perspectives. In this situation, off-route way finders may be able to choose between alternative paths by approaching landmarks that were temporally encoded as earlier in their trip or by remembering the direction they chose when they turned off path (Cornell *et al.*, 1999). In other words, to get back on route, places that are recognized sometimes need to be situated in a series of memories of travel.

Serial recall. When they are first learning a route, eight-year-old children remember the places and events at the beginning and end (Cornell, Heth, Kneubuhler and Sehgal, 1996). When children are nine to eleven years of age, early in route learning they also note some places where way finding decisions or turns are made (Doherty, 1984; Golledge *et al.*, 1985). Choice points that occur near the origin and terminus of a complex urban route are more likely to be remembered than those in the middle (Cornell *et al.*, 1992; Golledge *et al.*, 1992). For example, when eight- and twelve-year-old children were asked to point to the way to proceed at junctions while heading back along a 1km route around a university core, the pattern of correct choices was a downward bowed serial position curve (Cornell *et al.*, 1996). The bow was not deep, but reliable, and indicates that children tend to step off route at junctions midway during their attempts at reversing a new route. The projection of their errant travel into areas of the university was consistent with data from previous studies that followed children when they had stepped off route. Cornell *et al.* (1996) showed how the mathematical description of typical route errors could be incorporated into urban police search procedures.

Problem solving. Repeating or reversing a route is not a problem unless inattention or forgetting occurs. Hence, one lesson a child learns from inadvertently stepping off a previously travelled route is that something must be done to prevent such lapses. By six years of age, children can be taught prospective strategies that allow them to remember the paths that they walked on the way to their destination (Heth *et al.*, 2002). During outbound travel, the six-year-old children were repeatedly told at junctions to anticipate what they would see if they were to turn around. The children were then instructed to turn around and check that the landmarks would be there. By twelve years of age, children walking long and relatively unfamiliar routes independently learned to note landmarks at junctions where changes of direction could occur (Cornell *et al.*, 2001). They also independently learned to note landmarks in the skyline that could be seen from a variety of locations. This prospective attention indicated that twelve-year-old children are aware of information that allows inferences when they are way finding off route.

Way finding when lost can be thought of as goal-oriented problem solving. The goal is typically not to regain orientation, in the sense that most lost people, children or adults, may only incidentally seek to establish their whereabouts within a known frame of reference. The common goal when lost is to find the most direct route to a familiar place: the original paths, the origin of travel, places with people, home.

Syrotuck's (1977) analyses of a small number of case histories suggested that toddlers under the age of three are unaware of the concept of being lost. They may not feel alone when they are preoccupied with the activities of adventure and may not attempt to 'find mommy' for some time. When they do try to get back, they may wander circuitously for several hours. As a result, toddlers are likely to be found in the general area of the point last seen, sometimes hiding or sleeping. Urban search managers describe a '300 meter rule' for toddlers, recommending initial and detailed search within 300 m of the point last seen (ERI, 2001).

In contrast, Syrotuck (1977) suggested that children between the ages of three and six have a concept of being lost, will often make some effort to return home, but lack strategic way finding skills. As a result, they tend to use paths of least resistance and may wander progressively from the point last seen. For example, one five-year-old child was found 6.4 km down a gentle slope in hilly terrain surrounding the point last seen.

Although when alone many children older than six appear to move randomly as an initial reaction to being lost, most settle down and attempt a more effective response. Hill's (1999) interviews suggest that children use four of nine strategies that lost adults reported they had used 'for getting unlost'. Hill acknowledges that some of these strategies may not be unequivocally rational. For example, the strategy of path running sometimes occurs after children realize that they are disoriented or have not seen familiar cues for some time. They then hasten down the nearest path or least effort course. In some instances, the strategy is intended to find out quickly what the travel corridor leads to. Minimizing effort while seeking new information is a rational strategy. Paths are thought to go somewhere, there is the possibility that other people are on the path, and sights along the path may help to reestablish bearings. However, in their anxiety to achieve any of these ends, or because of systemic reactions to fear, children will often run to exhaustion and even though a path is fading or taking them farther into rugged new territory, they are unlikely to reverse their direction.

The other strategies recorded to be used by lost children are classified as *direction sampling, view enhancing,* and *staying put.* Direction sampling and view enhancing are brief excursions to obtain more information about the surrounding terrain. These strategies involve procedures to return to an anchor point once a bearing or view has been sampled and not found to be informative. As an example of direction sampling, in one urban incident two nine-year-old girls used a playground knoll as an anchor point for search for familiar cues. One girl watched on the knoll while the other walked down a street to stand on her toes and look for their school. She progressed to the farthest point she could while keeping her friend in view, then returned to the knoll. The girls took turns going out, moving clockwise around the knoll systematically to search adjacent streets (Cornell and Heth, 1983/1999). The view enhancing strategy is illustrated by a rural incident: a thirteen-year-old boy reported that he interrupted his walking to climb trees to scan for any house (Hill, 1999).

Notice in both the urban and rural incidents that the children's primary goal, to find their own way home, was recast as an immediate sub goal: to gain new information. The analytical decomposition of the problem had not been taught and the children's creation and execution of the strategies is striking. A full description of children's cognitive development could benefit from research on attention, memory and problem solving in these natural but extraordinary circumstances. Reciprocally, forecasting probable locations of lost children could benefit from research on their way finding strategies.

Staying put can be considered strategic behavior if the child has adopted the goal of being found. This is not an obvious goal for many children. Some youngsters have been instructed not to talk to strangers and will avoid searchers who are calling their name, while others do not realize that they are the object of search and will watch with curiosity as searchers sweep areas or police cars or helicopters pass by. Some youngsters lost in cities have hidden from the police because they believed that they were in trouble. These reactions help us to understand how children may be lost among people.

However, if the child understands that one solution to becoming unlost is to be found, he or she may go to a familiar or popular site. For example, there is a community police station within West Edmonton Mall, the largest shopping complex in the world. One of the effective police protocols for the almost daily incidents of lost children is to notify the staff at one of the two MacDonald's restaurants. The child is described and staff may have already noticed an anxious isolate. Staying put can be considered to be strategic if, when found, the lost children state that they were following parental instructions or they realized that their travel could lead them farther from home. In rural and wilderness incidents, some children have perched on promontories to wait, despite the exposure to weather (Cornell and Heth, 1983/1999). They state that this helps them to be seen or that this helps them to see large areas where somebody might come. Notice that these strategies require that the children take the perspective of a searcher.

Because young children who are wandering while lost typically are tired and frightened, they may not be staying put with the intention to be found when they are subsequently located asleep, hiding, or resting alongside a path. Lost persons rarely stay put, even though it is the course of action recommended by search and rescue experts and is commonly instructed by parents. Older children, adolescents, and adults will persevere with way finding for days, even though the daily distance they travel decreases with accumulating fatigue and exposure. These older individuals may have the wherewithal to organize their activities after episodes of panic and can be quite embarrassed by attributions of way finding incompetence.

Social context

Parental restrictions. Now, as in the past, one of the chief tasks of parents is to inhibit their youngsters from wandering out of supervised care (see also Derr, this volume). Fairy tales telling of dark woods, witches and wolves have been updated as urban myths telling of bad neighbourhoods, strangers and mean dogs. Less dramatically, while walking with their child in their neighbourhood, parents may caution or forbid and thereafter assume that their child is not attempting independent way finding. There is evidence that many children do not adhere to these admonitions (Cornell et al., 2001; Cornell, Heth, Faulkner and Marusiak, 2004; Hart, 1979; Valentine, 1997). Their activities outdoors suggest that even young children should be instructed about procedures for safe way finding and what to do when they think that they are lost.

Although typically not recorded as a childrearing variable, parent's regulation of their children's travel fits with the typologies of authoritative, authoritarian, permissive or uninvolved parenting (Maccoby and Martin, 1983). For example, Hart (1979) described negotiated and monitored range restrictions that are characteristic of authoritative parenting. Parents usually initiated control of outdoor travel by specifying the destination for each excursion. After showing that they would comply with restrictions, children would sometimes suggest a new place they could visit on their own. In addition, children would sometimes assume (but not ask) permission, and then go to familiar places and return home to report their activities candidly. Hart reported examples of children fooling their mothers concerning where they played, but usually not for long without being found out. While the reaction of most parents to rule breaking was to ground their child to home for some period, some parents treated the excursion as a sign that their child was capable; the parents subsequently loosened their range restrictions. Similarly, some parents reported that they allowed extraordinary travel because their children had visited distant sites before restrictions had been set (Cornell et al., 2004).

In general, children report that they go to more distant destinations when they have parental permission than when they are free ranging (travelling alone without having to ask or tell anyone where they are going; Hart, 1979; Matthews, 1992). Children also report that they go to their most distant destinations when their parents give them permission to be accompanied by older siblings or friends. These self-reports of unsupervised travel attest that children know that it is important to comply with parental regulations.

Vagaries of childhood. Nevertheless, urban police who are experienced search managers will be able to recount many incidents involving normally well-disciplined children. Some youngsters become intrigued with adventures of the moment and travel beyond their ability to find their way home. They may accompany friends or siblings to sites and inadvertently become separated from the group. Many will experience errant travel when exploring new routes or devising shortcuts to known sites (Cornell et al., 2001). Hart (1979) provides fascinating observations that independent children often go out of their way to take 'shortcuts' that are frequently longer and more hazardous than the original routes that they knew. There seems to be prestige associated with retelling these adventures and knowledge of secret routes. Certainly, cognitive prowess underlies efficient shortcutting; shortcuts require the child to rely on survey representations and strategies for way finding rather than specific route knowledge. When asked to make shortcuts by taking new paths in their neighbourhood, eight-year-old children travelled approximately 49 per cent farther than the shortest possible route, whereas twelve-year-old children walked only 14 per cent more than necessary (Cornell et al., 2001). Adults attempting shortcuts in an unfamiliar neighborhood walked about 28 per cent more than the least distance shortcut (Cornell, Sorenson and Mio, 2003).

Sometimes an uncharacteristic argument with peers or parents may cause children to travel beyond their abilities to find their way. Heth and Cornell (1998) found that case histories of runaways and despondents showed a unique distribution of crow's-flight distance between the point last seen and the point found. These subcategories of lost persons exhibited skewed distributions, with more records of distant travel. Upset children may be traveling in response to conflict rather than as part of recreational activities; they may hasten to get away from places, rather than intending to go to places. They are often preoccupied with social imbroglios and not attending to time, landmarks, or bearings. Even when they realize that they do not know how to return, they may avoid searchers until food or shelter takes priority.

Summary

Modern children living in cities and suburbs are supervised, bussed and driven. The child's independent travel to play sites and school is a gradual accomplishment, usually involving the showing of routes, accompaniment by competent peers and the child demonstrating knowledge of his or her address and phone number. Environmental design provides for ease of travel, elimination or isolation of hazards, and way finding aids such as distinguishable pedestrian, cyclist and vehicle routes and signage. Given these circumstances and an evolutionary history that selected for exploration, foraging, and the ability to return home, the problem of lost children is rare.

Nevertheless, hundreds of incidents do occur and communities have supported the readiness of police and search and rescue organizations. These groups are the real catcher in the rye. They have been deeply affected by their successes and failures and have learned to treat search as an emergency and an investigation. It is only as a last resort that search managers line volunteers shoulder-to-shoulder to blanket an area ploddingly. Instead, search managers first respond by prioritizing areas for search. To do so, they consider the victim's motivations, cognitive abilities and experience, and lost person behaviours in the context of the particular environment. Research in environmental psychology is beginning to help them.

Acknowledgment

We gratefully acknowledge research support from the Natural Sciences and Engineering Research Council and the Search and Rescue Secretariat of Canada.

References

Anderson, J. and Tindal, M. (1972). The concept of home range: New data for the study of territorial behavior. In W. Mitchell (ed.), *Environmental Design: Research and Practice* (pp. 1–7). Los Angeles: University of California Press.

Cornell, E. H., Hadley, D. C., Sterling, T. M., Chan, M. A. and Boechler, P. (2001). Adventure as a stimulus for cognitive development. *Journal of Environmental Psychology, 21,* 219–31.

Cornell, E. H. and Heth, C. D. (1983/1999). Report of a missing child. In K. Hill (ed.), *Lost Person Behavior* (pp. 31–44). Ottawa, Ontario: The National Search and Rescue Secretariat.

Cornell, E. H. and Heth, C. D. (1996). Distance traveled during urban and suburban walks led by 3- to 12-year-olds: Tables for search managers. *Response! The Journal of the National Association for Search and Rescue, 15,* 6–9.

Cornell, E. H., Heth, C. D. and Alberts, D. M. (1994). Place recognition and way finding by children and adults. *Memory and Cognition, 22,* 633–43.

Cornell, E. H., Heth, C. D., Faulkner, J. P. and Marusiak, C. W. (2004). *The rides of summer: How cycling leads to the expansion of home range in suburbia.* Unpublished manuscript, University of Alberta, Edmonton, Canada.

Cornell, E. H., Heth, C. D., Kneubuhler, Y. and Sehgal, S. (1996). Serial position effects in children's route reversal errors: Implications for police search operations. *Applied Cognitive Psychology, 10,* 301–26.

Cornell, E. H., Heth, C. D. and Rowat, W. L. (1992). Way finding by children and adults: Response to instructions to use look-back and retrace strategies. *Developmental Psychology, 28,* 328–36.

Cornell, E. H., Heth, C. D. and Skoczylas, M. J. (1999). The nature and use of route expectancies following incidental learning. *Journal of Environmental Psychology, 19,* 209–29.

Cornell, E. H., Sorenson, A. and Mio, T. (2003). Human sense of direction and way finding. *Annals of the American Association of Geographers, 93,* 402–28.

Dalley, M. (2002). *Canada's Missing Children: 2002 Annual Report.* Ottawa, Ontario: National Missing Children Services.

Doherty, S. E. (1984). *Developmental differences in cue recognition at spatial decision points.* Unpublished doctoral dissertation, Department of Geography, University of California, Santa Barbara.

ERI (Emergency Response Institute, 2001). *Search Management for the Initial Response Incident Commander*. Olympia, WA: ERI International.

Golledge, R. G., Gale, N., Pellegrino, J. W. and Doherty, S. (1992). Spatial knowledge acquisition by children: Route learning and relational distances. *Annals of the Association of American Geographers*, *82*, 223–44.

Golledge, R. G., Smith, T. R., Pellegrino, J. W., Doherty, S. and Marshal, S. P. (1985). A conceptual model and empirical analysis of children's acquisition of spatial knowledge. *Journal of Environmental Psychology*, *5*, 125–52.

Hart, R. A. (1979). *Children's Experience of Place*. New York: Irvington.

Heth, C. D. and Cornell, E. H. (1997). Differential use of landmarks by 8- and 12-year-old children during route reversal navigation. *Journal of Environmental Psychology*, *17*, 199–213.

Heth, C. D. and Cornell, E. H. (1998). Characteristics of travel by persons lost in Albertan wilderness areas. *Journal of Environmental Psychology*, *18*, 223–35.

Heth, C. D., Cornell, E. H. and Flood, T. L. (2002). Self-ratings of sense of direction and route reversal performance. *Applied Cognitive Psychology*, *16*, 309–24.

Hill, K. A. (1998). *Managing the Lost Person Incident*. Chantilly, VA: National Association for Search and Rescue.

Hill, K. A. (ed.) (1999). The psychology of lost. In K. Hill (ed.), *Lost Person Behavior* (pp. 1–15). Ottawa, Ontario: National Search and Rescue Secretariat.

Ledoux, J. E. (1996). *The Emotional Brain: The Mysterious Underpinnings of Emotional Life*. New York: Simon and Schuster.

Maccoby, E. E. and Martin, J. A. (1983). Socialization in the context of the family: Parent-child interaction. In E. Hetherington (ed.), *Mussen's Manual of Child Psychology* (4th edition, vol. IV, pp. 1–102). New York: Wiley.

Matthews, M. H. (1992). *Making Sense of Place: Children's Understanding of Large-scale Environments*. Hertfordshire, UK: Harvester Wheatsheaf.

Milne, R. and Bull, R. (1999). *Investigative Interviewing: Psychology and Practice*. New York: Wiley.

Montello, D. R. (1998b, September). *What it means to be lost*. Proceedings of the Search and Rescue Secretariat of Canada (SARSCENE), Banff, Alberta, Canada.

Syrotuck, W. G. (1977). *Analysis of Lost Person Behaviour: An Aid to Search Planning*. Westmoreland, NY: Arner Publications.

Tindal, M. A. (1971). *The home range of black elementary school children: An exploratory study in the measurement and comparison of home range*. Unpublished master's thesis, Clark University, Worcester, MA.

Valentine, G. (1997). 'Oh yes I can.' 'Oh no you can't': Children and parents' understandings of kids' competence to negotiate public space safely. *Antipode*, *29*, 65–89.

3 Children's understanding of environmental representations: aerial photographs and model towns

Beverly Plester, Mark Blades and Christopher Spencer

We experience the world around us in two ways. By direct experience of living in, travelling through or manipulating our environment, and most of the chapters in this book are concerned with children's and adolescents' direct experience of their environments. But we also learn about the world through secondary sources – for example from spatial representations like maps, from written descriptions, such as guide books, and from visual images like films. These are particularly important sources of knowledge for environments that we have not had the opportunity to experience directly. Compared to the research into children's direct experience and activity in their local environments, there is little research into how children learn about places from secondary sources, and even less into how children combine information from experience and from secondary sources.

In this chapter we will discuss how young children understand one secondary source of information – aerial photographs. In particular we will consider how children relate aerial photographs to real places, in other words how they use photographs to interpret the immediate environment. And we will also consider the reverse issue – what types of environmental experience contribute to children's ability to interpret aerial photographs.

Understanding spatial representations, such as maps, models, and map-like photographs, has at least two functions, for children and adults alike. First, such representations can serve as compact, durable and portable representations of large areas of the world. Representations like aerial views taken by photographers, or maps drawn by cartographers are part of adult cultural images that children have to learn to interpret and use. Second, such representations extend our senses beyond our inherent physical limitations and allow us to see, at least in metaphoric or symbolic form, aspects of the physical world in which we live that would otherwise have to be experienced sequentially and piecemeal. For a young child, whose independent exploration of the world may be restricted (see Rissotto and Giuliani, this volume) representations are one way to learn about the physical world beyond their own limited direct experience (Uttal, 2000).

In this chapter we review the previous research into young children's understanding of aerial photographs. As we will point out, previous researchers have nearly always investigated children's understanding of photographs of unfamiliar places, and therefore the assessment of children's abilities has focused on how children interpret an aerial photograph. We will discuss the cognitive competences that might underpin the interpretation of aerial photographs. Then we will describe some of our research testing children's understanding of aerial photographs when the children are in the actual environments portrayed in the photograph. In such a context the children not only need to interpret the photograph, but also need to relate the photograph to their immediate surroundings. This adds a further dimension to children's understanding of environmental representations.

Children's understanding of aerial photographs: early research

Blaut (1991, 1997) claimed that understanding environmental representations such as aerial photographs was a natural, untrained ability in young children. This suggestion was based on studies such as Stea and Blaut (1973). They asked Puerto Rican five-year-olds from four types of community to interpret 1:5000 scale vertical aerial photographs of these communities, the photographs being centred on the children's schools. The children in all groups gave more accurate identifications of features than inaccurate ones, and so Blaut and Stea concluded that the children had no difficulty 'reading' the content of the photographs. In another study, Blaut, McCleary and Blaut (1970) tested five to seven-year-old children in both Puerto Rico and the United States, using black and white vertical aerial photographs of scales 1:2000 and 1:3000 respectively. The children identified features, and then were asked to trace a map on acetate from the photograph, then identify the features they had drawn, and to plot a route on their maps. Most of the children successfully completed these tasks. Spencer, Harrison and Darvizeh (1980) used the same photographs with children in the UK and found similar results, even though in this case, the areas were of unfamiliar landscapes.

To examine the implications of recognizing aerial photographs on children's understanding of other representations Muir and Blaut

(1969) conducted an educational experiment with five- and six-year-old American children. The children saw vertical black and white aerial photographs, at a scale of 1:2700, including photographs of the schools attended by the children, to find out whether learning about the aerial photographs would lead to increased ability with interpreting and constructing maps. Muir and Blaut found that children taught with aerial photographs demonstrated the map abilities better than an untaught control group. Taken together these early studies demonstrated that young children have some ability to identify features on aerial photographs and that the benefits of looking at photographs transfer to other representations like maps.

Although Liben and Downs (1997) acknowledged the successes of young children found by other researchers, they drew more cautious conclusions and emphasised the limitations, as well as the abilities, of young children. For example, Liben and Downs (1989) showed three to six-year-old children a black and white vertical aerial photograph, with scale 1:12,000, of an unfamiliar city, and in other work (Liben and Downs, 1992) children were shown aerial photographs of their own city. In these studies, Liben and Downs found limitations in the children's interpretations of aerial photographs, including 'scale errors' indicating that the children had not applied the appropriate size transformation needed, for instance thinking that boats on a lake could be fish; or confusions over the representational function of the photograph, when children suggested that a field could not be grass because it was not depicted in green. However, errors of these kinds, although intriguing, are usually exceptions to young children's overall representational competency, and indicate incomplete understanding, rather than complete misunderstanding.

Liben and Downs (1997) emphasized the need to track the development of spatial representation skills through childhood, so we now turn to theoretical models of this development (e.g. Liben, 1999; 2002). Then we will turn to more recent research investigating children's understanding of aerial photographs.

Understanding an aerial photograph

To understand an aerial photograph as a representation of an area, and in particular to use that photograph to solve problems in the depicted real space, we must accomplish several cognitive tasks. We must recognize the representational nature of the photograph, that it is 'of' something; then we must identify correspondences between the features of the photograph and the features in the referent space. Another kind of correspondence must also be acknowledged; spatial relations among features in the photograph need to be maintained among the referent features in the real space. To do that with an aerial photograph, we need to make not only a scale transformation to the size of the real space, but also a transformation to the viewpoint of the photographer. If we are situated in the real space at the time, we need to keep those transformations available for use as we consider the information available from both the photograph and the real space, so that we can go on to solve problems in that space using the combined information.

Understanding spatial representations

Liben (1999) considered the development of an incremental set of cognitive abilities that underlie the understanding of spatial representations, and proposed six basic competencies that must be achieved before a child can be said to understand a spatial representation.

Referential content

This competence indicates that the child must know that the pattern of colour and shapes perceived represents something, although there may be confusion about what difference there is between the representation and the environment. For example, DeLoache, Strauss, and Maynard (1979), using gaze monitoring, documented infants' understanding of pictures as more similar to their referents than to other possible referents by five months of age, but there was no indication that the infants had an understanding of the symbolic, representational nature of the picture.

Global differentiation

This competence refers to the implicit knowledge that a representation is separate from the environment it represents, but it does not explicitly address the representational relationship. Children of three years differentiate between a model room and the real room it represents (DeLoache, 1989). But three-year-olds have difficulty with dual representation (e.g. Gopnik and Rosati, 2001). In other words they have difficulty considering a model as a model (toy) and as a representation at the same time. When DeLoache (1995) explained to two-and-a-half-year-olds that a model room was the real room, made smaller by a 'shrinking machine', it relieved the children of the need for dual representation, and thus increased their ability to find a hidden toy whose location they knew from the real room. However, Liben (1999) has argued that this might no longer be a case of a representation, but of an identity. Liben suggested that infants begin to achieve global differentiation, and toddlers appear largely to have achieved it, but this is an aspect of development that continues into the pre-school period.

Representational insight

The third competency refers to understanding that a representation stands for the environment, and generally appears by about three years of age, although some development may continue during early school years. To achieve this competency, children must acknowledge that the representation does stand for the place it represents, not just treat it differently. As described above, pre-schoolers have shown representational insight, in many cultural settings, acknowledging that aerial photographs do represent a real space (e.g. Muir and Blaut, 1969; Blaut and Stea, 1974; Blades and Spencer, 1987a; Blades et al., 1998). However, children in these studies did not always acknowledge that the photograph represented a particular real space.

As DeLoache (2000: 329) has pointed out 'achievement of representational insight (with respect to symbolic artifacts) is not an across-the-board, stage-like acquisition with respect to symbols in general, but rather depends on the particular stimuli and situation'. The factors that might influence representational insight include the characteristics of the child, such as their experience with symbolization generally and their domain knowledge of the particular task; and characteristics of the stimulus such as the iconicity of symbols, salience of the materials, and the possibilities they afford for achieving a particular task. Other factors that affect representational insight are the social context of the task, such as instructions given, or the expressed intention to make the representation symbolic of the referent; and the strategic behaviour of the child in the situation. All these factors feed into the achievement of representational insight.

Attribute differentiation

Liben (1999) proposed that pre-school children can achieve this competency, but development may continue throughout the primary school years. Where representational insight indicates that children acknowledge the similarities between an aerial photograph and real space, attribute differentiation indicates that children must also acknowledge differences. The most important differences in the case of aerial photographs are scale and projection.

One attribute dissimilarity that appears incompletely understood by young children is the scale relation of representation to referent. For example, Liben and Downs (1992) described a child rejecting a tiny rectangle on a large scale map as a representation of his father's office building because his office was 'as big as this whole map!' (1992: 162). However, it should be emphasized that such scale errors are not universally present when young children interpret aerial photographs. Blades et al. (1997) found only a very small proportion of scale errors with children from three and a half years to five years of age, using an aerial photograph of 1:1300 scale. Further, Blades et al. (1998), found little evidence that young children were unable to make the scale and perspective transformations required to describe features in large scale maps.

The children in Blades et al. (1998), Liben and Downs (1992, 1997), and Spencer et al. (1980) were shown aerial photographs of unfamiliar environments. They were asked to describe features in the photographs, but were not asked to relate the photographs to the environments that they represented. Uttal (1996, 2001) assessed children's memory for spatial relationships in tasks in which they had to recall layouts of objects. Uttal found that young children preserved the configuration of objects in a layout without preserving metric accuracy, indicating the children's difficulty in maintaining scale. If this is the case then children who are asked to apply information from an aerial photograph to the area it represents, might well make scale errors in such tasks, and this will be discussed below.

Correspondence mastery

To reach this fifth competency, children must understand the systematic rules by which representations correspond to their referent spaces while differing from them. There are two essential correspondences: feature correspondence between individual objects or places (that a tree on a photograph represents a particular tree in the environment), and geometric correspondence of spatial relationships (e.g. that the distance between the tree and a building represents that distance on the ground). The importance of understanding both feature and geometric correspondences when using representations has been made by several authors (Blades and Cooke, 1994; Liben, 1999; Newcombe and Huttenlocher, 2000).

Feature correspondence develops before geometric correspondence (Blades and Cooke, 1994), and we suggest that geometric correspondence may develop in phases, with children understanding direction before distance. This would be plausible because direction can be ascertained by reference to an egocentric projective spatial relation (Piaget and Inhelder, 1956) between self and a distal landmark. This is compatible with Uttal's (1996, 2001) findings, and with Leplow *et al.* (2003) who found that children as young as three years of age were able to search for hidden objects and use projective relations to remember their locations.

Meta-representation

This last competency proposed by Liben (1999) takes the understanding of the rules of correspondence from particular types of representations to general principles of spatial representation. This reflects Piaget and Inhelder's (1956) position that mature spatial representation has reference to abstract frames of reference, in two- and three-dimensional geometric space. As we are concerned in this chapter with one domain, aerial photographs, a broader understanding of the purposes of various other representation types does not need to be addressed here, but we mention it to complete the model.

Recent research with aerial photographs

To illustrate the development of these representational competencies by children in pre-school and through the school years, we turn to recent research using aerial photographs. Blades *et al.* (1998) used a variety of aerial photographs with four-year-old children in five countries and found a widespread ability across cultures to 'read' the aerial photographs meaningfully. Representational insight and attribute differentiation were generally in evidence, and we might conclude, from the small number of scale errors and misinterpretations reported, that these young children showed considerable development toward correspondence mastery, to use Liben's (1999) phrase.

In contrast to the small scale, black and white photographs of unfamiliar environments used in some research (e.g. Liben and Downs, 1992), other researchers have attempted to scaffold children's growing competence with the use of more 'friendly' materials. These include the use of larger scale, colour photographs, often of familiar areas, and the results from the use of these materials show the positive effects of these more perceptually salient images.

Blades, Hetherington, Spencer and Sowden (1997) compared four- and five-year-olds' understanding of a vertical photograph with an oblique one, at a scale of 1:1100 and in colour. They reported very few scale errors or misinterpretations, and found that identification of features was improved with the oblique projection. Their second experiment compared children familiar with the referent space with children unfamiliar with the space, and demonstrated that familiarity further improved accuracy. They also reported anecdotal evidence that familiarity was acknowledged explicitly and spontaneously by some of the children, indicating that they understood the photograph to be a representation of not just 'real space', but a particular real space. Blades and Uttal (1999) reported generally good understanding of features, and also reported an effect for the scale of the photograph, because larger scale was associated with marginally more accurate interpretation, and here again, children familiar with the space interpreted the photograph more accurately than those unfamiliar with it. Plester *et al.* (2001) also reported a marginal positive effect of a larger scale photograph.

Blades *et al.* (1997) also investigated children's understanding beyond comprehension of feature correspondences, with a proposed navigation task, asking children to draw a proposed route over the photograph from one place to another, using either a familiar or unfamiliar real space. Children familiar with the space were considerably better at plotting a plausible route. Where the latter work is important for assessing the functional aspects of the children's understanding of representations of familiar and unfamiliar spaces, it falls short of fully assessing the children's pragmatic ability to make use of that understanding in real environments. Simple maps have been used with young children in small spaces, like a room, with some success (e.g. Bluestein and Acredolo, 1979; Liben and Yekel, 1996; Blades and Spencer, 1987b), but children have not been tested for their ability to use aerial photographs. In contrast to these earlier studies, the research we review below considers children in the much larger, perceptually rich referent spaces using aerial photographs as aids to carry out tasks involving navigation, finding hidden objects, and placing objects in the space.

Using aerial photographs to solve problems in the referent space

Plester, Richards, Blades and Spencer (2002) used aerial photographs with four- and five-year-olds to identify features and search for hidden objects in the large spaces of their school playgrounds. These children showed, as Blades and Spencer (1987a) and Blades *et al.* (1998) had found, few misinterpretations or scale errors in reading the photographs, showing clear representational insight, good attribute differentiation, and notable progress toward correspondence mastery.

When searching for the hiding places that were marked on the photographs, the type of hiding place was an important factor in success. Distinctive targets, marked both on photograph and in the real space by proximity to landmarks, required only feature correspondence for success, and almost all of these hiding places were found.

Non-distinctive, marked targets were used near landmarks that needed to be picked out from a set of similar landmarks, such as sets of windows, several similar trees or a line of fence posts. These required both feature correspondence and correspondence of projective spatial relations to other features to disambiguate the correct landmarks. The majority of these targets were found, showing some progress in correspondence mastery, at least with regard to this type of target.

A third type of target was also used, non-distinctive and unmarked in the real space, part of the way along a hedge or solid fence. The targets were indicated only by marks on the photographs, and therefore geometric correspondence was essential to find these targets in the playground. These targets were found less than half of the time, showing that the concept of correspondence mastery was still in need of further development at the ages of four or five.

In a third investigation, Plester et al. (2002) found that the use of an oblique aerial photograph enhanced children's success in finding targets when they later used a map drawn from the photograph. Plester et al. suggested that the greater perceptual iconicity of the photograph enabled easier feature correspondence using the map, and the application of geometric correspondence as needed, making the analogical mapping between representation and referent clearer.

Research described by Plester, Blades and Spencer (2003) used an object placement task, to reduce the extent to which random search could lead to success, and focused on the non-distinctive, unmarked type of target. Children from five to ten years, and adults, were shown an aerial photograph and asked to place an object (a toy dog) in the open space of a large playground, at locations marked by dots on the photograph. These target locations were several metres from any landmark on the ground, so there were no nearby landmarks, only the distal landmarks provided by the peripheral features around the playground.

Plester et al. (2003) found that the use of distal landmarks was demonstrated by children of all ages, and even the youngest children appeared to subdivide the large space by reference to peripheral landmarks as far as forty metres away. There was steady improvement in accuracy of placements with age with children reaching adult levels by eight or nine years of age. This matches reports of an adult-like profile in a variety of spatial tasks by approximately this age (e.g., Leplow

Figure 3.1. A child using an aerial photograph to place a toy dog in a large playground. The location for the dog was marked on an aerial view of the playground, and children were asked to place the toy dog in the playground at the location that corresponded to the one marked on the photograph.

et al., 2003; Choi and Silverman, 2003; Sandberg, 2000; Sandberg, Huttenlocher and Newcombe, 1996).

Accuracy of placements was assessed in terms of both distance and direction measures. These two dimensions resulted in the use of different strategies by different age groups. All participants used distal landmarks (identified from the photograph) to determine direction of approach in the playground, and the accuracy of direction judgments increased gradually with age. In contrast, judgments of distance by the younger children who focused just on one distant landmark were comparatively poor. But many of the older children and adults used two or more landmarks in more than one direction to work out the location of the target and this resulted in more accurate placements.

These results show that even young children have the ability to apply knowledge learnt from an aerial photograph to the environment that it represents. The strategies used to apply this knowledge in a progressively more accurate way develop with age, but children by about eight or nine years of age have achieved a sophisticated understanding of correspondence mastery.

Using toys to represent environmental knowledge

In this section we return to the abilities of the youngest children, who demonstrated some understanding of correspondence. Such an achievement in the absence of any formal teaching or experience begs the question – what sort of environmental experience do young children need before they can start to interpret an aerial photograph?

We can assume that children do, of course, need experience of real environments if they are going to understand aerial photographs. It should go without saying that children need to know what a tree, a road, or a building looks like in a real environment before they can recognize the same features in an aerial photograph. But Blaut and Stea (1974) also made an intriguing suggestion that children may learn about maps and aerial photographs, not just from direct environmental experience, but also from activities like toy play. They argued that by playing with toys and model layouts young children could develop a view of the world as seen from above that might help them understand more formal representations of the world, like maps.

Blaut and Stea (1974) reported that children from three to six years of age used model houses, roads, and other features, to make coherent landscapes. Blaut and Stea took this to mean that young children possessed cognitive maps of relatively large areas, constructed through their experiences. Generic toys cannot represent details of specific neighbourhoods, so we assume that the children's layouts in Blaut and Stea's study reflected general environmental schemata.

However, in contrast to Blaut and Stea's (1974) results from young children, when Dijkink and Elbers (1980) asked older children (seven-year-olds and above) to make model towns the children had difficulty creating coherent representations of an urban landscape. Dijkink and Elbers provided the children with all the necessary elements to make a town (e.g. different types of buildings, shops, houses, roads, railway tracks). But many of the children just spread the items out in an apparently random way and did not create layouts that could be interpreted as a town. Given the contrasting results in previous studies, we carried out a series of experiments with three to six-year-olds in which we asked the children to use toy items to make a model town (Blades, Spencer, Plester and Desmond, 2003).

We found that few of the children, and virtually none of the three- and four-year-olds produced models that could be coded as ones representing the layout of a town. Most of the younger children only placed the toy items in a pile, or just grouped all the houses together, and then all the road pieces and then the other features. In contrast to Blaut and Stea's (1974) results, we did not find any evidence that very young children spontaneously made representations of places. However, as we have noted in the previous sections, children of this age can interpret, and to some extent use, aerial photographs. In other words, the ability to understand aerial photographs precedes children's ability to make representations in toy play. This result does not support Blaut's (1991) suggestion that activities such as toy play and model making contribute to children's ability to interpret aerial photographs and maps. But rather the result does support Uttal's (2000) argument that maps (and photographs) might be one way that children learn about the world.

Conclusions

Young children's understanding of aerial photographs, and their representational competencies have been demonstrated in problem-solving tasks in the large, familiar spaces they inhabit daily. We have seen the development of correspondence mastery, with feature correspondence and then geometric correspondence, including direction; then with distance correspondences, being achieved during the early school years. For this reason we support the practice of aerial photographs being introduced early in school geography and environmental studies courses. Young children's use of aerial photographs in navigational tasks would tap into early perceptual and symbolic competence, and give children the opportunity to develop their mastery of representations through active participation. In turn this will lead to more mature spatial understanding, as Liben (2001), Uttal (2000) and Blaut (1991) have all suggested.

In this chapter we have focused on children's understanding of aerial photographs. Children do, of course, learn about the world not only from direct experience or from aerial photographs, but from any number of different representations of the world – whether these representations are maps, photographs, drawings, television, film or computer games. How young children combine all the knowledge of the world they gain from direct experience of the environment with all the environmental images they receive from secondary sources is still an issue that requires much more investigation.

References

Blades, M. and Cooke, Z. (1994). Young children's ability to understand a model as a spatial representation. *Journal of Genetic Psychology, 155*, 201–18.

Blades, M. and Spencer, C. (1987a). Young children's recognition of environmental features from aerial photographs and maps. *Environmental Education and Information, 6*, 189–98.

Blades, M. and Spencer, C. (1987b). The use of maps by 4–6-year-old children in a large-scale maze. *British Journal of Developmental Psychology, 5*, 19–24.

Blades, M. and Uttal, D. H. (1999). The development of children's understanding of aerial photographs. *Paper presented to Society for Research in Child Development Biennial Meeting*, Albuquerque, New Mexico, April 1999.

Blades, M., Hetherington, D., Spencer, C. and Sowden, S. (1997). Can young children recognize aerial photographs? *Paper presented to Society for Research in Child Development Biennial Meeting*, Washington, DC, April 1997.

Blades, M., Spencer, C., Plester, B. and Desmond, K. (2003). Young children's recognition and representation of urban landscapes: From aerial photographs and in toy play. In G. Allen (ed.), *Human Spatial Memory: Remembering Where*. Mahway, NJ: Erlbaum.

Blades, M., Blaut, J. M., Darvizeh Z., Elguea, S., Sowden, S., Soni, D., Spencer, C., Stea, D., Surajpaul, R. and Uttal, D. (1998). A cross-cultural study of young children's mapping abilities. *Transactions of the Institute of British Geographers, 23*, 269–77.

Blaut, J. M. (1991). Natural mapping. *Transactions of the Institute of British Geographers, 16*, 55–74.

Blaut, J. M. (1997). The mapping abilities of young children: Children can. *Annals of the Association of American Geographers, 87*, 152–8.

Blaut, J. M. and Stea, D. (1974). Mapping at the age of three. *Journal of Geography, 73*, 5–9.

Blaut, J. M., McCleary, G. S. and Blaut, A. S. (1970). Environmental mapping in young children. *Environment and Behavior, 2*, 335–49.

Bluestein, N. and Acredolo, L. (1979). Developmental changes in map reading skills. *Child Development, 50*, 691–7.

Choi, J. and Silverman, I. (2003). Processes underlying sex differences in route-learning strategies in children and adolescents. *Personality and Individual Differences, 34*(7), 1153–66.

DeLoache, J. S. (1989). The development of representation in young children. *Advances in Child Development and Behaviour, 22*, 1–39.

DeLoache, J. S. (1995). Early symbol understanding and use. *The Psychology of Learning and Motivation, 33*, 65–114.

DeLoache, J. S. (2000). Dual representation and young children's use of scale models. *Child Development, 71*, 329–38.

DeLoache, J. S. (2002). Early development of the understanding and use of symbolic artefacts. In *Handbook of Childhood Cognitive Development*. Oxford: Blackwell.

DeLoache, J. S., Strauss, M. S. and Maynard, J. (1979). Picture perception in infancy. *Infant Behaviour and Development, 2*, 77–89.

Dijkink, G. and Elbers, E. (1980). The development of geographic representation in children. Cognitive and affective aspects of model-building behaviour. *Tijdschrift voor Economische en Sociale Geografie, 72,* 2–16.

Gopnik, A. and Rosati, A. (2001). Duck or rabbit? Reversing ambiguous figures and understanding ambiguous representations. *Developmental Science, 4(2),* 175–83.

Huttenlocher, J., Hedges, L. V. and Duncan, S. (1991). Categories and particulars: Prototype effects in estimating spatial location. *Psychological Review, 98,* 352–76.

Leplow, B., Lehnung, M., Pohl, J., Herzog, A., Fersti, R. and Mehdorn, M. (2003). Navigational place learning in children and young adults as assessed with a standardized locomotor search task. *British Journal of Psychology, 94* (3), 299–317.

Liben, L. S. (1999). Developing an understanding of external spatial representations. In I. E. Sigel (ed.), *Development of Mental Representation.* Mahwah, NJ: LEA.

Liben, L. S. (2001). Thinking through maps. In M. Gattis (ed.), *Spatial Schemas and Abstract Thought.* Boston: MIT.

Liben, L. S. (2002). Spatial development in childhood: Where are we now? In U. Goswami (ed.), *Handbook of Childhood Cognitive Development.* Oxford: Blackwell.

Liben, L. S. and Downs, R. M. (1989). Understanding maps as symbols: The development of map concepts in children. *Advances in Child Development and Behaviour, 22,* 145–201.

Liben, L. S. and Downs, R. M. (1992). Developing an understanding of graphic representations in children and adults: The case of GEO-graphics. *Cognitive Development, 7,* 331–49.

Liben, L. S. and Downs, R. M. (1997). Can-ism and can'tianism: A straw child. *Annals of the Association of American Geographers, 87,* 159–67.

Liben, L. S. and Yekel, C. A. (1996). Preschoolers' understanding of plan and oblique maps: The role of geometric and representational correspondence. *Child Development, 67,* 2780–96.

Muir, M. and Blaut, J. (1969). The use of aerial photographs in teaching mapping to children in the first grade: An experimental study. *The Minnesota Geographer, 22,* 4–19.

Newcombe, N. S. and Huttenlocher, J. (2000). *Making Space.* London: MIT.

Piaget, J. and Inhelder, B. (1956). *The Child's Conception of Space.* London: Routledge.

Plester, B., Blades, M. and Spencer, C. (2003). Children's understanding of aerial photographs. *Children's Geographies, 1(2),* 281–93.

Plester, B., Richards, J. and Howard, J. (2001). Aerial photographs as treasure maps: Four studies for four- and five-year-olds. *Poster presentation at the Biennial Meeting of the Society for Research in Child Development,* Minneapolis, MN, April, 2001.

Plester, B., Richards, J., Blades, M. and Spencer, C. (2002). Young children's ability to use aerial photographs as maps. *Journal of Environmental Psychology, 22,* 29–47.

Sandberg, E. H. (2000). Cognitive constraints on the development of hierarchical spatial organization skills. *Cognitive Development, 14,* 597–619.
Sandberg, E. H., Huttenlocher, J. and Newcombe, N. (1996). The development
of hierarchical representation of two-dimensional space. *Child Development,
67,* 721–39.
Spencer, C., Harrison, N. and Darvizeh, Z. (1980). The development of iconic
mapping ability in young children. *International Journal of Early Childhood,
12,* 57–64.
Stea, D. and Blaut, J. M. (1973). Some preliminary observations on spatial
learning in school children. In R. M. Downs and D. Stea (eds.), *Image
and Environment: Cognitive Mapping and Spatial Behavior.* Chicago: Aldine.
Uttal, D. H. (1996). Angles and distances: children's and adults' reconstruction
and scaling of spatial configurations. *Child Development, 67,* 2763–79.
Uttal, D. H. (2000). Seeing the big picture: Map use and the development of
spatial cognition. *Developmental Science, 3,* 247–86.
Uttal, D. H. (2001). Scaling and relational thinking in five-year-olds' reconstructions of spatial configurations. *Paper presented to Society for Research in Child
Development Biennial Meeting,* Minneapolis, MN, April 2001.

4 Children's knowledge of countries

Martyn Barrett, Evanthia Lyons and Alison Bourchier-Sutton

In this chapter, we review the research literature on children's geographical knowledge about countries. During the course of their development, children acquire a large body of knowledge about countries: they learn about the existence, location, size and shape of many different countries, they learn about the natural and man-made features (e. g. mountain ranges, rivers, coastlines, cities, etc.) which characterize some of these countries, and they learn about some of these countries' climates and their flora and fauna. This chapter reviews the research which has been conducted into children's acquisition of such knowledge. We begin by discussing children's knowledge of the geography of their own country.

Children's knowledge of their own country

Piagetian research

Piaget (1928; Piaget and Weil, 1951) was the first researcher to conduct research in this field. His investigations, conducted with four to fifteen-year-old Swiss Genevan children, led him to propose that children's large-scale geographical knowledge exhibited three stages of development (following a pre-stage of ignorance before five years of age). The first stage lasted from five to seven–eight years of age: between these ages, Piaget and Weil found that children were able to name their own country, and were able to state when questioned verbally that the city in which they lived was located within this country. However, these children were unable to depict the correct spatial inclusion relationship between the city and the country in their drawings (typically drawing them side by side, rather than one within the other), and failed to understand the conceptual inclusion relationship that they themselves were simultaneously both Genevese and Swiss. Piaget and Weil proposed that stage 2 lasted from seven–eight to ten–eleven years of age. Between these ages, the children fully understood the

57

spatial-geographical relationship between their own city and country, and were able to express this relationship both verbally and in their drawings. However, they still denied that they themselves were both Genevese and Swiss. Finally, Piaget and Weil postulated that stage 3 began at ten–eleven years of age; this represented a mature level of understanding, as the children now grasped both the spatial inclusion relationship and the conceptual inclusion relationship between being Genevese and Swiss.

There are a number of aspects of this account which make it compatible with Piagetian stage theory. For example, the changes at age seven–eight coincide with the transition to concrete operational understanding, while the changes at age ten–eleven coincide with the transition to formal operational understanding. However, subsequent research by Jahoda (1963, 1964) has shown that Piaget and Weil's description of children's development is over-schematized and neglects much of the individual variation in development which actually occurs in practice.

In his study, Jahoda interviewed Glaswegian Scottish children aged between six and eleven years old. The children were asked a range of questions about Glasgow, Scotland and Britain. In addition, the children were given a construction task, in which rectangular pieces of plastic were used to represent Scotland, England and Britain, and a disc to represent Glasgow; the children were asked to assemble these units correctly in relationship to each other. Jahoda found four stages of spatial-geographical understanding. In the first stage, the children had no conception of Glasgow as a unitary whole. Instead, the children thought of it as some vague entity nearby. In the second stage, the children had a conception of Glasgow as the city in which they lived, but no conception of this city as being spatially included within Scotland. In the third stage, the children had a conception of Glasgow as being spatially included within Scotland, but had no conception of Scotland as being spatially included within Britain. Finally, in stage 4, children understood the full spatial-geographical relationship between Glasgow, Scotland and Britain.

Although Jahoda found all four stages were exhibited by the children in his sample, he discovered that these stages were not linked to particular ages. For example, the six–seven-year-olds were distributed across all four stages of development, while the ten–eleven-year-olds were distributed across the second, third and fourth stages. Contrary to the claims of Piaget and Weil, then, spatial-geographical understanding is not related clearly to age *per se*. However, Jahoda did find that there was a greater probability of older children exhibiting higher stages of development than younger children. In addition, there was a social class difference: middle class children were more likely to exhibit higher stages of development than working class children.

As part of the interview, Jahoda also asked the children whether they were Scottish, and whether they were British. Jahoda found that about a quarter of the children showed understanding of the conceptual inclusion relationship between being Scottish and being British, without showing any understanding of the spatial-geographical inclusion relationship between Scotland and Britain. According to Piaget and Weil, this pattern should not occur, because concrete spatial understanding is always acquired before the more abstract conceptual understanding. Jahoda (1964) concluded that Piaget and Weil's account oversimplifies the actual complexities of the developmental process.

Although Jahoda's study undermines the credibility of the specifics of Piaget and Weil's description, more recently other researchers have proposed that a discontinuity does nevertheless occur in the development of children's large-scale geographical knowledge at about the age of seven when they make the transition from pre-operational to concrete operational understanding. These researchers are therefore arguing for a more general Piagetian position, namely that children's geographical understanding is dependent upon their domain-general cognitive capabilities.

One such researcher is Piché (1981). She examined five to eight-year-old London children's large-scale geographical knowledge. She found that the youngest children construed geographical places in terms of their own personal activities, as the individual locations where things happen, rather than within an integrated geographical frame of reference. At a slightly later age, the children began to name places, and to describe them in terms of their more general use, but these young children were still unable to integrate these places into a coherent framework. When the transition to concrete operations commenced, however, continuity of the land finally began to be conceptualized, and the children at last started to construct place hierarchies such as home-London-England. At the same time, they conceptualized the continuity of the land in terms of travel times. Piché argued that the children's geographical representations only became properly integrated at about eight years of age, with the full achievement of concrete operational understanding, when the children finally became able to tackle complex mapping problems and analytical questions.

Other studies have confirmed that at least some aspects of children's understanding of the geography of their own country are linked to the acquisition of concrete operational thinking. For example, Downs, Liben and Daggs (1988) and Wilberg (2002) both report studies which examined young children's understanding of spatial-geographical inclusion relationships (e.g. between the child's own city and country) and their performance on Piagetian concrete operational tasks. Both studies found that the children's geographical understanding was correlated with performance on class inclusion tasks, and Downs *et al.* also found that such understanding was correlated with performance on a transitive reasoning task. In other words, the development of children's understanding of geographical inclusion relationships does appear to be related to the development of their general cognitive capabilities between four and eight years of age.

Post-Piagetian research on children's knowledge of their own country

Gould (1973) pursued a different approach, using the notion of mental maps. He examined the mental maps of Sweden which were held by seven-, nine-, eleven- and thirteen-year-old Swedish children. These children lived in the town of Jönköping in the centre of southern Sweden between the cities of Stockholm, Göteberg and Malmö. The children were asked to write down, in exactly five minutes, the names of all the villages, towns and cities in Sweden which they could remember. Gould found that at the age of seven, information was at a very low level, with the children only knowing about Jönköping itself and, to a lesser extent, Stockholm, Göteberg and Malmö. At the age of nine, local knowledge was still the most prominent, supplemented by lesser knowledge of the three major cities. However, between these cities and Jönköping, a filling-in process had begun to occur, with some knowledge about intermediate locations having been acquired. The children had also begun to exhibit some knowledge about the island of Öland, one of the main holiday resorts for families in southern Sweden, and about some of the locations between Jönköping and Öland. However, the children still exhibited very little knowledge about the north of the country, with only a few children exhibiting any knowledge of Umeå (the northern capital). By eleven years of age, the filling-in process had continued further, with the children having acquired more knowledge of the north, although middle Sweden still remained a blank. Finally, by the age of thirteen, some additional infilling of information had taken place, although Gould notes that some sort of saturation level was being reached by this age. Thus, the overall developmental process appears to be one in which information about the child's own local area and larger national cities is first acquired, and then, gradually, information about intermediate locations is acquired which links these initial nodes up into a more coherent mental map. Gould found that the amount of information which children held about a location was a function of the size of the population of that location coupled to its distance away from Jönköping, with holiday regions and locations receiving heavy attention in the media forming the main exceptions.

Nugent (1994) also examined the representations which children held of their own country. He tested a slightly older range of children than Gould, asking ten-, twelve-, fourteen- and sixteen-year-old Irish children to write down their thoughts and feelings about Ireland. The ten-, twelve- and many fourteen-year-olds produced descriptions of Ireland largely in terms of its man-made places, its natural physical geography, and its flora and fauna. However, there was a notable shift in the contents of the children's narratives between fourteen and sixteen years, with the sixteen-year-olds instead producing descriptions in terms of Ireland's history, culture, traditions, and the Irish 'personality', and way of life. Nugent also examined the types of emotional attachments to their country which had been expressed by the children in their narratives. He found that the ten-year-olds tended to display unilaterally positive and unqualified attachments to Ireland's geographical features. However, the twelve- and fourteen-year-olds were more defensive in their attitudes, tending to compare Ireland with other countries and arguing for its comparative superiority. The sixteen-year-olds, by contrast, tended to recognize the value of Ireland being unique as opposed to being the 'best'. This study therefore suggests that there may be a shift in the way in which children spontaneously think and feel about their own country round about fifteen years of age.

Possible links between children's geographical knowledge of their own country and their levels of national identification were examined more directly by Barrett and Whennell (1998). They measured five to eleven-year-old English children's knowledge of the geography of the UK (including knowledge of cities, regions, surrounding seas, rivers and islands) and the children's strength of national identification. They found that the children's degree of identification with being British (i.e., whether the child felt very, a little bit or not at all British) was positively correlated with factual geographical knowledge of the UK. Barrett and Davey (2001) tested five to ten-year-old English children, looking at the relationship between these children's ability to differentiate between photographs of typically English versus non-English landscapes and their strength of national identification. They found that the

children's strength of national identification (both their degree of identification with being English, and the importance which they attributed
to being English) was positively correlated with their ability to differentiate between the two sets of photographs. The findings of these two
studies therefore suggest that there is a relationship between children's
geographical knowledge of their own country and their strength of
national identification. We will return to the issue of the relationship
between knowledge and affect in the geographical domain later on,
but first we will look at the research which has been conducted into
children's knowledge of foreign countries.

Children's knowledge of foreign countries

The studies by Jahoda and Wiegand

In an early study, Jahoda (1962) asked six to eleven-year-old Glaswegian
Scottish children to name any foreign countries which they had heard
about. He found that there was a significant increase in the number of
countries which were named by the children at eight years of age.
Amongst the six to seven-year-olds, 42 per cent of the children could
not name a single foreign country even after they had been given an
example, and only 10 per cent could name more than five foreign
countries in total. By comparison, only 10 per cent of the eight to
nine-year-olds could not name a single foreign country, and 50 per cent
of these older children could name more than five other countries (the
corresponding figures amongst the ten to eleven-year-olds were 2 per
cent and 71 per cent).

After having named these foreign countries, the children were asked
to say which countries they liked best and which, if any, they disliked.
Jahoda found that at six–seven years of age, preferences were based
upon either the appeal of the unusual and the exotic or the presence
of relatives in a country. At eight–nine years of age, the children typically liked more familiar countries most (i.e. holiday destinations and
America), and these preferences tended to be justified by reference to
stereotypical images of the distinctive physical features of those countries (e.g. sun, snow, skyscrapers, etc.). At ten–eleven years of age,
preferences were justified in terms of the positively evaluated characteristics of the population or of the country itself. Although a significant minority of the children did not express any dislikes, amongst
those who did, Germany was singled out for particular dislike because
of past wars. Finally, Jahoda found that the middle class children

were more advanced in their geographical knowledge and in their patterns of reasoning about other countries than working class children, at all ages.

More recently, Wiegand (1991a, 1995) has conducted two studies examining English children's knowledge of foreign countries. In the first study (Wiegand, 1991a), two groups of children, aged seven–eight and ten–eleven years old, were tested; the sample included both middle class and working class children, as well as both ethnic majority and ethnic minority (Indian and Pakistani) children. The children were asked to write down the names of all the foreign countries they knew, and then to circle the names of the places they had visited. The children's travel experiences were followed up in interviews. Consistent with the findings of Jahoda (1962), the seven to eight-year-olds were able to name about five or six countries. By contrast, the ten to eleven-year-olds were able to name fifteen different countries on average. In addition to these age-related differences, Wiegand found both social class and ethnic group differences in the children's knowledge. The working class children named only half the number of countries that were named by the middle class children, while the children of Indian and Pakistani ethnicity exhibited more extensive knowledge of the Indian subcontinent, the Middle East and Africa, and less knowledge of Western Europe, compared with their white English peers. These children of South Asian origin often had substantial travel experience, with one third of them having been to India or Pakistan for six–twelve weeks; however, relatively few of the Asian children had been to other Western European countries. Amongst the white children, only the middle class children had travelled abroad, with over half of these children having been to France and Spain, and a large minority having also been to the USA.

In a subsequent study, Wiegand (1995) examined English children's knowledge of foreign countries using drawings (rather than verbal methods). He asked four to eleven-year-olds to draw a map of the world. Not surprisingly, the quality of the maps improved with age. The youngest children tended to draw equal-sized individual circles randomly scattered across the page to represent countries, with the names of the countries written inside them. As the children got older, countries began to acquire distinctive shapes and sizes, and the maps tended to become better organized. Rudimentary knowledge of the distinctive shapes of countries, and of the correct spatial locations of countries relative to one another, were only really displayed from about eight–nine years of age onwards. The most capable of the ten to eleven-year-old children produced maps which were highly accurate in their attention to shapes, locations and names (albeit with many omissions).

Social group differences in children's knowledge of other countries, and the factors which are responsible for these differences

Both Jahoda and Wiegand found differences in children's geographical knowledge of foreign countries not only as a function of age but also as a function of social class and, in the case of Wiegand's study, ethnicity as well. Other investigations have confirmed the existence of systematic differences in children's knowledge of foreign countries as a function of age (with older children displaying more knowledge than younger children: Axia, Bremner, Deluca and Andreasen, 1998; Barrett, 1996; Barrett and Farroni, 1996; Barrett, Lyons, Purkhardt and Bourchier, 1996), social class (with middle class children exhibiting more knowledge than working class children: Barrett et al., 1996; Rutland, 1998), gender (with boys exhibiting more knowledge of other countries than girls: Barrett, 1996; Barrett and Farroni, 1996; Barrett et al., 1996), nationality (with British children exhibiting less knowledge of other countries than either Italian or Dutch children: Axia and Bremner, 1992; Axia et al., 1998; Barrett and Farroni, 1996; Jahoda and Woerdenbagch, 1982), and the child's own geographical location within the nation (with, for example, urban metropolitan children exhibiting higher levels of knowledge than rural children: Barrett et al., 1996; see also Axia et al., 1998, who found differences between northern and southern Italian children). These social group differences in children's knowledge of other countries probably stem from children's differential exposure to information about other countries through personal travel experience, the school curriculum, and the mass media, especially television.

The evidence pertaining to children's travel experience is actually somewhat mixed. For example, Moss and Blades (1994), Barrett (1996), Barrett and Farroni (1996) and Bourchier, Barrett and Lyons (2002) all failed to find evidence of consistent relationships between geographical knowledge of foreign countries and children's travel experience. However, Barrett et al. (1996), who tested English six to thirteen-year-olds, did find significant correlations between levels of travel experience and the children's geographical knowledge of Europe (including their knowledge of countries, cities, mountains, rivers and seas). They also found that older children, middle class children and urban children had had more extensive travel experience than younger children, working class children and rural children, respectively.

Consequently, the systematic differences in geographical knowledge which were found in this study as a function of age, social class and location are likely to have been, at least partially, a consequence of the enhanced travel experience of the former groups of children over the latter groups. Similarly, Wiegand (1991b) tested nine to eleven-year-old English children, and found that children who had travelled to India or Spain were able to provide much more detailed and diverse descriptions of these countries (including their climates, fauna, buildings, modes of transport, etc.) than children who had not visited them. Rutland (1998) also found correlations between travel experience and geographical knowledge in a group of six to sixteen-year-old English children.

As far as the effects of schooling on levels of geographical knowledge are concerned, Axia *et al.* (1998) found clear effects of formal educational instruction upon children's knowledge of other countries: ten-year-olds who had received formal instruction about Europe were able to draw more detailed and more accurate maps of Europe than ten-year-olds who had not. The fact that educational instruction does impact upon levels of knowledge may at least partially explain the existence of cross-national differences in levels of knowledge about other countries, as different nations operate different educational curricula and practices. In the case of Italy versus England, for example, the studies of Axia and Bremner (1992), Barrett and Farroni (1996), and Axia *et al.* (1998) all found that (northern) Italian children had higher levels of knowledge than English children. When these studies were conducted in the 1990s, different educational curricula were in place in these two countries. In England, the National Curriculum in Geography (Department of Education and Science, 1991) only required eleven-year-old English children to know the names of four European countries outside the British Isles, namely Spain, France, Germany, and Italy. By contrast, in Italy, the National Curriculum for Elementary Schools (Laeng, 1985) specified that ten to eleven-year-olds must learn about all of the countries of Europe and about their geographical, economic, political and social relationships with each other. It is therefore not surprising that the Italian children exhibited higher levels of knowledge than their English peers.

However, children do not only acquire their knowledge about other countries at school from formal teaching delivered through the curriculum. Stillwell and Spencer (1973) looked at nine-year-old English children's uptake of information about other countries from classroom posters and wall charts. They assessed children's knowledge about other countries, using interviewing, both before and after mounting displays of information about other countries on classroom walls for a period of one week. They found that the children acquired factual information from this incidental source without any explicit teaching.

The mass media (television, comics, magazines, books, etc.) are further sources of information which impact upon children's knowledge of other countries. There has been comparatively little research into this topic, but an intriguing study was conducted by Holloway and Valentine (2000). They asked British and New Zealand children to email each other with their impressions of the other country. They found that the children had picked up many aspects of their images of the other country from the mass media, particularly from television programmes and especially from soap operas. For example, the New Zealand children drew heavily upon 'Coronation Street' (a British soap opera which many of the New Zealand children said their mothers watched) to generate their impressions of Britain. The British children, however, did not have access to many media images of New Zealand, and they (mistakenly) drew upon and generalized from images of Australia instead, which are accessible in Britain through soap operas such as 'Neighbours' and 'Home and Away' and films such as 'Crocodile Dundee'.

Exposure to information about other countries through travel experience, schooling and the mass media is, of course, linked to precisely those social group memberships by which geographical knowledge has been found to vary in children. For example, travel experience varies according to children's social class (with more affluent middle class children travelling to other countries more frequently than working class children), ethnicity (with ethnic minority and majority group children travelling to different destinations abroad), and age (with older children having visited more countries than younger children). Schooling also varies according to children's age, nationality and social class, and sometimes their ethnicity as well (for example, in the case of children who attend faith schools). Finally, the programmes and the advertisements which children watch on television, and the comics, magazines and books which they read, also vary according to children's age, gender, nationality, ethnicity and social class. It is therefore not surprising to find that systematic differences arise in children's levels of knowledge about other countries as a function of these factors.

Children's feelings about foreign countries

Children's acquisition of geographical knowledge about foreign countries is often accompanied by the acquisition of strong feelings about those countries. The studies which have investigated this issue have employed a variety of measures to assess children's feelings, including verbal interviewing, rating scales and paired comparisons. As we have seen already, Jahoda (1962) used interviewing, and found that, before the age of eight, Scottish children expressed positive feelings for distant countries which were picturesque and exotic, or for countries where they had relatives; however, from the age of eight onwards, the children tended to like familiar countries more than unfamiliar ones, justifying their feelings by reference to stereotyped images of those countries. Recall, too, that Jahoda found that, at *all* ages, many of these Scottish children exhibited negative feelings towards Germany, a past 'enemy' nation. The same finding was obtained by Johnson (1966, 1973), who used a rating scale rather than interviewing to assess eight to ten-year-old English children's feelings about other countries. Johnson found that these children held negative feelings towards Germany, Japan and Russia. He additionally found that children who were regular readers of war comics liked the 'enemy' countries of Germany, Japan and Italy less, but liked the Allied countries of England, America, Australia and France more, than children who did not read these comics.

Johnson *et al.* (1970; Middleton *et al.*, 1970) also assessed the feelings of English seven-, nine- and eleven-year-olds towards a large number of countries. They found that, when mean ratings were considered, at all ages the children rated their own home country, England, more positively than any other country; furthermore, this preference for England strengthened with age. A mean preference for the home country at all ages was also found by Jaspers *et al.* (1972), who used a method of paired comparisons to assess seven to eleven-year-old Dutch children's relative degree of liking of different countries. These children also showed a significant increase in the degree of their preference for their own home country with age. However, conducting a more fine-grained analysis of the English data, Middleton *et al.* (1970) found that only 22 per cent of the seven-year-olds, 44 per cent of the nine-year-olds, and 56 per cent of the eleven-year-olds individually rated England higher than *all* other countries. In other words, while there often appears to be an overall mean preference for the home country over other countries from seven years of age onwards, and this preference seems to strengthen through middle childhood, many individual children may nevertheless continue to rate some other countries just as positively, if not more positively, than their own home country.

The fact that children can exhibit strong emotional responses to other countries at the same time as they are acquiring factual knowledge about those countries raises the possibility that there may be a relationship between children's affect and knowledge acquisition here.

For example, strong positive affect for a country might motivate the child to seek out factual information about that country, while strong negative affect might motivate the child to avoid such information. Alternatively, the causality might run in the opposite direction: children might come to like some countries more than others because they know more about them.

Early studies (e.g. Tajfel, 1966) suggested that children sometimes have very little knowledge of those countries about which they express negative feelings. Stillwell and Spencer (1973) also found a linear relationship between knowledge and affect in a group of nine-year-old English children. Using a test of factual knowledge, and a rating scale to measure affect, they found that children knew the most about countries which they liked, knew less about neutral countries, and knew least of all about disliked countries. However, Johnson *et al.* (1970), who investigated this issue using similar methods to Stillwell and Spencer, obtained different results with a group of seven to eleven-year-old English children. They found a curvilinear rather than a linear relationship between knowledge and affect: the children knew most about the countries they liked; they knew less about countries they disliked; however, the children knew least of all about the countries about which they felt neutrally.

Three more recent studies have also investigated this issue. In one study, Giménez *et al.* (1997) failed to find any consistent relationship between affect for individual countries and geographical knowledge about those countries in a sample of six to fifteen-year-old Spanish children. In a larger cross-national study involving 1,700 British, Spanish, and Italian six to fifteen-year-olds, Barrett *et al.* (1997) found, in the sample as a whole, small but statistically significant linear (not curvilinear) relationships between children's liking of, and geographical knowledge about, Britain, Spain and Italy (correlations ranged from 0.12 to 0.17), but found no significant relationship between affect towards and geographical knowledge about either Germany or France. However, in the most detailed study of this issue to date, Bourchier *et al.* (2002) failed to find any relationships at all between knowledge of, and affect towards, foreign countries. A notable feature of this study was that it employed multiple regression rather than differences in mean knowledge for liked versus neutral versus disliked countries (used by Johnson *et al.*, 1970, and Stillwell and Spencer, 1973) or simple bivariate analysis (used by Barrett *et al.*, 1997). Bourchier *et al.* found that, although significant bivariate correlations sometimes occurred between affect and factual geographical knowledge in the case of some specific countries, these correlations disappeared when these variables' covariance with other variables was controlled. Thus, this study suggests that there is no direct relationship between the amount of factual knowledge which children acquire about particular countries and the affect which those children display towards those countries.

Conclusions

From this review, it is apparent that children start to acquire geographical knowledge about their own country by the age of five. Knowledge of other countries starts to be acquired at a slightly later age, with a significant increase in such knowledge at about eight years of age. The organization of children's large-scale geographical knowledge is related to their general cognitive capabilities, and the overall developmental process appears to be one in which information about salient places is first acquired on an item-by-item basis, followed by the subsequent integration of this information into a more coherent mental map as further information is acquired and as the child's cognitive capacities develop. However, in addition, children's knowledge of foreign countries varies according to their social class, gender, ethnicity, nationality and geographical location within the nation. These social group differences are almost certainly a consequence of the differential exposure to information about foreign countries which occurs across different social groups through personal travel, the school curriculum and the mass media. Children's knowledge of their own home country is related to their strength of national identification (although the direction of the causality here remains ambiguous), while their knowledge of foreign countries does not appear to be systematically related to their feelings about those countries.

However, the studies which have been conducted in this area have differed in terms of the specific measures which have been used. Furthermore, with a few exceptions, the children who have been tested to date have tended to consist of *ad hoc* opportunity samples of children living in the local vicinity of the individual researcher. There is clearly a need for more systematic research to be conducted in this field, to assess the generality of the findings which have been obtained to date, to elucidate the full range of factors which can impact upon children's development in this domain, and to determine the details of the underlying psychological processes which are responsible for children's large-scale geographical knowledge acquisition.[1]

Note

1 For a more extensive discussion of the issues which have been covered in this chapter, see Barrett (in press).

References

Axia, G. and Bremner, J. G. (1992). Children's understanding of Europe: British and Italian points of view. Paper presented at the Fifth European Conference on Developmental Psychology, Seville, Spain, September 1992.

Axia, G., Bremner, J. G., Deluca, P. and Andreasen, G. (1998). Children drawing Europe: The effects of nationality, age and teaching. *British Journal of Developmental Psychology, 16,* 423–37.

Barrett, M. (1996). English children's acquisition of a European identity. In G. Breakwell and E. Lyons (eds.), *Changing European Identities: Social Psychological Analyses of Social Change* (pp. 349–69). Oxford: Butterworth-Heinemann.

Barrett, M. (in press). *Children's Knowledge, Beliefs and Feelings about Nations and National Groups.* Hove, UK: Psychology Press.

Barrett, M. and Davey, K. (2001). English children's sense of national identity and their attachment to national geography. Unpublished paper, Department of Psychology, University of Surrey.

Barrett, M. and Farroni, T. (1996). English and Italian children's knowledge of European geography. *British Journal of Developmental Psychology, 14,* 257–73.

Barrett, M., Lyons, E., Bennett, M., Vila, I., Giménez, A., Arcuri, L. and de Rosa, A. S. (1997). Children's beliefs and feelings about their own and other national groups in Europe. Final Report to the Commission of the European Communities, Directorate-General XII for Science, Research and Development, Human Capital and Mobility (HCM) Programme, Research Network No. CHRX-CT94–0687.

Barrett, M., Lyons, E., Purkhardt, C. and Bourchier, A. (1996). *English children's representations of European geography.* End of Award Report to ESRC, Research Grant No. R000235753. Guildford: University of Surrey.

Barrett, M. and Whennell, S. (1998). The relationship between national identity and geographical knowledge in English children. Poster presented at XVth Biennial Meeting of ISSBD, Berne, Switzerland.

Bourchier, A., Barrett, M. and Lyons, E. (2002). The predictors of children's geographical knowledge of other countries. *Journal of Environmental Psychology, 22,* 79–94.

Department of Education and Science (1991). *Geography in the National Curriculum.* London: HMSO.

Downs, R. M., Liben, L. S. and Daggs, D. G. (1988). On education and geographers: The role of cognitive developmental theory in geographic education. *Annals of the Association of American Geographers, 78,* 680–700.

Giménez, A., Belmonte, L., Garcia-Claros, E., Suarez, E. and Barrett, M. (1997). Acquisition of geographical knowledge. Poster presented at the 7th European Conference for Research on Learning and Instruction, Athens, Greece, August 1997.

Gould, P. R. (1973). The black boxes of Jönköping: Spatial information and preference. In R. M. Downs and D. Stea (eds.), *Image and Environment: Cognitive Mapping and Spatial Behaviour* (pp. 235–45). Chicago: Aldine.

Holloway, S. L. and Valentine, G. (2000). Corked hats and Coronation Street: British and New Zealand children's imaginative geographies of the other. *Childhood*, 7, 335–57.

Jahoda, G. (1962). Development of Scottish children's ideas and attitudes about other countries. *Journal of Social Psychology*, 58, 91–108.

Jahoda, G. (1963). The development of children's ideas about country and nationality, Part I: The conceptual framework. *British Journal of Educational Psychology*, 33, 47–60.

Jahoda, G. (1964). Children's concepts of nationality: A critical study of Piaget's stages. *Child Development*, 35, 1081–92.

Jahoda, G. and Woerdenbagch, A. (1982). Awareness of supra-national groupings among Dutch and Scottish children and adolescents. *European Journal of Political Research*, 10, 305–12.

Jaspers, J. M. F., van de Geer, J. P., Tajfel, H. and Johnson, N. (1972). On the development of national attitudes in children. *European Journal of Social Psychology*, 2, 347–69.

Johnson, N. (1966). What do children learn from war comics? *New Society*, 8, 7–12.

Johnson, N. (1973). Development of English children's concept of Germany. *Journal of Social Psychology*, 90, 259–67.

Johnson, N., Middleton, M. and Tajfel, H. (1970). The relationship between children's preferences for and knowledge about other nations. *British Journal of Social and Clinical Psychology*, 9, 232–40.

Laeng, M. (ed.) (1985). I Nuovi Programmi della Scuola Elementare (3rd edition). Rome: Giunti and Lisciani.

Middleton, M., Tajfel, H. and Johnson, N. (1970). Cognitive and affective aspects of children's national attitudes. *British Journal of Social and Clinical Psychology*, 9, 122–34.

Moss, N. and Blades, M. (1994). Travel doesn't broaden the mind. Poster presented at the Annual Conference of the Developmental Section of the British Psychological Society, Portsmouth, September 1994.

Nugent, J. K. (1994). The development of children's relationships with their country. *Children's Environments*, 11, 281–91.

Piaget, J. (1928). *Judgment and Reasoning in the Child*. London: Routledge and Kegan Paul.

Piaget, J. and Weil, A. M. (1951). The development in children of the idea of the homeland and of relations to other countries. *International Social Science Journal*, 3, 561–78.

Piché, D. (1981). The spontaneous geography of the urban child. In D. T. Herbert and R. J. Johnston (eds.), *Geography and the Urban Environment: Progress in Research and Applications*, vol. IV (pp. 229–56). Chichester: John Wiley.

Rutland, A. (1998). English children's geo-political knowledge of Europe. *British Journal of Developmental Psychology*, 16, 439–45.

Stillwell, R. and Spencer, C. (1973). Children's early preferences for other nations and their subsequent acquisition of knowledge about those nations. *European Journal of Social Psychology*, 3, 345–9.

Tajfel, H. (1966). Children and foreigners. *New Society*, *7*, 9–11.
Wiegand, P. (1991a). The 'known world' of primary school children. *Geography*, *76*, 143–9.
Wiegand, P. (1991b). Does travel broaden the mind? *Education*, *3*, 54–8.
Wiegand, P. (1995). Young children's freehand sketch maps of the world. *International Research in Geographical and Environmental Education*, *4*, 19–28.
Wilberg, S. (2002). Preschoolers' cognitive representations of their homeland. *British Journal of Developmental Psychology*, *20*, 157–69.

Part II

Children's experience of places

5 Learning neighbourhood environments: the loss of experience in a modern world

Antonella Rissotto and M. Vittoria Giuliani

Maria loves cakes. She can always tell you which local cake shop has the freshest whipped cream, the richest cheese cake, the vanilla slice which melts in your mouth or the lightest puff pastry. She also knows which of these shops is nearest to home and which is furthest away, yet she can't explain to her friend, who lives in another part of the town, which of them would be her nearest cake shop.

Anna often takes her dog for a walk and she likes to let him wander off the lead. On one of their walks she discovered a car-free track between two rows of houses: an excellent shortcut for walking to school.

It's always David who decides where he and his friends will play football in their neighbourhood: he not only knows where, but also when to play so that the neighbours don't complain about the noise.

Mark stopped wanting to go to school on his own because of a menacing drunk he always encountered on the way. When Louis showed him another route, frequented by more people and with fewer risks, he was very relieved.

These fictitious, but plausible, examples illustrate some of the types of skills which form part of environmental competence. They also show the different types of relationships which exist between children and their everyday environment. What does knowing your own neighbourhood or, on a wider basis, the environment in which one lives, mean? It obviously involves knowing the important landmarks and finding your way around; knowing the location of the things that interest you, how to reach them and evaluating the best route to use. It also means being able to pass on this knowledge to other people, who are perhaps in other places, and this implies in turn being able to view the area as a whole, independent of your position in it – in short, having a map of the environment in your head. But it also means knowing the rules and customs of places: knowing who can be found where, which places are better avoided, what you can do in one place but not in another, and when. Knowing your own neighbourhood also means being able to recognize what you like and what you would like to change; the needs of the other neighbourhood inhabitants – the list could probably be continued.

The aim of this chapter is to discuss some of the problems currently faced by children as they develop this knowledge. We will examine some of the significant contributions which have occasioned a re-evaluation of the role of the child in the city: from a developing individual, with imperfect skills, to an individual with specific competence and needs.

Autonomous movement and knowledge

During the last few decades social scientists, urban planners and environmental psychologists have highlighted the increase in traffic, the reduced number of public spaces and the declining sense of community which make our cities increasingly more difficult to live in. This progressive dehumanization of urban space has affected in particular children, who have seen their freedom of movement compromised. If we return to the examples given at the beginning of the chapter, how many children aged between six and eleven and living in cities in the Western world would recognize themselves in one of the above situations? Probably very few: research carried out during the last two decades in several European countries and both North America and Australia has in fact documented a sharp decline in children's independent mobility. This in turn has had a profound effect on the way in which they know their environment.

The size and scope of the restrictions which children experience on a daily basis led Gaster (1995) to maintain that the concept of home range is no longer applicable to the interaction between a child and his/her everyday environment.

One of the most widely used indicators to measure the level of children's freedom to travel independently is the unescorted home-school journey and its frequency. Children start to go to school unaccompanied by an adult during primary school, but surveys of English primary school children reveal that between 1971 and 1990 the number of seven- and eight-year-olds who went to school on their own dropped from 80 per cent to 10 per cent (Hillman et al., 1990). Recent studies (O'Brien et al., 2000) confirm this decline in children's independent mobility in Great Britain. In Italy, 400 seven to thirteen-year-old children living in Rome participated in research on the use of the neighbourhood space. Of those interviewed, only 14 per cent always went to school on their own; 68 per cent were always accompanied by an adult and 18 per cent occasionally went to school unescorted (Giuliani et al., 1997). A few years later, interviews with the mothers of seven to twelve-year-olds from the same city in different kinds of neighbourhoods confirmed these results (Prezza et al., 2001). In Sweden the situation appears to be less serious, but this country has also experienced an increase in traffic, with a concomitant decrease in freedom of movement and thus greater isolation (Bjorklid, 1994). Indeed, Finland would seem to be the only European country in which children still enjoy a high level of independent mobility (Kittä, 1997), and one which is certainly greater than that enjoyed by the children of Great Britain, Italy, Portugal (Arez and Neto, 1999), and Australia (Tranter, 1993).

Parents wishing to justify the restriction of movement illustrated above most frequently mention concern for their children's safety, both in terms of road safety and of protection from strangers. But there are probably several other reasons, whether linked to the physical environment or to changes in lifestyle, such as an increasingly car-oriented society with growing time pressures, a falling birth rate, and a change in parental models. In fact, Boggi (2000) argues that recent decades have witnessed a growth in the idea that a good parent is one who gives greater importance to the protection, rather than to the independence, of his/her child. This concept of the parental role may bear almost no relation to the real dangers of the child's environment and to the child's own capacity to live autonomous experiences. Furthermore it is also possible that new concepts, such as that of the 'parent-friend' who wants to share his/her child's experiences, have led to far more parents accompanying their children to school. As Solomon (1993) argues: 'Some parents actually enjoy taking and collecting their children from school. For those who are interested in what their child has been doing, going home with them (preferably walking) is a very good time to find out' (p. 84).

An inverse relationship between the child's freedom of movement and the socio-economic and cultural level of his/her family was found in a follow up study undertaken in several Italian towns in order to assess the effectiveness of city councils' initiatives to promote children's autonomous mobility (Tonucci, 2001).

Whatever the underlying reason behind it, this restriction of children's mobility seems to have direct and adverse consequences on the child's development of spatial skills. Furthermore, children who do not travel independently are most frequently taken by car to their destination. This in itself unites two potentially negative situations: first, they are denied the possibility of using their own skills to independently identify where they want to go and how to get there; second, on a more basic level, the possibility of acquiring sensor-motor information through physically active moving is reduced, and this, in particular in young children, is needed to integrate internal and external spatial information.

The development of spatial cognition

Developmental theorists almost unanimously argue for the natural progression of understanding from action to concept. In accordance with this, the ability to form a coherent spatial representation would develop from the experience of moving within a space, to an abstract configuration of the spatial relationships within it. Siegel and White (1975) argued that locomotor movement within a large-scale environment leads to a more accurate and flexible spatial representation than that produced by physically passive experiences. Actively moving through the environment brings the individual into contact with the multiple perspectives of the space, facilitating the integration of views and the co-ordination of percepts with motor experiences. This is not the place to re-examine the theoretical models which have guided research into the formation of children's knowledge of their environment: comprehensive reviews are already provided for example by Hart and Moore (1973) or Heft and Wohlwill (1987). However, it is worthwhile examining some empirical research which shows the relationship between the active exploration of the environment, and its cognition.

Since the 1970s numerous experiments have investigated the age at which different spatial skills are acquired. These have shown that Piagetian theory considerably underestimated the abilities of the young child. Contemporary developmental theory now views models of development as more flexible than was previously thought, and assigns a more critical role to the way in which knowledge is acquired and to the characteristics of the environment than to the developmental stage.

A major emphasis in empirical research has focused on the effect of children's mode of travelling to school and independent mobility on the development of spatial cognition. In general, children who walk to school draw more detailed and correctly oriented maps than those who are driven by car or by bus. Hart (1981) reported that the first ones included more natural elements in their maps, while the second ones tended to include more roads. In addition, children of under eight years of age who were driven to school were less able to estimate the distance between home and school when compared to those who walked. Cycling allows children and adolescents to extend their home range and results in a larger space included in their maps, but also in a less accurate representation of their living space (Andrews, 1973; Brown and Broadway, 1981).

Children who walk to school show higher performance in spatial cognition tests, not only because walking allows them to develop perceptual and motor skills which facilitate the construction of spatial schemes, but also because of the active relationship with the environment which this involves. Spencer and Darvizeh (1981) showed that three to five-year-olds who walked to nursery school had better route-finding skills than those who were passively taken there by bus. The authors' explanation was that active travellers have a more developed tendency to look for, and remember, landmarks and sequences on their routes. On the basis of these results Spencer and Darvizeh suggested that children who are allowed to explore their neighbourhood in an active way will widen their environmental capabilities. Conversely, children without the opportunity to experience their local environment may not develop these skills to the same degree.

Malucelli and Maass (2001) have shown that there is a concrete relationship between traffic levels and spatial memory tasks: traffic may have adverse effects on the development of spatial skills through the loss of autonomous exploration of the environment. The authors chose three sites in the same municipality that differed from each other in traffic intensity (the car-free historical centre of Venice; Marghera, with some car-free spaces; and Mestre with a high density of cars) and thus also differed in the degree of children's autonomous mobility. They then investigated what impact these conditions might have on the development of spatial skills. Two hundred and sixty-four children between the ages of eight and ten were required to complete a questionnaire on their autonomy of movement, and to perform two spatial memory tasks.

Greater autonomy and freedom to explore the neighbourhood without adult supervision (directly related to low level of traffic) was associated with better performance on a spatial memory task, the correct positioning and orientation of rulers, as well as on a task involving path drawing, while memory for landmark recognition was not affected. It should be noted that the tests investigated the ability to learn and memorize new environments, not the child's local neighbourhood, and this implied that basic skills in spatial cognition were affected.

Rissotto and Tonucci (2002) investigated the local environment knowledge of forty-six children aged between eight and eleven years in a large Italian city. The children's way of travelling to school (on their own, accompanied by an adult, on foot or by car) and freedom of movement in the neighbourhood were assessed through a questionnaire. The tasks to be completed by participants included a sketch map of the route from home to school and the drawing of the route on a blank map of the neighbourhood. In order to investigate the role of autonomy in the development of a full understanding of the everyday environment, the children were asked to use landmarks to find their way around a blank map of the neighbourhood and to mark on the map the

Figure 5.1. Drawing of the route from home to school by a girl aged ten, who is driven to school by car.

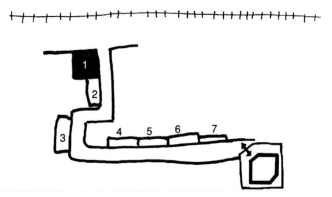

Figure 5.2. Drawing of the route from home to school by a boy aged ten who goes to school on his own. The numbers 1 to 7 refer to the number of locations indicated by the child: his house, the house of a friend, a coffee shop, a grocery, a pizzeria, a stationer's shop, and a bank.

position of important components of their environment. Children who went to school on their own achieved the best results, both in making a sketch map of the route and in drawing their movements on the blank map of the neighbourhood, thus confirming that freedom of movement has an impact on acquiring, processing, and structuring environmental knowledge.

In Spain, Goluboff *et al.*, 2002 have analyzed both the way in which eleven-year-olds conceptualize spatial information on their home-school route and also how they configure the urban space as a whole. Twenty-nine children drew the route they took from home to school and located on the map fifteen of the town's landmarks most commonly cited by the sample children. The results showed that children who walk to school conceptualized space in a different way from those who are taken by car. The former perceived the town's landmarks as a continuum, they remembered them more accurately, and they showed a greater capacity to structure the urban space. On the other hand, the children who travelled by bus or by car had a poorer perception, they tended to group the city's landmarks together and have a less structured memory which in turn produces less continuous impressions.

Evidence somewhat inconsistent with previous findings is provided by Joshi *et al.* (1999) in an empirical study that assessed spatial skills, knowledge, and perceptions of the environment in ninety-three children aged between seven and twelve years. Spatial ability was measured in terms of performance in abstract tasks in close-body space, and knowledge of the environment was measured in terms of the representation of the local area. To assess the more general perception of the environment, children were invited to respond to four sets of drawings depicting hypothetical routes home and one set of photographs depicting possible play areas.

Joshi *et al.*'s results did not support the idea that children's spatial ability is disadvantaged by travelling to school with an adult, on foot or by car. In fact, in the map-drawing task, children who were accompanied to school used more landmarks than those who were unaccompanied. Yet children who had greater freedom to travel without an adult on non-school journeys also used more landmarks in their maps than those who enjoyed less freedom. According to Joshi *et al.* an explanation for this may relate to Solomon's (1993) comment that accompanying children on the journey to school may have some advantages such as promoting parent-child communication.

These conflicting findings, probably due in part to the different types of spatial cognition tasks which the children faced (declarative versus procedural and configurational), seem less striking when one considers the freedom of movement the children enjoyed away from the home-school run. In fact, both in Joshi *et al.* (1999) and in Rissotto and Tonucci (2002) this was associated with better performance. Indeed it should be pointed out that given that the departure and arrival points are fixed, and that there are restrictions on the journey time, the home-school journey can only in part be considered an autonomous exploration exercise. Giuliani *et al.* (1997) found that the fear of arriving late was one of the major worries of those children who had started to go to school on their own. This fear can inhibit the independent exploration which is one of the prerequisites for the acquisition of adequate environmental knowledge.

Being taken to school is in fact only one indicator of the overall reduction in the freedom to explore the local environment independently. Undoubtedly an extension of the activity range would be a more suitable measure of a child's autonomous mobility. Several studies have shown how a broader activity range results in a more extensive knowledge of the environment. Munroe and Munroe (1971) reported that the amount of active exploration of the environment among five to eight-year-olds in rural Kenya was positively correlated to their performance in spatial tasks. Torell and Biel (1985) asked children aged between six and ten years to draw sketch maps of their local environment and data on how children used their environment were gathered through diaries and interviews with the children and their parents. Results show that there was a significant correlation between the size of the area covered by the sketch maps and the size of the activity range. It was quite normal for younger children to know a smaller part of their neighbourhood than older children, one exception being a six-year-old girl who played with her older brother. This girl's activity range was wider than that of most of the ten-year-olds and the size of the map she drew was comparable to those drawn by the latter.

Way-finding activities outside the usual home range (Cornell *et al.*, 2001) show that children are capable of developing new and more advanced strategies: the 'adventure' is not just a source of fun, but also stimulates cognitive development.

From spatial to environmental cognition

It should be noted that the scope of cognitive mapping and the nature of representations are closely related to the goals the individual has during his/her spatial activity. Many of the researchers who have investigated the importance of local experience approach the issue exclusively in terms of the acquisition of spatial cognition, as if the children's knowledge of their environment was an end in itself rather than part of the problems and practical objectives of their everyday actions.

On the one hand, it is this very stress on acquisition that defines a clear arrival point, towards which a child is supposed to proceed and which then constitutes the principal measure of the child's level of knowledge. Whether one talks of acquisition in terms of an ontogenetic or microgenetic process, 'attainment of configurational knowledge (is considered) as the final level of achievement, with a fully coordinated, Euclidean spatial representation reflecting at once the ideal cognitive structure and the standard against which all other forms of environmental knowledge are judged' (Heft and Wohlwill, 1987: 178).

On the other hand, the same Heft and Wohlwill (1987) questioned the 'inclination to explain all forms of environmental knowledge in terms of underlying cognitive representation' and looked forward to 'a consideration of psychological processes from a more contextualist point of view, and a recognition of the influence of factors such as preference and affect' (p. 199).

With reference to the first point, some studies have questioned whether the progression from landmark to route to configurational knowledge represents an improvement in the quality of the knowledge which is independent of the task and of the nature of the environment (Gärling and Golledge, 1989; Anooshian, 1996; Rossano and Reardon, 1999). In navigational tasks and in particular settings, for instance, a survey representation did not prove to be the most efficient.

Denis *et al.* (1999) in an experimental study on navigational instruction in Venice found that the tendency to use a survey-representation versus a route-representation is largely dependent on the individual's cognitive preferences and the characteristics of the environment. In Venice, a city characterized by an intricate street structure, navigation anchored to salient visual landmarks resulted in better performance than attempts to build comprehensive survey representations (p. 171). In Malucelli and Maass' research (2001) mentioned above, the authors found that children who lived in Venice tended to prefer a route-representation of their way from home to school while children living in Mestre (a town with a much more regular street structure), mainly drew survey-representations, and this tendency was consistent across all age groups.

We can similarly imagine that if children living in Manhattan and Perugia were tested on their ability to identify the cardinal direction of their neighbourhood streets, the former would perform more successfully, without this necessarily implying a more sophisticated spatial knowledge on their part. In fact the cardinal directions form an integral part of Manhattan topography, to the extent that they are included in many of the street names, but how could this information interest a child who lives in a medieval city where a street can change direction numerous times in a hundred metres?

With reference to the second point, Gauvian (1993) suggests considering the acquisition of environmental knowledge as an active process of problem solving. For experimental reasons it has been useful to think of this knowledge as something which can be expressed in cognitive maps, descriptions of the route or answers to geographical tests. However, it should be borne in mind that these are only some of the representations of some of the aspects of environmental knowledge. In fact, the development of spatial skills includes the ability to use a space effectively, whether to resolve problems or to pursue meaningful activities on an individual basis; the ability to pass this knowledge on to others and the possibility of learning to use cultural tools and customs from within the children's own culture. As Cohen and Cohen (1985) argue, 'any motor activity in space operates in the service of other cognitive and social cognitive and social concerns. We do not walk (or ride) to a shopping mall in order to walk (or ride). There is a purpose to the activity. This purpose provides a conceptual theme to the activity, which aids not only in the enactment of the theme but also in the use of spatial information in the service of the theme'. (p. 217).

The studies undertaken by Hart (1978), Bjorklid (1982), Moore (1986), Torell and Biel (1985), Matthews (1992) have clearly shown that the acquisition and structure of the knowledge in a child are correlated to the functional meaning of the places and thus to their potential usability. Spatial information is coupled to social information. Experiencing their environment, children 'learn where different behavior settings are, where to go to find things, people, personal involvements or help. They learn who some of the other people are in the community and thus become aware of the range of the social, physical and behavioral differences that people in the community represent to them. They develop normative expectations about social life and social forms'. (Siegel and Cousins, 1985: 361).

Participation and the specificity of children's knowledge

If the stage in the progression towards an abstract representation of space is not a suitable tool to measure *environmental* cognition in the wider sense described above, what other tools could be used to evaluate the complexity and richness of children's knowledge of their everyday environment?

The ever more widespread participatory experiments (Hart, 1997; Chawla, 2002; Matthews, 2001; Alparone and Rissotto, 2001; Paba, 2000, see also Sutton and Kemp, and Francis and Lorenzo, both in this volume) in which children participate in the planning and decision-making process of the urban environment remain as a promising avenue for future research. The ability to think up innovative projects or to suggest changes in the urban structure implies the possession of various skills: a knowledge of the spatial physical characteristics, their function and hence their worth; the ability to evaluate the condition of the environment and its potential; the ability to formulate a dynamic representation of the environment and to understand the systemic relationships between different spaces and between components of an environment. In fact, researchers who have run experiments of this kind testify that children possess the above skills, and sometimes to a high level.

The analysis of focus groups of ten to twelve-year-olds involved in participatory experiments led Spencer, Woolley and Dunn (1999) to conclude that 'the children express strong civic values [. . .] have strong aesthetic and sensual appreciation of the cityscape, whilst being outspoken critics of poor design and maintenance. They [. . .] can give vivid accounts of perceived threats to their well being and safety: from some adults on the street, from older adolescents, and often from groups from out of town' (p. 16).

Cosco and Moore (2002) report how they used two fourteen-year-old Argentine boys as 'consulting experts' on a field trip into a neighbourhood with a particularly bad reputation. The two boys, and many of their friends of the same age, were able to provide reliable and clear information, both on the physical space of the neighbourhood and on the community dynamics. Namely, 'they knew every square meter of it, who lived there, who their friends were, areas to avoid because of drug dealing and violence' (p. 42). According to the authors, the children's expertise also relied on their being 'rooted in a particular place, feeling part of that place, knowing that 'this is where I live so I know what I'm talking about' (p. 43).

Children's knowledge is not only extensive and articulate, it is also specific. Horelli (1994) compared the plans drawn up by children with those produced by experts for the same green space and highlighted the existence of differences which had spatial and behavioural consequences. It was the children's plans, rather than those of the experts, which promoted the possibility of different types of meeting and interchange either between peers or between adults (see also Horelli, this volume). These differences can reasonably be attributed to a greater degree of specificity in the children's knowledge of the area in question and of the future users' needs.

What is most striking is that the awareness of children's environmental competence is probably more widespread among designers and planners than among developmental psychologists. For example, the Italian town planner Paba (2000), reviewed children's experiences of urban participation in a number of Italian cities. Paba acknowledged that the transformation of a city certainly required technical and administrative expertise, but also pointed out that a positive outcome to such transformations depended increasingly on the ability to make use of the different skills of the population, starting with the child's viewpoint.

Research into preferences is another field which promises to deepen our understanding of the knowledge children have of their surroundings (Korpela, 2002). Developmental shifts in the place preferences of boys – from land use and activity orientation to appreciation of the aesthetic and cognitive value of places – could be related, according to Malinowsky and Thurber (1996), to an increasing capacity to shed an egocentric orientation and to acquire an abstract view of the world.

Changing lifestyles and the understanding of spatial surroundings

The decrease in children's freedom of movement which was discussed at the beginning of this chapter is not the only important change to have occurred during the last decades in the relationship between a child of the Western world and his/her everyday environment. Other changes such as the progressive 'urbanization' of the lifestyles of small and rural towns; the increasing popularity of travel abroad, especially from adolescence onwards, and the familiarity with different environments through the media; the availability of new tools and ways to acquire environmental knowledge, including the greater availability of illustrated descriptive material, allow children to extend their experience, whether directly or through other means, to include environments far beyond their local surroundings and on a different scale.

In emphasising only the negative impact of reduced autonomy on the development of children's environmental knowledge there is a risk of giving a distorted and restrictive view of these changes, biased by a romantic image of the past. Knowledge is accumulated not only through the acquisition of new information, but also through the integration and restructuring of various types of information.

Among the various factors which influence the environmental preferences of children, Malinowski and Thurber (1996) mentioned the variety of environments to which a child is exposed, as well as indirect familiarity via different media and peer preferences. These are all factors that can be affected by the changes discussed above.

Especially significant is Uttal's (2000) discussion of the relationship between the development of spatial cognition and children's use of maps and models. His theoretical perspective is based on the assumption that the relationship between maps and the development of spatial cognition is reciprocal in nature, namely 'maps provide a perspective that can be difficult to acquire from direct experience navigating in the world [and] the development of mental representations of large scale space is affected by the symbolic representation of spatial information on maps' (p. 247). Extending this reasoning, he argues that the conception of space is culturally biased, and the map-like representation of the large scale space of the Western societies is a map-influenced model of the world.

Finally we should bear in mind that during recent decades the cognitive and social demands faced by children have also changed. We do not mean to question the role of experience in the acquisition of spatial cognition. But we suggest that research into children's environmental knowledge could benefit from investigating the relationship between new ways to acquire information, and the kind of environmental competence needed in contemporary society.

References

Alparone, F. R. and Rissotto, A. (2001). Children's citizenship and participation models: participation in planning and Children's Councils. *Journal of Community and Applied Social Psychology*, *11*, 421–34.

Andrews, H. F. (1973). Home range and urban knowledge of school-age children. *Environment and Behavior*, *5*, 73–86.

Anooshian, L. J. (1996). Diversity within spatial cognition – strategies underlying spatial knowledge. *Environment and Behavior*, *28*, 471–93.

Arez, A. and Neto, C. (1999). The study of independent mobility and perception of the physical environment in rural and urban children. *XIV World Conference of International of IPA*, Lisbon, 13–17 June.

Björklid, P. (1982). *Children Outdoor Environment*. Stockholm Institute of Education.

Björklid, P. (1994). Children–traffic–environment. *Architecture and Behaviour*, *10*, 399–406.

Boggi, O. (2000). Portare i bambini in città. A scuola ci andiamo da soli. In C. Baraldi and G. Maggioni (eds.), *Una Città con i Bambini* (pp. 123–51). Rome: Donzelli.

Brown, M. A. and Broadway, M. J. (1981). The cognitive maps of adolescent: confusion about inter-town distances. *Professional Geographer*, *33*, 315–25.

Chawla, L. (ed.) (2002). *Growing up in an Urbanising World*. London: Earthscan and Paris: UNESCO Publishing.

Cohen, S. L. and Cohen, R. (1985). The role of activity in spatial cognition. In R. Cohen (ed.), *The Development of Spatial Cognition* (pp. 199–223). London: Lawrence Erlbaum Associates Publisher.

Cornell, E. H., Hadley, D. C., Sterling, T. M., Chan, A. M. and Boechler, P. (2001). Adventure as a stimulus for cognitive development. *Journal of Environmental Psychology*, *21*, 219–31.

Cosco, N. and Moore, R. (2002). Our neighbourhood is like that! Cultural richness in Boca-Baraccas, Buenos Aires. In L. Chawla (ed.), *Growing up in an Urbanising World* (pp. 35–56). London: Earthscan and Paris: UNESCO Publishing.

Denis, M., Pazzaglia, F., Cornoldi, C. and Bertolo, L. (1999). Spatial discourse and navigation: an analysis of route directions in the city of Venice. *Applied Cognitive Psychology*, *13*, 145–74.

Gärling, T. and Golledge, R. G. (1989). Environmental perception and cognition. In E. H. Zube and G. T. Moore (eds.), *Advances in Environment, Behavior, and Design*, vol. II (pp. 203–36). New York: Plenum Press.

Gaster, S. (1995). Rethinking the children's home range concept. *Architecture and Behaviour*, *11*, 35–42.

Gauvian, M. (1993). The development of spatial thinking in everyday activity. *Developmental Review*, *13*, 92–121.

Giuliani, M. V., Alparone, F. R. and Mayer, S. (1997). Children's appropriation of urban spaces. *Urban Childhood International Conference*, Trondheim, 9–12 June.

Goluboff, M., Garcia Mira, R. and Garcia Fontan, C. (2002). Perception of urban space from the perspective of pedestrians and passengers. In R. Garcia Mira, J. M. Sabucedo Camaselle and R. J. Martinez (eds.), *Psicologia y medio ambiente: Aspectos psicosociales* (pp. 149–58), educativos y metodologico, A Coruña, Unidad de investigacion persona-ambiente.

Hart, R. A. (1978). *Children's Experience of Place: A Developmental Study*. New York: Irvington Publishers.

Hart, R. A. (1981). Children's spatial representation of the landscape: lessons and questions from a field study. In L. Liben, A. H. Patterson and N. Newcombe (eds.), *Spatial Representation and Behaviour Across the Life Span* (pp. 195–233). New York: Academic Press.

Hart, R. A. (1997). *Children's Participation: The Theory and Practice of Involving Young Citizens in Community Development and Environmental Care*. London, Earthscan and New York: UNICEF.

Hart, R. A. and Moore, G. T. (1973). The development of spatial cognition: a review. In R. M. Downs and D. Stea (eds.), *Image and Environment* (pp. 246–88). Chicago: Aldine Publishing Company.

Heft, H. and Wohlwill, J. F. (1987). Environmental cognition in children. In D. Stokols and I. Altman (eds.), *Handbook of Environmental Psychology*, vol. I (pp. 175–203). New York: John Wiley and Sons.

Hillman, M., Adams, J. and Whitelegg, J. (1990). *One False Move. . . A Study of Children's Independent Mobility*. London: Policy Studies Institute.

Horelli, L. (1994). Children as urban planners. *Architecture and Behaviour*, *10*, 371–7.

Joshi, M. S., MacLean, M. and Carter, W. (1999). Children's journey to school: spatial skills, knowledge and perceptions of the environment. *British Journal of Developmental Psychology*, *17*, 125–39.

Kitta, M. (1997). Children's independent mobility in urban, small town, and rural environments. In R. Camstra (ed.), *Growing up in a Changing Urban Landscape* (pp. 41–52). Assen: Van Gorcum.

Korpela, K. (2002). Children's environments. In R. B. Bechtel and A. Churchman (eds.), *Handbook of Environmental Psychology* (pp. 363–74). New York: John Wiley and Sons.

Malinowsky, J. C. and Thurber, C. A. (1996). Developmental shifts in the space preferences of boys aged 8–16 years. *Journal of Environmental Psychology, 16*, 45–54.

Malucelli, E. and Maass, A. (2001). The development of spatial abilities: growing up with or without cars. *Bulletin of People-Environment Studies, 18* (Spring), 6–9.

Matthews, H. (2001). *Children and Community Regeneration: Creating Better Neighbourhoods.* London: Save the Children.

Matthews, M. H. (1992). *Making Sense of Place: Children's Understanding of Large Scale Environments.* Hemel Hempstead: Harvester.

Moore, R. (1986). *Childhood's Domain.* London: Croom Helm.

Munroe, R. L. and Munroe, R. H. (1971). Effect of environmental experience on spatial ability in an East African society. *Journal of Social Psychology, 83*, 15–22.

O'Brien, M., Jones, D., and Sloan, D. (2000). Children's independent spatial mobility in the urban public realm. *Childhood, 7*, 257–77.

Paba, G. (2000). Partecipare per costruire la città in Ministero dell'Ambiente (ed.), *Le bambine e i bambini trasformano le città: progetti e buone pratiche per la sostenibilità nei comuni italiani* (pp. 24–30). Firenze: Litografica.

Prezza, M., Pilloni, S., Morabito, C., Sersante, C., Alparone, F. R. and Giuliani, M. V. (2001). The influence of psychological, social and urban factors on children's independent mobility and relationship to peer frequentation. *Journal of Community and Applied Social Psychology, 11*, 435–50.

Rissotto, A. and Tonucci, F. (2002). Freedom of movement and environmental knowledge in elementary school children. *Journal of Environmental Psychology, 22*, 65–77.

Rossano, M. J. and Reardon, W. P. (1999). Goal specificity and the acquisition of survey knowledge. *Environment and Behavior, 31*, 395–412.

Siegel, A. W. and Cousins, J. H. (1985). The symbolizing and symbolized child in the enterprise of cognitive mapping. In R. Cohen (ed.), *The Development of Spatial Cognition* (pp. 347–68). Hillsdale, NJ: Lawrence Erlbaum Associates.

Siegel, A. W. and White, S. H. (1975). The development of spatial representations of largescale environments. In H. W. Reese (ed.), *Advances in Child Development and Behavior*, vol. X (pp. 51–83). New York: Academic Press.

Solomon, J. (1993). Escorting: balancing the advantages and the disadvantages. In M. Hillman (ed.), *Children, Transport and the Quality of Life* (pp. 82–6). London: Policy Studies Institute.

Spencer, C. and Darvizeh, Z. (1981). The case for developing a cognitive environmental psychology that does not underestimate the abilities of young children. *Journal of Environmental Psychology, 1*, 21–31.

Spencer, C., Woolley, H. and Dunn, J. (1999). Participating in their towns: Children feel ignored. . .. *Streetwise, 10*, 16–18.

Tonucci, F., Prisco, A., Renzi, D. and Rissotto, A. (2001). *L'autonomia di movimento dei bambini italiani, Quaderno n. 1 del progetto La città dei bambini.* Rome: Istituto di Scienze e Tecnologie della Cognizione del CNR.

Torell, G. and Biel, A. (1985). Parental restrictions and children's acquisition of neighborhood knowledge. In T. Garling and J. Valsiner (eds.), *Children Within Environments. Toward a Psychology of Accident Prevention* (pp. 107–18). New York: Plenum Press.

Tranter, P. (1993). *Children's Mobility in Canberra: Confinement or Independence?* Monograph Series no. 7, Canberra, Department of Geography and Oceanography, University College, Australian Defence Force Academy.

Uttal, D. (2000). Seeing the big picture: map use and the development of spatial cognition. *Developmental Science, 3,* 247–86.

6   The classroom environment and children's performance – is there a relationship?

Sandra Horne Martin

Introduction

When we go into a classroom, what do we see? Busy people, some chaos and a lot of activity like sitting, standing, moving, and talking, some might be in silence, writing, drawing, pointing, singing, fidgeting, crying, laughing, whispering, or sleeping. But one person (the teacher) seems to be dominating the setting and communication seems to be always present, either by talking or writing, or through gestures like the raising of an arm (Adams and Hiddle, 1970). A classroom environment is much more than a place to house books, desks, and resources. It is a place for learning.

This chapter will examine the current literature on the impact of the classroom environment on performance. There still seems to be a lack of research in educational settings that looks into the school environment and children's performance. The investigation into the physical environment's influence on learning outcomes has been largely ignored, or maybe avoided, in favour of research into other areas within the school, for instance, pedagogical, psychological, and social variables. What is surprising though, is that children spend most of their waking hours in school and that should in itself prompt investigation into the impact the physical environment has on them.

Since 2001 the UK Government seems to be finally recognizing the importance of the environment in raising standards (Clark, 2002). Clark cited the following by David Blunkett, Secretary of State for Education and Employment:

Getting the basics right is not just about literacy and numeracy – it also means putting the right facilities in place so that teachers can teach and children can learn. (January 2001)

Since then some initiatives have been developed but there is still a lot to be done in order to understand why and how the school environment influences performance. One of the limitations about this kind of research is defining what a desirable outcome is and how it can be measured (Dick, 2002). Presently the only measurable variable seems to be results from standardized tests. However, both educators and society as a whole are now questioning the validity of these results and, consequently, it is difficult to quantify and measure improvement in areas such as interactions, creativity and thinking. It is a difficult task to isolate physical factors and measure their effect on learning but if links can be identified, investments can be made where they will have the maximum effect (Clark, 2002). An important aim is to integrate educational goals with the design of buildings and spaces, but as Clark points out, school buildings are often created without reference to changes in education, and changes in education do not adequately recognize the impact of the physical environment on any new approach.

The literature offers a varied body of work although quite fragmented and we will examine here a range of what the literature has to offer currently in the subject of classroom, school and performance.

Function

Schools, like all physical settings, serve a variety of functions. The most obvious function is the school's responsibility to educate. In addition, schools at different times in history have been expected to assume the responsibility for socialization, transmitting ideas and values of society, and preparing children for their adulthood. All of these functions have been emphasized at different points in time while others have been played down. The same happens with the emphasis given to areas of the school curriculum. At different times educators have focused on literacy, practical and manual skills, numeracy, rote learning, independent learning, the arts, the basics, vocational skills and health, among others (Rivlin and Weinstein, 1984). But whatever focus is given at a certain time, all built environments for children should serve certain common functions with respect to children's development: to foster personal identity; to encourage the development of competence; to provide opportunities for growth; to promote a sense of security and trust; and to allow both social interaction and privacy (Weinstein and David, 1987).

The function of a room is partially defined by the purpose of a larger system. A classroom is part of a school that already places constraints on the behaviour occurring there. The type of influence on behaviour will also depend on the kind of room – a lecture hall, a science lab, a small seminar room or a general classroom (Heimstra and Macfarling, 1978).

In the processes of teaching and learning, the physical environment arranged by the teacher provides the setting for learning and at the same time acts as a participant in teaching and learning. According to Loughlin and Suina (1982), there are two major interacting elements in a classroom that will either strengthen or limit the environment's contribution to education. One is the *architectural facility* and the other is the *arranged environment*. Each is essential and each influences behaviour and learning, but each has different functions and characteristics.

The architectural facility provides the setting for all the interactions among people and materials. It establishes the basic space of the environment, organizing access to external spaces and resources, and it determines basic conditions of light, sound, temperature, and interactions between groups of people. For example, we find qualities like colour, texture, floor levels and their softness or hardness. The *architectural* facility is the beginning of the learning environment and forms the framework in which the teacher will establish the *arranged* environment (Loughlin and Suina, 1982). The teacher within the spaces provided by the architectural design arranges the learning environment. The arranged environment rests upon understanding the relationships between the physical settings and behaviour.

Room organization

The amount and arrangement of space in educational settings is important for classroom performance and behaviour. Classroom layout affects the social interaction of both teachers and students (Gifford, 1987). The design and arrangement of space and furniture are factors in implementing educational goals (Gump, 1987; Proshansky and Wolfe, 1975). Physical and spatial aspects of a learning environment communicate a symbolic message about what is expected to happen in a particular place. The atmosphere is readily apparent when one enters the classroom and is reflected by subtle cues in the physical arrangement as well as by the style of teaching. The arrangement of classroom space can communicate expectations for behaviour that are reinforced by institutional policies (Weinstein and David, 1987).

The effective arrangement and management of space can facilitate the learning process, while the unplanned ineffective use of space can result in unforeseen and unexpected interference, and may even serve to instigate conflicts. The teacher sometimes does not realize that certain behaviours occur in the classroom as a result of how the room has been arranged (Proshansky and Wolfe, 1975). When children exhibit puzzling behaviour, the environment should be checked. Turning furniture around or re-routing traffic are some ways to change patterns of behaviour in a classroom (Loughlin and Suina, 1982). Placing chairs in a circle, instead of in rows and columns, for instance, makes it clear that discussion and interaction are involved (Gump, 1987). Rivlin and Rothenberg (1976) examined the distribution of furniture and activity in elementary school classrooms throughout the school year and found that the physical layout of the classroom remained quite stable over the course of the year. This means that although teachers were free to make changes, these changes were not made during the year, a point confirmed in later research by Horne (1999).

Loughlin (1982) states that teachers can use spatial organization to design settings that stimulate children's work. The arranged environment can work in partnership with the teacher. Spatial organization is the task of arranging furniture to create appropriate spaces for movement and the learning activities that the teacher works to pursue. Teachers accomplish this task by defining spaces within the environment, planning traffic patterns, and arranging furniture. Room arrangement is more than a casual responsibility or a matter of aesthetics, because spatial organization influences so many behaviours. New spaces are created each time a piece of furniture is put in place or moved. Spaces and their relationships will influence behaviour, whether planned or not (see Figures 6.1a–6.1c).

Spatial organization requires clear perceptions of the space, and an understanding of the particular effects of space on movement and activity patterns. Teachers who perceive classroom space in informed ways can use deliberately organized space to facilitate children's movement and support learning (Horne, 1999).

Rivlin and Weinstein (1984) described a study made in preschools which compared the behaviour and cognitive development of randomly arranged classrooms and planned classrooms. Equipment, furniture, and materials in the classrooms were the same but in one the set up was casual and the other, the set up was thoughtfully and intentionally organized to promote specific learning outcomes. Scheduling, activity choices, and interaction patterns were similar in all rooms. The findings were clear. In the planned room, children engaged in more manipulative activities and they also produced more complex work. The most striking finding was that conservation of knowledge was achieved earlier and by a greater number of children in the spatially planned rooms. Moore (1986), in a similar study, found that spatial definition of behaviour settings is related to cognitive development, degree of engagement and exploratory behaviour. The built environment is not to be considered the major influence on the developing child but it would appear that the developmental process can be influenced by characteristics of the physical setting (Weinstein and David, 1987).

Figure 6.1. Three different classroom layouts, with different expectations of behaviour.

Movement is a normal accompaniment to learning experiences for children. The environment can facilitate the movement that is important for working and learning. Movement provides communication. When spatial organization encourages movements and other behaviours that conflict with the teacher's wishes, the productivity and communication of classroom movement are reduced. Circulation patterns surrounding activities encourage children to look around and see what is available, and fluid traffic patterns provide a means for better communication (Loughlin and Suina, 1982; Moore and Lackney, 1995). Where traffic patterns are not clear, disruptive behaviour may occur. It is easy to assume that the problem lies with the children, but the teacher-arranged environment may also be at fault when this happens. Teachers can unknowingly, through the environmental messages sent by the setting, encourage children to act quite differently from the expected ways by the arrangement of classroom furniture. When this happens, much energy and time must be spent enforcing behaviour expectations that contradict the behaviour suggestions made through spatial organization (Loughlin and Suina, 1982).

The ambient environment

Noise

Gifford (1987) found evidence that strongly suggests that noise interferes with learning both while it occurs and after the noise is gone (if the learner is exposed to noise for long periods). Whether quietness is necessarily conducive to learning remains to be determined. However, if a classroom were completely free of noise, learners would be likely distracted by the smallest sound (even their breathing). The Educational Facilities Laboratories (1960) reported that an acoustically dead room is nearly as bad for some purposes as a noisy one. At certain times, some sounds or noises are pleasant, or at least not distracting. At other times, the same sounds will be intrusive and frustrating. Regardless, excessive sounds have proved to be inhibitors of efficient and effective hearing (physiological process) and listening (psychological process). Excessive noise has been shown to have an adverse effect upon reading comprehension, memory, and retention (Ledford, 1981; Silverstone, 1981).

Zentall (1983) reports that the effects of noise on children may be harmful. The effects depend on the level and duration of noise exposure, as well as the degree to which the noise involves conversations. Other factors present in the classroom also contribute to the stimulation of noise, for instance, the difficulty of the task being performed or the density of the classroom. Noise distracts depending upon the activity; a high noise level in a workshop activity is not nearly as distracting as similar noise in a study session. Noise distracts depending upon its content. Students report much higher distraction from overheard social conversations than from subject matter talk within a lesson. Noise distracts even more when conditions are crowded. Reflection on these findings by Zentall indicates that noise cannot be equated with annoyance or distraction. Noise moderation might be necessary or not, depending upon who the inhabitants are, their current activity, and conditions within and around the noise (Krovetz, 1977). Activities within the classroom have been found to contribute highly to the ambient sound level, although the teacher typically controls noise (Wohlwill and Heft, 1991). Teachers tend to report more problems from the effects of noise than pupils (Gump, 1975; Krovetz, 1977; Wohlwill and Heft, 1991; Zentall, 1983) and they suggest it may adversely influence educational activities.

Noise in classrooms often makes children struggle to hear and concentrate. Noise can come from different sources: outdoors, building mechanical systems, noise generated within the classroom, other classrooms, road traffic, trains, aircrafts, etc. (Lyons, 2001; Rubida Research, 2001). It is clear that excessive noise levels influence stress, verbal interaction, reading comprehension, blood pressure, cognitive task success, feelings of helplessness, inability to concentrate, and lack of extended application to learning tasks (Cohen, Evans, Krantz, and Stockols, 1986; Gifford, 1987; Rubida Research, 2001). The research linking noise to learning is consistent and indicates that good acoustics are fundamental to good academic performance (Schneider, 2002).

Lighting

Fletcher (1983) found that research on classroom lighting generally indicates that lighting (either natural or artificial) seems to have some effect on children's behaviour, cognitive performance and visual fatigue. It is generally accepted that good lighting, both natural and artificial, can contribute to the aesthetic and psychological character of a learning space. Medical studies have shown that light is critical to the regulation of the circadian rhythm of the body in adjusting to night and day (Rubida Research, 2001). Lighting can affect learning, through mental attitude, class attendance, and performance (Lyons, 2001). Consensus of lighting studies is that appropriate lighting improves results, reduces off task behaviour, and plays a significant role in students' achievement (Schneider, 2002).

Figure 6.2. A cold room can lead to lack of attention and 'fidgeting' – the classroom's temperature illustrated above was 7°C and children's behaviour was severely disrupted.

Temperature, circulation and air quality

Schools have an average of four times as many occupants per space unit as offices, and they can contain a host of pollution sources such as chemicals, cleaning supplies, chalk or dust. The US Environmental Protection Agency states that asthma is a leading cause of school absences due to chronic illness (Lyons, 2001). Various American studies in the 1990s have established a positive relationship between academic achievement and school building conditions (Clark, 2002; Rubida Research, 2001; Tanner and Jago, 1999). Schools need especially good ventilation because children breath a greater volume of air in proportion to their body weight than adults do (Kennedy, 2001; McGovern, 1998; Moore, 1998) and because schools have much less floor space per person than found in most office buildings, for instance (Crawford, 1998).

Colour

Colour has been found to have an influence on blood pressure and behaviour. Taylor and Gousie (1988) found that warm colours increase the blood pressure and muscular activity, while cool colours lower both. Other studies have also found that the use of nature's colours can create a comfortable and relaxed atmosphere (Hathaway, 1987). Although no quantitative measures have been identified in the published research, colour is believed to influence student attitudes, behaviours and learning, particularly student attention span (Rubida Research, 2001; Sinofsky and Knirck, 1981). It is also suggested that carefully planned colour schemes can influence attendance, promote positive feelings about the school and also muscular tension and motor control (Gimbel, 1997; Pile, 1997; Rubida Research, 2001).

Other environmental factors

Density

Density has no inherent psychological meaning while crowding is a psychological state, a personal, subjective reaction that is based on the feeling of too little space (Heimstra and Macfarling, 1978; Moore, 1979; Steele, 1973). High density may affect learning in situations where the activity involves physical movement around the classroom or when learning is dependent on some resource that is not increasing as fast as the number of learners. Also when a particular situation seems crowded to a particular learner or when the concept to be learned is complex, high density may affect the learning (Gifford, 1987).

Moore and Lackney (1994) found considerable evidence that characteristics such as school size and classroom size make a difference in academic achievement. They found that high-density conditions (number of students per space unit) lead to increased aggression and hostility, and decreased social interaction. Evans, Saegert and Harris (2001) agree with these results and added that consequences of children's chronic exposure to high density has generally resulted in lower academic performance. In addition, it was found that as pupil density increased, so did movement and distraction (Lackney, 1994). In classrooms with fewer students, teachers can have more interactions with each pupil providing a richer array of interactions, establishing learning centres and teaching strategies that improve the quality of interactions with each pupil. It is argued that these effects may lead to increased educational performance, though no study has been found that clearly established this increased performance.

Maxwell's (2003) review established that smaller schools led students to participate more in extra curricular activities, demonstrated more positive self-images, showed greater personal responsibility and were more sensitive to the needs of other students (Barker and Gump, 1964). Garbarino (1980) noted a lower incidence of crime and less serious student misconduct. Moos (1979) found that classes with fewer students can foster positive attitudes such as an increased emphasis on friendship while Moore and Lackney (1993) believe that increased student participation and positive student and teacher attitude may mediate higher achievement levels. An investigation on classroom density by Ahrentzen (1981) found that teachers reported more distractions from physical contacts and difficulty in moving about in denser classrooms.

Abransom (1991) found higher achievement in lower-density schools than high-density schools. Research by Wohlwill and van Vliet (1985) found that high density conditions cause excess of stimulation; stress and arousal; a drain on the resources available; considerable interference; reductions in desired privacy levels; and loss of control. Crowding causes behaviour problems and increased maintenance costs.

The relationship between density and pupil achievement is remarkably strong. Large reductions in class size promise learning benefits of a magnitude commonly believed not within the power of educationalists to achieve (Glass, Cahen, Smith, and Filby, 1982).

Participation

It would be beneficial if the education specifications were an iterative, interactive, performance based process rather than a recipe (Lang, 2002). Central to the participatory process is the gradual building consensus and ownership that creates a sense of community and shared intentions. People feel more attached to an environment they have helped to create; they will therefore manage and maintain it better, reducing the likelihood of vandalism, neglect and costly replacements in the future (Architecture Foundation, 2000; Lackney, 2000).

In schools, pride in creating, and being listened to, increases pupils' sense of respect for their environment and stimulates a sense of community which in turn creates a sense of well-being and enhances potential for learning (OECD, 1988). Although it is argued that there are financial implications to participation, there is also the argument that user participation produces a better, more sustainable building and that a building process that costs more in the short term can save money over the long term (Clark, 2002; Seymor, Cottam, Comely, Annesley, and Lingayah, 2001).

Environmental awareness and competence

Beyond general tidiness and classroom displays, many educators may not be accustomed to thinking about their physical environments as an active medium contributing to learning behaviours, and tend to make a distinction between 'education' and the physical setting in which this takes place (Clark, 2002). There is enough evidence that the active engagement with the school environment by school users can enhance the potential in supporting learning (Clark, 2002; Horne-Martin, 2002).

The users of the building, the staff and pupils, should be assisted and trained in understanding the possibilities buildings can offer (OECD, 1988). The shape and layout of most classrooms still in use today is a seemingly fixed and immutable factor, designed for traditional teaching and learning. Increasingly, a variety of learning methods demand a variety of spaces. Many classrooms therefore depend on the ability, awareness and imagination of teachers to be adaptable (Clark, 2002; Horne, 1999).

Loughlin and Suina (1982) found that it is common for teachers to look at their classrooms and only see part of the available space, overlooking the rest. Although teachers are different and see spaces in different ways, some kinds of spaces are more likely to be invisible to teachers' eyes than others and these areas are the most often neglected areas in spatial organization. Lackney and Jacobs (1999) established that teachers may have a real or perceived lack of efficacy over their physical classroom. The learning environment can be a powerful teaching instrument at the disposal of the teacher, or it can be an undirected and unrecognized influence on the behaviours of both children and teachers (Horne, 1999). As Loughlin and Suina (1982) state, informed attention to the arranged environment and the deliberate use of it to support teaching and learning, have not been widespread in schools, but understanding environmental influences is important for all teachers. Horne (1999) found that a great deal of attention is generally given to lesson plans but the room in which those lessons are going to be taught is not taken into consideration in the planning.

David's (1975) understanding is that in the absence of an active attitude towards the environment, teachers are reduced to defensive postures and attempts to traditionalize the environment. In a seminar report by the Organization for Economic Co-operation and Development (OECD, 1988) about the quality of the physical environment of the school and the quality of education, participants reported that teachers are responsible for spaces for teaching and learning and should attempt to make them exciting and stimulating and be prepared to develop them. They also mentioned that a lack of awareness of the potential of an environment could be rectified through staff training in issues concerning the environment, including architecture and design. The participants speculated that by raising such standards amongst teachers, they would impart this knowledge to their pupils who, in later life, would apply this understanding in their own environments. In a study by Lackney (1997), it emerged that teachers feel that some environmental qualities are in part their responsibility even if they are unable to control them. This again raises questions about the need for educators to become more aware of the potential and opportunities that the physical setting presents to them. Knowledge of the relationships between physical surroundings and actions should be a practical tool the teacher can use. Loughlin and Suina (1982) believe that a well trained teacher can predict behaviour in classroom settings. This seems to be another piece of evidence leading to the need for teachers to understand space. Horne-Martin (2002) found that teachers who question their surroundings more have a tendency to be less satisfied with their environments. Horne-Martin argued that when a teacher does not recognize the role of the environment, it is unlikely that change will occur, and proposed that environmental awareness training should be part of the curriculum of teacher training and professional development. A pilot study on the impact of such training on teachers is currently under development.

Conclusion

There is enough evidence in research that states that physical aspects of the environment can either enhance or impede learning. For instance, colour can either increase or lower blood pressure. A room that is uncomfortably hot or cold can lower thresholds for frustration that can affect the acoustical environment (Schneider, 2002). Considerable evidence was found on physiological effects of specific environmental variables but these tend to be small scale and focus on isolated variables.

Nevertheless, many researchers conclude that there is an explicit relationship between the physical characteristics of school buildings and educational outcomes. Poor school conditions make it more difficult for teachers to deliver, affect their health and increase the likelihood that teachers will leave the teaching profession (Schneider, 2003).

Physical settings can affect both teacher and student behaviour (such as attendance and concentration) and attitudes (such as motivation and self-esteem). The impact of the physical environment on the behaviour and attitudes of teachers and students has a mediating effect on student achievement. Although it seems to be difficult to identify a direct causal effect relationship between the school environment and educational outcomes through quantitative research, qualitative research on the indirect influences of school buildings on student learning and behaviour is helpful and constructive. The evidence enhances our understanding of indirect influences such as how motivation and self-esteem affect behaviour, which in turn is likely to affect performance.

Decisions about school facilities have to be translated into bricks and mortar (Price Waterhouse Coopers, 2000). These decisions are based on tradition, available technology, experience, and changing needs. Architectural facilities are designed in terms of a generalized prediction of behaviours, activities, functions, and teaching styles. Research on the effects of school buildings on performance allows professionals to sort through the findings productively and can help produce long term, positive effects on academic outcomes.

The influence of the environment is continuous, and how well the environment communicates with the users will depend on how well the environment is planned. However, a variety of teachers with specific and very different groups of pupils will subsequently inhabit and inherit these spaces. Each teacher and each group of pupils is different, and teachers must develop the generalized environment for specific purposes and groups. When a new building is complete and the architect hands it over to the teacher, the classroom can only be a *finished beginning* in which adaptations will occur. It seems reasonable to suggest that the arranged environment can be used as a deliberate part of the teaching strategy; complementing and reinforcing other strategies the teacher uses to support children's learning and consequently, results.

There is a need for investigation into school buildings at a national level. Practical and research-based projects involving interdisciplinary partnerships should be a recognized area for the awarding of grants by funding bodies. Rather than seeking a definite correlation between the built environment and educational outcomes, future research should adopt a more holistic approach to the examination of the factors responsible for student achievement. A participatory approach to changes in school organization and use of space should be developed.

An important topic would be to incorporate environmental awareness and use of the built environment into teacher training and professional development. Architects and associated professionals should become trained in understanding pedagogical and curricular requirements before embarking on the development of an educational setting. Evaluation of accommodation needs in schools should be an on going process in order to accommodate the changes in curriculum, teaching styles and groups of children. The school setting should be fluid and dynamic and never be allowed to remain static in an environment where change and growth are the only constant. The studies examined identify a relationship between the classroom environment and performance and should be extended and developed in order to better inform authorities on how the environment can be planned and used to support children's learning more effectively.

References

Abramson, P. (1991). Making the grade. *Architectural Review, 29*(4), 91–3.

Adams, R. S. and Hiddle, B. J. (1970). *Realities of Teaching – Explorations with Video Tape.* USA: Holt, Rinehart and Winston, Inc.

Ahrentzen, S. (1981). The environmental and social context of distraction in the classroom. In R. A. Findlay (ed.), *Design Research Interactions* (pp. 241–50). Ames, IA, USA: Environmental Design Research Association.

Architecture Foundation (2000). *We cherish out homes; we aspire to beautiful places of work: why should our schools be different? School Works: A secondary schools design initiative.* London: Architecture Foundation/Arts Council.

Barker, R. G. and Gump, P. V. (1964). *Big School, Small School.* Stanford, CA: Stanford University Press.

Clark, H. (2002). *Building Education – The Role of the Physical Environment in Enhancing Teaching and Research*: Institute of Education, University of London.

Cohen, S., Evans, G. W., Krantz, D. S. and Stockols, D. (1986). *Behaviour, Health and Environmental Stress.* New York: Plenum.

Crawford, G. N. (1998). Going straight to the source. *American School and University, 70*(6), 26–8.

David, T. G. (1975). Environmental literacy. In B. D. Wright (ed.), *Learning Environments* (pp. 161–79). Chicago: University of Chicago Press.

Dick, J. A. (2002, Winter 2002). The built environment's effect on learning: applying current research. *Montessori LIFE*, 53–6.

Educational Facilities Laboratories (1960). *The Cost of a Schoolhouse.* USA: EFL.

Evans, G. W., Saegert, S. and Harris, R. (2001). Residential density and psychological health among children in low-income families. *Environment and Behavior, 33*, 165–80.

Fletcher, D. (1983). Effects of classroom lighting on the behavior of exceptional children. *Exceptional Education Quarterly, 4*(2), 75–89.

Garbarino, J. (1980). Some thoughts on school size and its effects on adolescent development. *Journal of Youth and Adolescence, 9*(1), 19–31.

Gifford, R. (1987). *Environmental Psychology – Principles and Practice.* Newton, MA: Allyn and Bacon, Inc.

Gimbel, T. (1997). *Healing With Colour.* London: Gaia.

Glass, G. V., Cahen, L. S., Smith, M. L. and Filby, N. N. (1982). *School Class Size – Research and Policy.* USA: Sage.

Gump, P. V. (1975). *Ecological Psychology and Children*. Chicago/London: University of Chicago Press.

Gump, P. V. (1987). School and classroom environments. In I. Altman (ed.), *Handbook of Environmental Psychology* (vol. I, pp. 691–732). USA: Wiley-Interscience Publication.

Hathaway, W. E. (1987). Effects of light and colour on pupil achievement, behaviour and phisiology. *Educational Facility Planner*, 25(2).

Heimstra, N. W. and Macfarling, L. H. (1978). *Environmental Psychology* (2nd edn.). CA: Wadsworth Publishing Company.

Horne, S. C. (1999). *The Classroom Environment and its Effects on the Practice of Teachers*. Unpublished PhD, London: Goldsmiths University of London.

Horne-Martin, S. (2002). The classroom environment and its effects on the practice of teachers. *Journal of Environmental Psychology*, 22, 139–56.

Kennedy, M. (2001). Into thin air. *American School and University*, 73(6), 32.

Krovetz, M. (1977). Who needs what when: design of pluralistic learning environments. In D. Stokols (ed.), *Perspectives on Environment and Behavior* (pp. 251–72). New York: Plenum Press.

Lackney, J. (1997). *Who is Managing What?: Placemaking and Facility Management of Environmental Quality in School Environments*: Unpublished paper poster presented at the Environmental Design Research Association Conference 28 in Montreal, May 7–11, 1997.

Lackney, J. A. (1994). *Educational Facilities: The Impact and Role of the Physical Environment of the School on Teaching, Learning and Educational Outcomes*. Milwalkee, WI, USA: Publications in Architecture and Urban Planning – University of Wisconsin-Milwaukee.

Lackney, J. A. (2000). *Thirty-three Educational Design Principles for Schools as Comunity Learning Centers*. Starkville, MS: Mississippi State University, Educational Design Institute.

Lackney, J. A. and Jacobs, P. J. (1999). *Teachers as placemakers: investigating teachers use of the physical setting in instructional design*, Council Educational Facility Planners.

Lang, D. C. (2002). *Teacher Interactions within the Physical Environment*. Unpublished PhD, University of Washington.

Ledford, B. (1981). Interior design: impact on learning achievement. In D. M. Rockwell (ed.), *Designing Learning Environments* (pp. 160–73). New York: Longman.

Loughlin, C. E. and Suina, J. H. (1982). *The Learning Environment: an Instructional Strategy*. New York: Teachers College Press.

Lyons, J. B. (2001). *Do School Facilities Really Impact a Child's Education?* Scottsdale, AZ: Council of Educational Facility Planners International.

Maxwell, L. E. (2003). Home and school density effects on elementary school children. *Environment and Behavior*, 35(4), 566–78.

McGovern, M. A. (1998). A breath of fresh air. *School Planning and Management*, 37(10), 14.

Moore, D. (1998). Improve your school's atmosphere. *School Planning and Management*, 37(10), 18.

Moore, G. and Lackney, J. (1993). School design: crisis, educational performance and design applications. *Children's Environments*, 10(2), 99–112.

Moore, G. T. (1979). Environment-behaviour studies. In A. J. Catanese (ed.), *Introduction to Architecture* (pp. 46–71). New York: McGraw-Hill Book Company.

Moore, G. T. (1986). Effects of the spatial definition of behavior settings on children's behavior: a quasi-experimental field study. *Journal of Environmental Psychology*, 6, 205–31.

Moore, G. T. and Lackney, J. A. (1994). *Educational Facilities for the Twenty-First Century: Research Analysis and Design Patterns*. Milwaukee, WI: University of Wisconsin-Milwaukee.

Moore, G. T. and Lackney, J. A. (1995). Design patterns for American schools: responding to the reform movement. In A. Meek (ed.), *Designing Places for Learning* (pp. 11–22). Alexandria, VA: ASCD.

Moos, R. H. (1979). *Evaluating Educational Environments*. San Francisco: Jossey-Bass.

OECD (1988). The quality of the physical environment of the school and the quality of education. In OECD (ed.), (pp. 21). France: Organisation for Economic Co-operation and Development.

Pile, J. (1997). *Colour in Interior Design*. New York: McGraw-Hill.

Price Waterhouse Coopers (2000). *Building Performance – An Empirical Assessment of the Relationship Between School's Capital Investment and Pupil Performance*. UK: HMSO.

Proshansky, E. and Wolfe, M. (1975). The physical setting and open education. In B. D. Wright (ed.), *Learning Environments* (pp. 31–48). Chicago: University of Chicago Press.

Rivlin, L. G. and Rothenberg, M. (1976). The use of space in open classrooms. In L. G. Rivlin (ed.), *Environmental Psychology – People and Their Physical Settings* (pp. 479–89). New York: Holt, Rinehart and Winston.

Rivlin, L. G. and Weinstein, C. S. (1984). Educational issues, school settings, and environmental psychology. *Journal of Environmental Psychology*, 4, 347–64.

Rubida Research Pty Ltd. (2001). *Schooling Issues Digest: The Impact of School Infrastructure on Student Outcomes and Behaviour*. Australia: Commonwealth Department of Education, Science and Training.

Schneider, M. (2002). Do school facilities affect academic outcomes? Washington DC: *National Clearing House for Educational Facilities*.

Schneider, M. (2003). *Linking School Facility Conditions to Teacher Satisfaction and Success*. Washington DC: National Clearing House for Educational Facilities.

Seymor, J., Cottam, H., Comely, G., Annesley, B. and Lingayah, S. (2001). *School Works Toolkit*. London: School Works.

Silverstone, D. M. (1981). Considerations for listening and noise distractions. In P. J. Sleeman and D. M. Rockwell (ed.), *Designing Learning Environments* (pp. 75–86). New York: Longman.

Sinofsky, E. and Knirck, F. (1981). Choose the right colour for your learning style. *Instructional Innovator*, 26(3), 17–19.

Steele, F. I. (1973). *Physical Settings and Organization Development*. USA: Addison-Wesley Publishing Company.

Tanner, K. and Jago, E. (1999). *The Influence of School Facility on Student Achievement.* Washington DC: University of Georgia.

Taylor, A. and Gousie, G. (1988). The ecology of learning environments for children. *Educational Facility Planner, 26*(4), 23–8.

Weinstein, C. S. and David, T. G. (1987). *Spaces for Children – The Built Environment and Child Development.* New York: Plenum Press.

Wohlwill, J. and Heft, H. (1991). The physical environment and the development of the child. In I. Altman (ed.), *Handbook of Environmental Psychology* (vol. I, pp. 281–328). USA: Wiley-Interscience Publication.

Wohlwill, J. F. and Vliet, W. V. (1985). *Habitats for Children: The Impacts of Density.* Hillsdale, NJ: Lawrence Erlbaum Associates.

Zentall, S. S. (1983). Learning environments: a review of physical and temporal factors. *Exceptional Education Quarterly, 4*(2), 90–115.

7   'Sometimes birds sound like fish': Perspectives on children's place experiences

Tori Derr

Over the past few years, studies of children's environments have increasingly recognized the *variation* in children's experiences in shaping their learning, social development, and play (Holloway and Valentine, 2000; Matthews *et al.*, 2000a; Matthews *et al.*, 2000b; Punch, 2000). These studies remind us that children who grow up within a particular physical environment will not all share the same experiences or emotional responses to a place. Punch (2000) emphasizes that children themselves play a significant role in shaping their own experiences even within similar physical and social environments.

With the recognition that children shape their own place experiences has come a growing number of studies with children in urban environments (Berg and Medrich, 1980; Katz, 1993; Kong, 2000; Lynch, 1997; Moore, 1986; Ward, 1978), rural environments (Derr, 2001; Hart, 1979; Jones, 2000; Matthews *et al.*, 2000a; Nabhan and St Antoine, 1993; Punch, 2000; Sobel, 1993; Ward, 1990), and within a variety of cultural contexts (Beazley, 2000; Derr, 2001; Katz, 1993; Kong, 2000; Matthews, 1995; Punch, 2000; Robson, 1996). As this body of literature continues to grow, some trends emerge as to the importance of these places in children's development. In this chapter I develop these trends through a framework that emerged from my own research with children, aged nine to eleven, living in rural and urban towns of northern New Mexico in the United States.

This research explored children's sense of place in northern New Mexico by working with eighty-nine children in three communities that represented a gradient from urban to rural. Santa Fe was the most urban community, Dixon intermediate, and Mora, the most rural. All the children created basic maps and essays and participated in semi-structured interviews about their place use. From this initial data set, I developed four themes, which I explored in depth with twelve case study children and families (Derr, 2001, 2002). These themes represent over-arching ways that children interact with and learn from their environment and are presented in Table 7.1.

Table 7.1. *Themes generated from childrens' place experiences*

Four wheelers, ramps, and rites of passage	Children learn through adventure and risk-taking, exploration, and many self-created rites of passage.
Fort-makers	Children experience imagination, escape, safety, and creativity through active place-making and place attachment.
Learning care	Children learn nurturance, companionship, respect from animals, ethnobotany, gardening.
The Web	Children experience a cultural place, giving context to the meanings and attachments they feel toward a place.

Figure 7.1. Leo, age ten, from Mora, New Mexico, standing in front of 'My Big Green Mountain'.

'Four wheelers, ramps, and rites of passage' and 'Fort-Makers' are themes where children's individual preferences and developmental needs figure highly. 'Learning Care' and 'The Web' are themes where experience is particularly influenced by the guidance of family, adults, community, and culture. By examining the growing body of research on children's environments within this thematic framework, I hope to provide a structure that allows contextual understanding of children's experiences and that allows children's voices to become part of academic understandings of their experiences.

Four wheelers, ramps, and rites of passage: children's exploration

'Vrrooomm!! And I ride my bike. Brrooom, vrrrooom . . . and sometimes there's a big hill, and I go Whoom! And then I come back up . . . and I go to the top again and WHOOM!' – Michael, age 10 (Derr, 2001:172)

In most cultures throughout the world, rites of passage have been and continue to be significant periods of time when children demonstrate the mastery of their physical environment necessary to be self-sufficient. Play has been an important means for children to learn this mastery. In many societies, these rites have become less formal, yet children still incorporate many aspects of these passages into their play. For example, in Mora, a rural mountain village in New Mexico, children learn to track animals from scat and tracks, to hunt, to maintain irrigation ditches, to collect wild foods and grow domesticated plants, and other skills that promote self-sufficiency at an early age (Derr, 2001). These more formal rites often involve older adults who provide context for the experience. But children also create many informal rites of passage, which they share among peers. For example, like many children, Michael (above) 'ramped' dirt bikes and four-wheelers. Mastery of these vehicles provided peer-acceptance as well as mobility necessary to traverse the mountains (Derr, 2001).

For children of both rural and urban areas, exploration provides many of these same benefits. Children use exploration to expand their view of the world, to test boundaries, and sometimes to incorporate these physical experiences with place into their sense of identity. An important aspect of exploration is the freedom necessary to achieve it. Many parents place restrictions on children that limit their home range considerably (Derr, 2001; Hart, 1979; Matthews et al., 2000a; Moore, 1986). Without the freedom to roam, children have greater difficulty accessing new places to truly explore. Katz (1993) and Punch (2000) both found that rural children in Sudan and Bolivia, respectively, were able to travel far from home as part of their daily chores, and this sanctioned travel provided more opportunities for play and exploration away from home. This was also true for children in northern New Mexico. Rural children with many chores, such as collecting medicinal plants or fuel wood, had many more opportunities to travel into the mountains, find special remote places, and develop experiences that led both to greater freedom and greater mastery of the environment (Derr, 2001).

While some urban children have more limited ranges because of parental fears for safety (Derr, 2001; Katz, 1993; Kong, 2000; Moore, 1986; Punch, 2000, and see Matthews and Tucker, this volume), this is not always the case. Sometimes rural children are similarly restricted. For example, Matthews and others (2000a) found that many rural children were less able to roam about than their peers who lived at the edge of town. Berg and Medrich (1980:330) found that children in densely populated neighbourhoods of Oakland, California enjoyed the greatest freedom whereas children in more physically attractive neighbourhoods with generous lots and wooded open space felt 'painfully isolated from the spontaneous and unplanned life cherished by children in the other neighbourhoods studied'.

For children in New Mexico who were able to explore, a diversity of natural places were most significant in facilitating this experience. In remote Mora, the mountains were significant for nearly three-quarters of both boys and girls. Other places for exploration included abandoned buildings and fields around children's homes. In contrast, in more urban Santa Fe, children listed mountains as places to explore about one-eighth of the time, and close-to-home nature nearly half of the time (Derr, 2001). Other authors have similarly found that children seek out natural places for play (Hart, 1979; Moore, 1986; Sobel, 1993). Some authors (Kellert, 1997, 2002; Orr, 2002; Pyle, 1993, 2002) suggest that these experiences with nature are particularly important in children's intellectual and affective development. However, these ideas are typically based on adults reflecting on their childhood rather than on studies during childhood itself (e.g., Francis, 1995; Hoffman, 1992; Sebba, 1991). For example, Sebba (1991) found that while nearly all adults recalled outdoor places as important in their childhood development, only half of the children named the outdoors as being important. Some have referenced this discrepancy as part of the 'rural idyll', in which adults can romanticize these experiences and detract from children's realities (Holloway and Valentine, 2000; Jones, 2000; Matthews et al., 2000a).

I found that outward exploration was particularly important for some children regardless of the natural elements present in a place. For example, Melissa grew up in Santa Fe and explored the old buildings around its historic plaza. She talked of places that scared her, places that inspired her imagination, and places that were simply fun. Many of these places were associated with a particular person, and this influenced Melissa's feelings toward the place. For Melissa, these places were important for her social development, for development of greater independence, and for inspiring creativity. In contrast, Leo and Marcos explored the mountain areas near their homes. For both, the natural features of the landscape provided an important context for mastery of the physical environment and the self-confidence that stemmed from this. For Marcos, nature was especially important in helping him cope with difficult family situations (Derr, 2001).

These three children provide important contrast and show that exploration can take different shapes and can play different roles in children's lives in both urban and rural environments. The children who seemed to most value exploration as an activity did also seem to gain certain social or emotional benefits from the experience. Similarly, Punch (2000) emphasized that greater spatial autonomy allowed rural Bolivian children greater control over their time and how it was spent, providing them with greater independence and choice.

Hart (1979) referenced the 'spontaneous play' of many children in rural Vermont. In walking about, children found new areas to explore. In my experience, the more interesting features a place could provide, the more likely it was to be explored (Derr, 2001). Similarly, Punch (2000) found that rural Bolivian children explored many areas as they combined work with play away from home. For example, girls would look for plants that could be braided in doll hair or would play games searching for the prettiest flowers. Many studies support this further, that the spontaneous aspect of exploration, whether in places close to home or far away, in nature or cities, is one of the most significant for children (Hart, 1979; Jones, 2000; Lynch, 1997; Moore, 1986; Punch, 2000).

Fort-makers: children's special places and place-making

'I see you've found the King's Chair' – Marcos, age 10 (Derr, 2001a:167)

In contrast to children's outward exploration, children sometimes use place-making as a means of looking inward, of establishing something of their own and developing a sense of self. Marcos (above), created a 'Mighty Jungle' of rocks and trees, where crevasses became caves, and large moulded boulders, chairs. For some children, forts and other special places were also important for 'escaping' – getting away from siblings or parents, centring oneself, and clearing the mind. Like Sobel (1993), I found that children used special places for a variety of needs – some social, some developmental, and some as physical departures for outward exploration (Derr, 2001).

Special places also can be important to children for the creative manipulation of space (Jones, 2000; Lynch, 1997; Moore, 1986; Sobel, 1993). Jones (2000: 42) describes children's 'opportunistic exploitation'

Figure 7.2. Marco, age ten, from Dixon, New Mexico, hanging out in
'The Mighty Jungle', a second generation fort also used by his mother.

of places as being 'remarkably responsive, with a fantastical mixing
of the material and the imaginary'. Chawla (2002) also describes
'magic relationships' that, while not universal to all children, can be an
important way for some children to interact imaginatively with natural
places.

Sobel's (1993) research found that eight to eleven-year-old boys in
Grenada were most interested in 'bush houses' located farther from
home and that few were interested in places closer to home. The boys

in all three New Mexico communities lend further support to this: only a handful of boys regularly spent time in a close-to-home fort or clubhouse. Most boys had special places further from home (Derr, 2001a). These places were important because they were located far enough away from home that exploration and play could be controlled by children alone. While Punch (2000) does not reference any physical structures that children created, she does suggest that rural Bolivian children also valued play spaces farther from home so that they could have greater control and freedom over their play activities.

In New Mexico, many girls created little houses, *casitas*, that were closer to home and were frequently used for social activities with other friends (Derr, 2001). This is also consistent with Sobel's Grenada findings, where girls had less use of or interest in 'bush houses' and more interest in 'playshops' (Sobel, 1993). Children's special places most often did not reflect the romantic notion of natural bowers made of leaves and greenery that Sobel (1993) or Nabhan (1994) depict. Instead, many houses were constructed of scraps of wood or other random materials. Some children did incorporate elements of nature into their places for aesthetics or shade. Many girls decorated their casitas with pictures, flowers, or found objects such as old glass bottles or potshards (Derr, 2001).

Like Jones (2000), I found that children did invest creativity and imagination into their place-making and other place interactions. This could be in the form of a rural Mora boy who created a make-believe Disney land in his clubhouse. This space was important for transporting him from what he saw as the sometimes boring rural life and for escaping from a large number of older brothers and sisters (Derr, 2001). Other children seemed to have 'magic relationships' that Chawla (2002) described, with some children holding strong beliefs in *la llorona*, a mythical weeping woman who haunts river areas, some pretending to be Ewaks from Star Wars, and others creating a sense of harmony with their special places. For example, Rosa (age 10) described her secret place that's 'pretty cuz of the way the river sounds . . . [and] because there's all these birds there, and flowers, and . . .sometimes the birds sound like the fish moving in the water' (Derr, 2001: 194). For Rosa, this special place seemed particularly important in having a quiet place of her own, to read, to think, and to begin to construct her own identity away from family.

For children such as Rosa, special places seemed to play a significant role in her personal well-being. For many children, however, the places seem to be less important than the *act* of place-making (Derr, 2002; Hart, 1979; Lynch, 1997). While special places were important to some

New Mexican children, they were not as universal as others have perhaps suggested (e.g., Nabhan, 1994; Sobel, 1993). In each community, children preferred going to friends' or families' homes, and sometimes to their rooms, more than to a special place (Derr, 2001). In these cases, social experience with friends and family were more important than physical places. This is supported by Hidalgo and Hernández (2001) who found that social attachments were greater than physical attachments in defining people's place attachments in a Spanish city. Children did seem to use their place-making experiences as a way to gain mastery or control over their environment, in ways similar to that which Punch (2000) describes.

It is possible that in New Mexico, place-making plays a reduced role in children's lives for at least three reasons. One possibility is that children in the New Mexico study, who were generally ten or eleven years old, may have already progressed from the developmental stage that Sobel describes for children aged eight to eleven (Sobel, 1993). It is possible that at ages eight to nine, place-making plays a more significant role than at ages ten to eleven. A second possibility is that if parents or other family members do not put much interest in experiencing places, then the children are also less likely to do so. And a third possibility is that many children spend more time indoors, watching television or playing video games, and do not participate in place construction at any age. This latter reason was especially true for children from each community who were raised by a single, working parent without extended family. These children often spent much time indoors (Derr, 2001).

Learning care: children's respect for places and nature

'[We still eat canned food from the garden . . .] like corn, green peas, peaches, pears, apples. . . and we used to get up at 4 o'clock in the morning, and [my grandma] used to wake me up, and we used to go to markets with our food . . .' – Marcos, age 10 (Derr, 2001:165).

Extended family care, once common throughout the world, is still a part of many children's lives. The daily experiences Marcos relates with his grandmother (above) were significant and common to many New Mexico children. These relationships helped ground children in the place where they lived – not just physical spaces, but also social places with a family and cultural history. Grandparents and extended family played an important role in passing on knowledge and respect for the places to their children (Derr, 2001).

The ways children learn care, through direct experiences and adult relationships, has been much less studied than other aspects of children's place experiences. Moore (1986:86–8) suggests that 'caring for animals provides . . . an ideal for children to develop a sense of responsibility and accomplishment', and Myers (1998, 2002) documents the importance of experience with animals in children's social and moral development. Kong (2000) stresses the importance of young Singaporean children not only having interactions with animals and nature, but also *learning care* for them. For many children, it is not just the direct experiences that comprise care, as described for *Rites of Passage* and *Fort-Making* above, but also the interaction with adults within these places. Children and adults frequently form attachments to places because of the social experiences that occur there more than the physical features of a place (Derr, 2001a,b; Hidalgo and Hernández, 2001).

Significant Life Experience (SLE) research suggests that frequent contact with natural places and with adults who teach respect are among the most important factors in developing environmentally caring people (Palmer, 1993; Palmer *et al.*, 1999; Sward, 1999; Tanner, 1980). As an example, Peña (1998:25–6) stresses the importance of his grand-mother's lessons in his long-term understanding toward treatment of other animals. He tells how as a boy he hunted for birds with his uncle:

On our return home, bloody prize trophies in hand, my grandmother Margarita strongly admonished us for this display of indecent behaviour . . . I felt shame but did not understand why. I could see that my grandma thought it was wrong to kill another living being. But maybe a preadolescent boy, anxious to prove his worthiness as a companion to older male kin, is too perplexed with his place in the family to worry much about ethical implications of such behaviour.

Peña describes a balancing act between the social rites of passage that were important in his immediate life, with the longer term lessons his grandmother, in the end, succeeded in passing on. The experiences of children in New Mexico lend further support to SLE research, that it is important not only for children to have direct experiences with plants and animals, but that there be a guiding adult to model respect. For example, one Santa Fe child spoke of watching ravens fledge each year, lowering her voice as she retold the event, demonstrating an active internalization of behaviours she learned from her father. A second child boasted loudly of his interactions with coyotes outside his house and how he wished he could catch the animal to show his cousins (Derr, 2001). To my knowledge, no studies to date have examined the extent that adult messages stay with children in their own play, or how this may vary by child and their relationship to adults. Like Peña, the children I worked with in New Mexico were likely to learn quite different messages from family members of different genders, ages, and values. Relatives who were closer in age, older cousins for example, provided role models more similar to those Peña describes for his uncle, than to the guiding instruction of his grandmother.

Sometimes New Mexico children's learning of care and respect for plants and animals was tied to a larger land ethic, held by a family or community, and sometimes it was not. For example, one Mora boy told of a family story, passed down from his grandfather, of how the horse, whose labour helps feed the family, always eats first. Another Mora boy spoke of wild cats, and how his immediate family did not think it right to trap them, but how his uncle, a rancher, would (Derr, 2001). When the concept of respect was tied to broader cultural ethics, it seemed that children could more rapidly internalize and understand these values because they were tied to a way of life.

Similarly, when children felt ownership over a place, whether because it was part of a family property, or because they personally had created the place, they were much more likely to be concerned about protecting it (Derr, 2001). This concept is supported by Low (1992) and Hay (1998) who both suggest that some form of ownership is an important dimension to place attachments. Tapsell (1997) found that children who lived near a river saw restoration activities as positively influencing play space, and Chawla (1998) also suggests that direct experiences with degraded or polluted environments have begun to play a role in shaping children's awareness and sensitivity to the environment.

The web: children's experience of cultural place

'Sometimes we go visit "Grandma" Lita. . . She's a medica,[1] and she's 90 . . . We all sit on her porch and listen to her tell stories of when she was a girl. . . Leo says, "I wish I were her grandson, I would learn it all". . .' – Maria, mother of Leo, age 10 (Derr, 2001)

When children live in and experience culture as a part of the place where they live, the lessons they learn are often tied to a way of life and a larger landscape. I call these integrated experiences part of a 'cultural web' – where stories, histories, and places all converge. For example, the stories Grandma Lita told Leo and others in their tiny mountain town (above) were part of a larger narrative that could influence children's experiences. When I walked with Leo through the fields near his home, he looked for medicinal plants, showed them to me, and told stories about them (Derr, 2002). Stories are an important form of place knowledge, common to many cultures throughout the world (e.g., Basso, 1996; Nabhan and St. Antoine, 1993). Ong (1982:41) explains the way oral cultures 'regard highly those wise old men and women who specialize in conserving [knowledge], who know and can tell the stories of the days of old'. And Cronon (1992:1375) suggests 'the stories we tell change the way we act in the world'. Many researchers lend further support to this by demonstrating ways that narrative is a qualitatively different form of learning (Devoscori, 1993; Fivush, 1995; Meichenbaum, 1993; Singer, 1995; Sutton-Smith, 1986; Yussen *et al.*, 1988; Zwann, 1995).

Singer (1995) suggests that narrative forms of memory are more closely associated with people's personality framework: stories help to tell us who we are. These stories, from 'the old ones' in New Mexico, were important in imbuing places and place experiences with meaning for children. Many cultural stories in the Hispanic Southwest consist of ghost stories, such as *la llorona*, or of moral lessons, which pass on values for plants and animals (Atencio, 2000). Though it was much harder to track, New Mexican children were influenced by these tales in constructing their own place experiences. *La llorona*, the weeping woman who is thought to haunt many rivers in New Mexico, was invoked by adults when they wanted to coerce children into certain behaviours. Yet this story also directly influenced children's place experiences: *la llorona* became a real figure at the river, yielding greater fear and excitement to these places in the evening. While some sought out these places, others avoided riversides altogether for fear of seeing this weeping woman.

I also found that children's place experiences were influenced by stories in rural Gambia, West Africa. These children avoided playing in the bush for fear of elves that were common in their folklore (Derr, 1996). It is possible that these elves were similar in function to *los duendes* that Punch (2000) described for Bolivian parents and children. While there is much greater documentation of stories in many cultures, less studied is the interaction between children's place experiences and these stories. Yet cultural and family stories do shape the locations and types of place experiences children have at least some of the time (Chawla, 2002; Derr, 1996; Derr, 2001).

'The web' consists of more than stories, it embodies an entire social relationship with extended family and community. While not all children feel a connection to 'community' (Derr, 2001; Matthews *et al.*, 2000a), some children do. For example, Leo, at age ten, was concerned with the career he might take so that he could remain in Mora, at his family's ranch. 'The web' provided children with a sense of ownership and attachment, and a more integrated sense of the place where they lived. When this is absent, children sometimes lose important nurturing and mentoring experiences that come from elders in a community. The ways children learn about and experience place matters because these more intimate, ongoing, everyday kinds of experiences that combine family and community with place are those that children hold on to and are more likely to integrate into their own identity (Derr, 2001).

Discussion

As a growing body of literature shows us, children gain much from their experiences with places. Exploratory places allow a sense of freedom, control, and self-sufficiency. Special places provide opportunities for creativity, imagination, and getting away from others to centre oneself. Activities that allow children to learn care also can help develop a sense of responsibility, respect, and empathy toward other living things. And family and community interactions help children position some place experiences into broader cultural meanings. All these place experiences help shape a child's identity and may help form attachments to place.

Those who study children's experiences with the environment tend also to advocate for unstructured, spontaneous play in spaces (e.g., Jones, 2000; Kong, 2000; Moore, 1986; Moore and Wong, 1997), and many champion the need for children to experience natural places as part of their development (e.g., Chawla, 2002; Kellert, 1997, 2002; Kong, 2000; Moore and Wong, 1997; Orr, 2002; Pyle, 1993, 2002). Spontaneous play is a common aspect to children's play (Derr, 2001; Hart, 1979; Jones, 2000; Moore, 1986; Punch, 2000) and places that support this kind of exploration need to be safe-guarded. Orr (2002:287) calls attention to a 'kind of obliteration' that results when children's places fall victim to adults' unknowing planning and 'development'. It is important for children's concerns and voices to be increasingly involved in planning and development projects that affect their lives (see also Sutton and Kemp, this volume).

Yet some authors remind us that it is also important to approach these issues with caution (Hart, 1997; Holloway and Valentine, 2000; Moore, 1986). If planning or education becomes too prescriptive, then spontaneity is lost. This is also true for many of the social interactions that influence children's place experiences. Time with grandparents or extended family, informal stories and lessons cannot be maintained in a structured way. Hart (1997:3) suggests that 'too many children are naively parroting clichés from someone else's agenda . . . entirely removed from their own experiences'. We need to continue to understand children's experiences from their own perspectives, and also to strive to make sure that environmental planning and education meet children's real needs and interests, so that children will have a sense of ownership and connection to what they experience and learn.

Note

1 A *medica* or *curandera* is a woman who practices traditional, herbal medicine.

References

Atencio, E. (2000). Environmental justice and public lands ranching in northern New Mexico. *The Quivira Coalition, 4*(1), 1, 16–21, 23. Santa Fe, New Mexico.

Basso, K. (1996). *Wisdom Sits in Places: Landscape and Language Among the Western Apache.* Albuquerque: University of New Mexico Press.

Beazley, H. (2000). Home sweet home? Street children's sites of belonging. In S. L. Holloway and G. Valentine (eds.), *Children's Geographies: Playing, Living, Learning* (pp. 194–210). London: Routledge Press.

Berg, M. and Medrich, E. A. (1980). Children in four neighborhoods: the physical environment and its effect on play and play patterns. *Environment and Behavior, 12*(3), 320–48.

Chawla, L. (1998). Significant life experiences revisited. *Journal of Environmental Education, 29*(3), 11–21.

Chawla, L. (2002). Spots of time: manifold ways of being in nature in childhood. In P. H. Kahn, Jr. and S. R. Kellert (eds.), *Children and Nature: Psychological, Sociocultural, and Evolutionary Investigations* (pp. 199–225). Cambridge, MA: MIT Press.

Cronon, W. (1992). A place for stories: nature, history, and narrative. *Journal of American History, 78*(4), 1347–76.

Derr, V. (1996). Stories that teach: human–environment relations in Gambian folktales. The spirituality of place in children's and adolescent literature. *Nebraska English Journal, 41*(1), 6–17.

Derr, V. (2001). *Voices from the Mountains: Children's Sense of Place in Three Communities of Northern New Mexico.* Ann Arbor, MI: Bell Howell Learning Company.

Derr, V. (2002). Children's sense of place in northern New Mexico. *Journal of Environmental Psychology, 22*, 125–37.

Devoscori, A. (1993). Joint-reading a picture book: verbal interaction and narrative skills. *Cognition and Instruction, 11*(3–4), 299–323.

Fivush, R. (1995). Language, narrative, and autobiography. *Consciousness and Cognition, 4*(1), 100–03.

Francis, M. (1995). Childhood's garden: memory and meaning of gardens. *Children's Environments, 12*(2), 183–91.

Hart, R. (1979). *Children's Experience of Place.* New York: Knopf.

Hart, R. (1997). *Children's Participation: The Theory and Practice of Involving Young Citizens in Community Development and Environmental Care.* New York: UNICEF.

Hay, R. (1998). Sense of place in developmental context. *Journal of Environmental Psychology, 18*, 5–29.

Hidalgo, M. C. and B. Hernández (2001). Place attachment: conceptual and empirical questions. *Journal of Environmental Psychology, 21*, 273–81.

Hoffman, E. (1992). *Visions of Innocence*. Boston: Shambhala.

Holloway, S. L. and Valentine, G. (2000). Children's geographis and the new social studies of childhood. In S. L. Holloway and G. Valentine (eds.), *Children's Geographies: Playing, Living, Learning* (pp. 1–28). London: Routledge Press.

Jones, O. (2000). Melting geography: purity, disorder, childhood and space. In S. L. Holloway and G. Valentine (eds.), *Children's Geographies: Playing, Living, Learning* (pp. 29–47). London: Routledge Press.

Katz, C. (1993). Growing girls/circles: limits on the spaces of knowing in rural Sudan and U.S. cities. In C. Katz and J. Monk (eds.), *Full Circles: Geographies of Women Over the Life Course*. London: Routledge Press.

Kellert, S. R. (1997). *Kinship to Mastery: Biophilia in Human Evolution and Development*. Washington DC: Island Press.

Kellert, S. R. (2002). Experiencing nature: affective, cognitive, and evaluative development in children. In P. H. Kahn, Jr. and S. R. Kellert (eds.), *Children and Nature: Psychological, Sociocultural, and Evolutionary Investigations* (pp. 117–52). Cambridge, MA: MIT Press.

Kong, L. (2000). Nature's dangers, nature's pleasures: urban children and the natural world. In S. L. Holloway and G. Valentine (eds.), *Children's Geographies: Playing, Living, Learning* (pp. 257–71). London: Routledge Press.

Low, S. M. (1992). Symbolic ties that bind: place attachment in the plaza. In I. Altman and S. M. Low (eds.), *Place Attachment* (pp. 165–85). New York: Plenum Press.

Lynch, K. (1997). *Growing Up in Cities*. Cambridge, MA: MIT Press.

Matthews, H. (1995). Culture, environmental experience, and environmental awareness: making sense of young Kenyan children's views of place. *Geographical Journal*, *161*(3), 285–95.

Matthews, H., Limb, M., and Taylor, M. (2000b). The 'street as thirdspace'. In S. L. Holloway and G. Valentine (eds.), *Children's Geographies: Playing, Living, Learning* (pp. 63–79). London: Routledge Press.

Matthews, H., Taylor, M., Sherwood, K., Tucker, F., and Limb, M. (2000a). Growing up in the countryside: children and the rural idyll. *Journal of Rural Studies*, *16*, 141–53.

Meichenbaum, D. (1993). Changing conceptions of cognitive behavior modification: restrospect and prospect. *Journal of Consulting and Clinical Psychology*, *61*(2), 202–04.

Moore, R. C. (1986). *Childhood's Domain: Play and Place in Child Development*. Berkeley, CA: MIG Communications.

Moore, R. C. and Wong, H., (1997). *Natural Learning: Creating Environments for Nature's Way of Teaching*. Berkeley, CA: MIG Communications.

Myers, O. E., Jr. (1998). *Children and Animals: Social Development and Connections to Other Species*. Boulder, CO: Westview Press.

Myers, O. E., Jr. and Saunders, C. D. (2002). Animals as links toward developing caring relationships with the natural world. In P. H. Kahn, Jr. and S. R. Kellert (eds.), *Children and Nature: Psychological, Sociocultural, and Evolutionary Investigations* (pp. 153–78). Cambridge, MA: MIT Press.

Nabhan, G. P. (1994). A child's sense of wildness. In G. P. Nabhan and S. Trimble (eds.), *The Geography of Childhood: Why Children Need Wild Places* (pp. 3–14). Boston, MA: Beacon Press.

Nabhan, G. P. and St. Antoine, S. (1993). The loss of floral and faunal story: the extinction of experience. In S. R. Kellert and E. O. Wilson (eds.), *The Biophilia Hypothesis* (pp. 229–50). Washington, DC: Island Press.

Ong, W. J. (1983). *Orality and Literacy: The Technologizing of the Word.* New York: Metheun.

Orr, D. (2002). Political economy and the ecology of childhood. In P. H. Kahn, Jr. and S. R. Kellert (eds.), *Children and Nature: Psychological, Sociocultural, and Evolutionary Investigations* (pp. 279–303). Cambridge, MA: MIT Press.

Palmer, J. A. (1993). Development of concern for the environment and formative experiences of educators. *Journal of Environmental Education, 24*(3), 26–30.

Palmer, J. A., Suggate J., Robottom I. and Hart P. (1999). Significant life experience and formative influences on the development of adults' environmental awareness in the UK, Australia, and Canada. *Environmental Education Research, 5*(2), 181–200.

Peña, D. G. (1998). Los Animalitos: culture, ecology, and the politics of place in the Upper Rio Grande. In D. G. Peña (ed.), *Chicano Culture, Ecology, Politics* (pp. 25–7). Tucson: University of Arizona Press.

Punch, S. (2000). Children's strategies for creating playspaces: negotiating independence in rural Bolivia. In S. L. Holloway and G. Valentine (eds.), *Children's Geographies: Playing, Living, Learning* (pp. 48–62). London: Routledge Press.

Pyle, R. M. (1993). *The Thunder Tree: Lessons from an Urban Wildland.* Boston: Houghton Mifflin Company.

Pyle, R. M. (2002). Eden in a vacant lot: special places, species, and kids in the neighborhood of life. In P. H. Kahn, Jr. and S. R. Kellert (eds.), *Children and Nature: Psychological, Sociocultural, and Evolutionary Investigations* (pp. 305–27). Cambridge, MA: MIT Press.

Robson, E. (1996). Working girls and boys: children's contribution to household survival in West Africa. *Geography, 81*, 403–07.

Sebba, R. (1991). The landscapes of childhood: the reflections of childhood's environment in adult memories and in children's attitudes. *Environment and Behavior, 23*, 395–422.

Singer, J. A. (1995). Seeing one's self: locating narrative memory in a framework of personality. *Journal of Personality, 63*(3), 429–59.

Sobel, D. (1993). *Children's Special Places: Exploring the Role of Forts, Dens, and Bush Houses in Middle Childhood.* Tuscon, AZ: Zephyr Press.

Sutton-Smith, B. (1986). The development of fictional narrative performances. *Topics in Language Disorders, 7*(1), 1–10.

Sward, L. (1999). Significant life experiences affecting the environmental sensitivity of El Salvadoran environmental professionals. *Environmental Education Research, 5*(2), 201–06.

Tapsell, S. M. (1997). Rivers and river restoration: a child's view. *Landscape Research, 22*(1), 45–65.

Tanner, T. (1980). Significant life experiences: a new research area in environmental education. *Journal of Environmental Education, 11*(4), 20–4.

Ward, C. (1978). *The Child in the City*. London: Architectural Press.

Ward, C. (1990). *The Child in the Country*. London: Bedford Square Press.

Yussen, S., Huang, S., Mathews, S. and Evans, R. (1988). The robustness and temporal course of the story schema's influence on recall. *Journal of Experimental Psychology: Learning, Memory, and Cognition, 14*(1), 173–9.

Zwann, R. (1995). Dimensions of situational model construction in narrative comprehension. *Journal of Experimental Psychology*, 386–97.

8   Is contact with nature important for healthy child development? State of the evidence

Andrea Faber Taylor and Frances E. Kuo

We know that children need nature . . . or do we? There are certainly many reasons to think that nature plays an important role in child development. For many of us, intuition emphatically asserts that nature is good for children. We hold intuitions such as, 'every kid needs a dog', 'children need a nice yard to play in', and 'children need "fresh air"'. Beyond these intuitions, there are also well-reasoned theoretical arguments as to why humans in general – and therefore children – might have an inborn need for contact with nature (e.g., S. Kaplan, 1995; Wilson, 1984). And there is a growing body of qualitative research consistent with this idea (Bardill, 1997; Hart, 1979; R. Moore, 1989; R. C. Moore, 1986; Nabhan, 1994; Sebba, 1991; Sobel, 1993; Titman, 1994). But what do we really *know* about the value of nature in promoting child development? What systematic evidence is there for or against this possibility? Is children's need for nature established fact, yet-to-be-substantiated folk theory, or simply myth?

The question of nature's role in healthy child development is increasingly urgent. A consistent concern among the researchers studying children and nature is that children's access to nature is rapidly diminishing (e.g., Kahn, 2002; Kellert, 2002; Pyle, 2002; Rivkin, 2000). Not only may there be less nature for children to access, but children's access of what remains may be increasingly sporadic. Some researchers suggest that parents are limiting children's freedom to roam more than in previous generations (Gaster, 1991; Hillman, Adams, and Whitelegg, 1990), partly for fear of traffic and crimes against children (for reviews see Spencer and Woolley, 2000; Valentine, 1997; and Rissotto and Giuliani, this volume). Children's lives are increasingly filled with programmed activities, leaving them with little time for exploring or free play outdoors (Davis, 1999; Rosenfeld, 2001). With the advent of video games, computers, and the Internet, children today may have more reasons to stay indoors than ever, and busy parents may be inadvertently modeling for their children a life in which nature activities have low priority.

Figure 8.1. The child's need for contact with nature: more than a romantic notion?

Does it really matter whether children have contact with nature? If children's need for contact with nature is simply a romantic notion, then we certainly cannot advocate spending precious resources on it. On the other hand, if contact with nature is as important to children as good nutrition and adequate sleep, then current trends in children's access to nature need to be addressed.

This chapter reviews the literature on children and nature with an eye to answering the question: does contact with nature promote healthy child development? Because the purpose of this review is to assess evidence of a causal link between contact with nature and children's development, the emphasis is on experimental and quasi-experimental studies, and to a lesser extent, correlational work. We focus on the ways in which nature in two broad realms – 'green space' and animals – fosters healthy psychological development.

Children and green space

A diverse array of studies has explored possible impacts of green spaces on healthy child development. These have examined the benefits of green spaces in a variety of forms, including wilderness programmes, outdoor education programmes with hands-on nature activities, and green space in neighbourhoods, play settings, and schools. The specific outcomes examined have been diverse as well, including cognitive, social, and emotional development, and the populations studied cover a wide range of socioeconomic groups, ages, housing conditions, and countries, though mostly developed ones (with the exception of Ratanapojnard, 2001) Research has included both children in clinical populations and children in the general population.

Overall, there is a great deal of encouraging evidence linking green space to important developmental outcomes. While a number of recurring methodological weaknesses in this literature limit the conclusions that can be drawn, this body of work also has notable strengths. It is encouraging that positive findings have come from studies employing different measures, research designs, and populations. To the extent that the findings reflect a real effect of green space on children's development, this effect would seem to be pervasive and generalizable to different populations and environments.

Impacts of wilderness programmes

Some of the most exciting findings of a link between contact with green space and developmental outcomes come from studies examining the effects of outdoor challenge programmes on children's self-esteem and sense of self. In one such study, in which over 400 youths were surveyed and interviewed, the majority reported an increased sense of personal autonomy, improved self-concept, a greater capacity for taking action and being decisive, and an improvement in their interpersonal skills after participating in wilderness challenge programmes (Kellert and Derr, 1998). There are similar findings from a study by R. Kaplan (1977) of over 200 youths. Here, close to half of nature programme participants showed an increase from low to high scores on a positive self-view scale (a component of self-esteem) from pre- to post-experience, whereas only a quarter of control group participants demonstrated such a change.

In another study, questionnaires and content analyses were used to assess the experiences of participants from twenty-five outdoor challenge groups. During their wilderness experience, the participants reported experiencing increased self-confidence and increased self-awareness; after their return to everyday life, they reported greater self-confidence and an improved sense of self-identity (S. R. Kaplan and Talbot, 1983). Similarly, pre- and post-experience surveys of youth and adult wilderness programme participants indicated an increase in psychological energy (including feeling self-confident, in control, and able to concentrate), positive outlook, and a decrease in feeling hassled after their wilderness experience (R Kaplan, 1984). Only one study examining self-esteem before and after an Outward Bound experience obtained null findings, but this null finding may have been due to the small sample size involved (R. Kaplan, 1974).

A few researchers have examined behavioural outcomes. In a study of teenage participants in a residential treatment programme based on wilderness camping, post-treatment parent and teacher reports showed that the majority of youths demonstrated improved interpersonal skills and school performance, but there was no improvement in delinquent behaviours compared to the pre-treatment ratings (Behar and Stephens, 1978). A study of troubled youths in a therapeutic wilderness programme showed an increase in scores on a measure of self-concept, and parent reports indicated a reduction in problem behaviours from pre- to six weeks, post-experience (Bandoroff and Scherer, 1994). Only weak support comes from a study in which Outward Bound participants with Attention Deficit Hyperactivity Disorder (AD/HD) and Conduct Disorder (CD) were rated as showing only slight reductions on measures of disruptive behaviours, inattention, and impulsivity, although no statistical tests were reported (Katcher, 2000). It is interesting to note that four studies included longitudinal measures and found that participants continued to report beneficial outcomes long after (ranging from six weeks to several years after) their nature experience (Bandoroff and Scherer, 1994; Behar and Stephens, 1978; R. Kaplan, 1977; Kellert and Derr, 1998).

These findings suggest that contact with green space may have benefits for children's development, but two methodological weaknesses make interpretation of these findings difficult. While this large volume of data (R. Kaplan, 1977; S. R. Kaplan and Talbot, 1983; Kellert and Derr, 1998) is almost entirely consistent with a systematic relationship between wilderness programmes and several developmental benefits, a limitation of many studies is the reliance on self-report measures. Such measures can be biased by participants' beliefs, by a desire to please the researcher or by wanting to support the programmes. Another limitation is the confounding of environmental experience with survival activities. Most of the effects seem plausibly attributable to the programme activities rather than the wilderness setting. Specifically, it seems likely that the need for participants to be self-reliant in unfamiliar and physically challenging environments is enough to promote increases in at least some, if not all, of the domains. At this point, we do not know if the reported effects are valid. To the extent that self-report is reliable and to the extent that the outcomes of wilderness experiences are attributable to the environment, these findings suggest that the potential benefits of wilderness for children's self-esteem, sense of self, and perhaps even their behaviour may be profound.

Impacts of outdoor education programmes

Several studies have findings consistent with the possibility that there is a systematic relationship between outdoor curricula in green space and learning. Of four studies comparing outcomes associated with outdoor versus indoor classroom curricula, three have found more learning after the outdoor classroom curricula. Children with outdoor classroom curricula scored higher on measures of knowledge transfer (Basile, 2000), performed better on standardized tests of academic achievement, earned higher grade point averages (Lieberman, 1998) and demonstrated greater knowledge gain (Ratanapojnard, 2001), than children with indoor curricula. One found children did not show greater learning in an outdoor classroom than those taught in a combination of indoor and outdoor classrooms or those taught in an indoor classroom (Howie, 1974). As in the wilderness programme research, contact with nature in these studies is confounded with activity – the outdoor curricula involved 'hands-on learning' while the indoor curricula followed a standard classroom format, making interpretation difficult. It is not clear to what extent the outcomes are caused by the different activities taking place in the different settings versus the settings per se. These cautions notwithstanding, the findings are consistent with the notion that outdoor education programmes may be widely effective in promoting learning.

Green space and children's play

Studies comparing patterns of play and creative play – important means of cognitive, social, and emotional development – in green versus built spaces are consistent with the notion that green space supports healthy child development. In one such study, children observed in a school yard with both green play spaces and built play spaces engaged in more creative forms of play in the green spaces than in the built spaces (Kirkby, 1989). In another study, children observed in green outdoor spaces engaged in more play and creative forms of play than children in barren outdoor spaces. In this same study children observed in green outdoor spaces also had more access to adults than children in barren spaces; while not a developmental outcome in itself, access to adults increases a child's potential for interaction with adults, which in turn fosters social development (Faber Taylor, Kuo, and Sullivan, 1998). However, a weakness of these studies is that children were self-selecting the spaces in which they played. Perhaps green space does not foster creative play, but rather when given a choice, children choose green spaces when they intend to engage in creative play.

Green space and attention

There is compelling evidence for a link between green space and enhanced capacity to pay attention in children. This link appears to hold when comparing different children's attentional functioning in, or after being in, different settings.

Two studies have compared different children in different settings, but did not employ random assignment. One study, compared two Swedish day nurseries, and found that children at the day nursery with a more natural school yard, which was incorporated into the curriculum allowing children to spend a great deal of time in it, were rated higher on a measure of concentration than children with a more built school yard, which was used in a more traditional manner (Grahn, 1997). Another study, found the greener the typical play-space of a child with AD/HD the lower their parental rating of overall symptom severity (Faber Taylor, Kuo, and Sullivan, 2001). Grahn (1997) was limited because only two spaces were compared, but in another study Faber Taylor *et al.* (2001) also compared multiple green and barren spaces and had similar findings. A weakness of both of these studies is that participants self-selected their settings. Well-functioning families, with potentially well-functioning children, may choose to send their child to a greener school, and children with AD/HD may choose to play in greener settings when they are in relatively high-functioning states.

Two other studies comparing different children in different settings help address the concerns about self-selection. Wells (2000) examined children who had moved from relatively barren housing to greener housing through a self-help housing programme; it is unclear how much, if any, influence participants had on their housing assignment. Those children whose moves involved the greatest increase in naturalness received the highest ratings on concentration by their parents after the move. Were parents' ratings influenced by their beliefs about the benefits of moving to a greener home? It seems unlikely, but a second study addressed this concern; using objective performance measures of concentration, Faber Taylor and colleagues examined view and concentration in children randomly assigned to architecturally identical apartments within the same development. The greener a girl's view from her apartment, the higher she scored on standardized performance measures of concentration. Boys showed no relationship between view and concentration. One interpretation of this latter finding is that in that public housing setting boys may not have been spending much time near their home and perhaps a measure of the greenness where they played would have been positively linked with their functioning (Faber Taylor, Kuo, and Sullivan, 2002). Indeed other research supports this interpretation (e.g., Faber Taylor et al., 2001).

Two studies have compared the same children under different settings and have also found links between green space and nature. In one study, parent ratings of activities' effects on their child's AD/HD symptoms indicated a greater reduction in symptoms after engaging in activities in green spaces compared to indoor and built outdoor spaces. Activities nominated by parents as helpful in reducing AD/HD symptoms were disproportionately likely to take place in green outdoor settings, and activities nominated as exacerbating symptoms were disproportionately likely to take place in non-green settings (Faber Taylor et al., 2001). A study of over 450 children with AD/HD also showed that parent ratings of activities' effects on symptoms indicated a greater reduction in attention deficit symptoms after engaging in activities in green outdoor spaces compared to indoor and built outdoor spaces. These findings were quite consistent across gender, age, child's severity of symptoms, co-morbid disorders, diagnosis, region of the United States, and community size (Kuo and Faber Taylor, 2004). But a weakness of these studies is that they are based on parent-report, making the findings susceptible to bias. Nonetheless, this set of findings strongly suggests viewing and being in relatively natural settings enhances attention in children and supports the idea that contact with nature is a valuable resource for children's healthy development.

Green space, conduct and well-being

Two studies focused on green space and children's conduct and well-being. Wells and Evans (2000) studied rural children and found that those with more nature near their home received lower maternal ratings on a measure of behavioural conduct disorders, anxiety and depression, indicating that they were less psychologically distressed than peers with less near-home nature. Children with more near-home nature also rated themselves higher on a global measure of self-worth than peers with less. This study also suggests that near-home nature buffered the effects of stressful life events on children's psychological distress. As described above, Faber Taylor et al. (2002) found that the greener a girl's view from her apartment the higher she scored on several standard psychological performance measures of impulse inhibition and delay of gratification. In addition, in that study when measures of concentration, impulse inhibition, and delay of gratification were combined as an index of self-discipline, the greener a girl's view from her apartment the higher she scored. However, in the same study, the boys' scores on measures of impulse inhibition, delay of gratification, and a self-discipline index did not correlate with greenness of their apartment view.

Both studies compared existing groups (i.e., subjects not fully randomly assigned to conditions). In Wells and Evans (2003) there is the possibility that psychologically more robust people may have self-selected to live in natural settings and this might explain why psychological distress is lower for those living in natural settings, and why the impacts of life stressors are less for those living in natural settings. However, this alternative explanation is less plausible in the case of Faber Taylor *et al.* (2002). This latter study also relied on existing groups, but the housing-assignment process was such that opportunities for self-selection into green or not-green housing were rare. With the exception of one set of null findings with a sample of boys, these studies' findings suggest a link between green space and children's conduct and well-being, and thereby add additional support to the notion that green space is a valuable resource for healthy child development.

Children and animals

The research on children's contact with animals includes two distinct groups of studies: on the impacts of contact with pets; and with animals trained for use in therapy such as dogs, horses, and dolphins. In our review of the literature, we did not find any empirical research focused on undomesticated animals such as urban wildlife. Like the research on green space, the studies on children and animals touched on cognitive, social and emotional development and involved diverse subpopulations of children. Overall, the evidence for contact with animals promoting healthy child development is promising. While there is ambiguity in the findings of individual studies, the persistence of positive findings across different studies with different methodological weaknesses lends confidence that this is a real effect.

Pet ownership/pet bond and development

A number of studies have examined the potential effects of pets on child development with mostly positive results with the exception of a few

Figure 8.2. Contact with animals may increase capacity for empathy.

null findings. Of the studies with pets, two studies have examined potential impacts on self-esteem or self-concept. Covet (1985) found teenagers who own pets scored higher on a measure of self-esteem than those who did not. Another study found that adults' self-concept was related to the age when they first had a bond with a pet; those who had a first pet during their teen years or when they were less than six years old scored higher on a measure of self-concept as an adult than adults who had a first pet between the ages of six and twelve (Poresky, Hendrix, Mosier and Samuelson, 2001). It is worth noting that two non-pet studies involving random assignment to conditions with and without animals also linked increased self-esteem/self-concept with animals. In Dismuke (1984), children interacting with horses during therapy sessions had a greater increase in scores on a measure of self-esteem than those receiving therapy without a horse. In Katcher (2000) youths who participated in a programme that incorporated hands-on learning with animals and natural ecosystems scored higher on a measure of self-concept than youths participating in the regular school programme.

Five studies with pets have examined their impact on children's social development. Guttman (1984) found that boys who owned a pet performed better on measures of their capacity for decoding non-verbal information, potentially making them better at communication, than boys who did not own a pet. Three studies found that young children with a strong bond or close relationship with their pet scored higher on a measure of empathy than children with a weak relationship to their pet (Poresky, 1990, 1996; Vidovic, Stetic, and Bratko, 1999) and children with no pet (Vidovic *et al.*, 1999). In Melson, Peet and Sparks (1991) five-year-old boys and fifth-grade boys and girls who were attached to a pet scored higher on measures of empathy, but for secondary school children in the study the findings were mixed or essentially null. Melson *et al.* also found that primary school children scores on a measure of perceived competence was related to their attachment to a pet. To date, the research on pets shows mixed evidence of a link between pets and child development. At present what is completely unclear is whether this link, if it exists, is due to pre-existing differences in the kinds of families who choose to have pets versus those who do not, or the kinds of children who form bonds with family pets versus those who do not. In other words, socially oriented, empathic children may be more likely to form bonds with pets, and socially oriented, empathic parents may be more likely to get pets for their children.

Companion animals and emotional self-regulation

Several findings are consistent with the notion that companion animals may support children's emotional self-regulation and thus may be valuable for healthy child development. Survey studies have found that the majority of pet owners turn to their pet for comfort when sad or upset (Covert, 1985; Rost, 1994; Triebenbacher, 1998). This raises the intriguing possibility that contact with pets might promote a later capacity for emotional regulation even when a pet is not available. Further, a study of children undergoing physical examinations found that those with a dog present in their exam room were rated as exhibiting less behavioural distress than those without a dog present, though there was a null finding with physiological measures of stress (Hansen, Messinger, Baun and Megel, 1999). In this study, however, raters were not blind to the presence or absence of a dog, and thus could have made biased ratings of the children's behaviours.

Animals in the context of therapeutic/educational interventions

A set of mixed findings comes from studies of animals in therapeutic and educational interventions, and thus are only somewhat consistent with the notion that animals contribute to children's cognitive and social functioning and development. These findings are difficult to interpret, because most have confounds and rely on potentially biased raters. In one such study, youths with AD/HD and CD in a programme involving hands-on-contact with animals were rated as displaying a greater reduction in inattention and impulsivity on a measure of symptom severity than the children in an outdoor challenge programme (Katcher, 2000). Another study found children with a dog incorporated into their classroom activities demonstrated greater improvement in their field independence, which plays a role in the development of autonomy, than children in a class without a dog present (Hergovich, 2002).

A few studies have examined whether the presence of animals enhances social behaviour. In Hergovich (2002), teacher ratings showed a greater increase in social integration among students and a greater decrease in children rated as aggressive after a dog was present in their classroom for three months than were found among comparable students without a dog in their classroom. However, there was one null finding with a performance measure of social intelligence. Limond (1997) found that children with Down's Syndrome displayed greater sustained focus towards and interaction with their therapist when a live dog was present than when a life-like imitation dog was present (Limond,

1997). Likewise, children with autism were rated as displaying an increase in pro-social behaviour directed at the therapist and a decrease in self-absorption after a dog was incorporated into therapy sessions. Children with mental disabilities were rated as engaging in more verbal responding to therapist's lessons with a dolphin present than when their favourite water toy was present (Nathanson and de Faria, 1993). Finally, youths in a programme with animals (described earlier) received better ratings on two measures of childhood conduct disturbances, indicating fewer aggressive behaviours and more cooperative behaviours, than the control group (Katcher, 2000).

It is important to note that two studies with more rigorous methodologies provide additional evidence of a link between the presence of animals and social outcomes and some evidence for cognitive and emotional outcomes. In Bailey (1987) exposure to animals in a classroom setting was found to impact children's capacity for empathy. Children with a puppy incorporated into a curriculum about pet care showed a greater increase in their ability to predict others' feelings and emotional states than children with the same curriculum without a puppy present or children in a control group. A longitudinal measure indicated a lasting change. In Dismuke (1984) children with learning disabilities and language disorders who were taught language skills in conjunction with horseback riding demonstrated increases on measures of complexity of language structure, appropriateness and efficient use of speech, and sensorimotor integration. In contrast, children who were taught the same language curriculum in a classroom setting without animals, but which included activities involving motor skills, only showed improvements in language complexity. However, a weakness in both these studies is that there is a chance that the outcomes were due to differences between teachers or therapists rather than contact with animals, as the animal and non-animal conditions did not have the same teacher or therapist. However, in both studies the strengths of children were randomly assigned to conditions and the raters were blind to the condition in which the children had been placed.

Animals as positive stimulation for infants

Findings from studies examining the impact of animals' presence on infants' behaviours are consistent with the possibility that a relationship exists between animals' and infants' cognitive behaviours. Kidd and Kidd (1987) found that infants spent more time observing and interacting with their family dog or cat than an interactive toy dog or cat. Ricard (1992) found infants spent more time observing and exploring in the presence of a live rabbit than they spent observing or exploring in the presence of a toy turtle (that lit up, made noises and moved) or in the presence of an unfamiliar woman. Unfortunately, in both studies the non-animal condition differed from the animal condition in ways other than just the presence or absence of an animal, and these differences make it difficult to determine if the group differences were attributable to the animal. In addition, raters were not blind to condition and thus could have given biased ratings.

Conclusion

Intuition commonly holds that nature is good for children. Does contact with nature really enhance children's functioning and development? While evidence in many forms of the relationship between nature and child development has been accruing, in this chapter we have focused on assessing the evidence of a causal link between nature and child development. With a few exceptions, most of the studies have methodological weaknesses that need to be addressed through future research. However, given the pattern of findings pointing in the same direction and persisting across different sub-populations of children and different settings, it is more parsimonious to accept the fact that nature can promote healthy child development. While we await more carefully controlled studies providing evidence of a causal relationship, current evidence suggests that the general hypothesis may be correct: contact with nature is supportive of healthy child development in several domains – cognitive, social, and emotional. Until proven otherwise, we can continue to assume, just as they need good nutrition and adequate sleep, children may very well need contact with nature.

To bolster the evidence for children's need for nature, additional qualitative and correlational studies are needed, but the greatest need is for controlled experimental studies. The current body of research, though relatively small and with limitations, seems consistent enough to encourage us to take the next step towards controlled studies. Future research should attempt to overcome weaknesses of the current body of research. This would include using random assignment of participants to conditions rather than using participants who self-selected conditions, and objective evaluations of outcomes, such as raters who are blind to conditions. Also keeping activity or programme characteristics constant across conditions is important. Future researchers should also try to show whether or not nature is uniquely necessary for healthy development. In other words, researchers might be able to show that not only does nature promote healthy development, but it also promotes healthy development more effectively than the activities and settings commonly used in place of nature. Finally, future researchers might answer questions such as, how much, in terms of quantity, richness, and type of interaction (passive vs. active), is enough for beneficial effects? Such quantified findings could provide a great deal of leverage in influencing policy makers' and the general public's beliefs about the value of nature for children. While taking the next step to conduct controlled studies and gather causal evidence will be expensive, such findings could have important impacts on the fight for preserving and increasing the amount of nature accessible to children.

Sometimes we get a glimpse of children experiencing nature, such as a child studying an intimate green space in search of 'treasures' – violets, insects, and the like. Or we see an infant who is plopped on a patch of lawn, or another infant tugging at a dog's woolly fur or pulling fine, cool grass. Children's obvious delight in nature, and the growing body of research evidence, should spur researchers onward to continue investigating the benefits of contact with nature, and verifying its impacts on children's development.

Acknowledgements

We gratefully acknowledge the invaluable support we received from Johanna Weber through her help in gathering relevant literature and providing insightful critiques of final drafts of the chapter. Also thanks go to Janet Zoch for her helpful technical assistance.

References

Bailey, C. (1987). *Exposure of preschool children to companion animals: Impact on role-taking skills.* (unpublished PhD dissertation), Oregon State University.

Bandoroff, S. and Scherer, D. G. (1994). Wilderness family therapy: an innovative treatment approach for problem youth. *Journal of Child and Family Studies, 3*(2), 175–91.

Bardill, N. and Hutchinson, S. (1997). Animal-assisted therapy with hospitalized adolescents. *Journal of Child and Adolescent Psychiatric Nursing, 10*(1), 17–24.

Basile, C. G. (2000). Environmental education as a catalyst for transfer of learning in young children. *Journal of Environmental Education, 32*(1), 21–7.

Behar, L. and Stephens, D. (1978). Wilderness camping: an evaluation of a residential treatment program for emotionally disturbed children. *American Journal of Orthopsychiatry, 48*(4), 644–53.

Covert, A. M., Whiren, A. P., Keith, J., and Nelson, C. (1985). Pets, early adolescents, and families. In M. B. Sussman (ed.), *Pets and the Family* (pp. 95–108). New York, NY: The Haworth Press.

Davis, J. (1999). No time to be a kid. *Illinois Issues, 25*.

Dismuke, R. P. (1984). Rehabilitative horseback riding for children with language disorders. In R. K. Anderson, B. L. Hart, and L. A. Hart (eds.), *The Pet Connection: Its Influence on Our Health and Quality of Life*, Minneapolis: CENSHARE, University of Minnesota, 131–40.

Faber Taylor, A., Kuo, F. E. and Sullivan, W. C. (1998). Growing up in the inner city: green spaces as places to grow. *Environment and Behavior, 30*, 3–27.

Faber Taylor, A., Kuo, F. E. and Sullivan, W. C. (2001). Coping with ADD: the surprising connection to green play settings. *Environment and Behavior, 33*(1), 54–77.

Faber Taylor, A., Kuo, F. E. and Sullivan, W. C. (2002). Views of nature and self-discipline: evidence from inner city children. *Journal of Environmental Psychology, 22*, 49–63.

Gaster, S. (1991). Urban children's access to their neighborhood: changes over three generations. *Environment and Behavior, 23*(1), 70–85.

Grahn, P., Martensson, F., Lindblad, B., Nilsson, P. and Ekma, A. (1997). Outdoors at daycare. *City and Country, 145*.

Guttman, G. (1984). The pet: a tutor to social skills. *Journal of the Delta Society, 1*(1), 37–38.

Hansen, K. M., Messinger, C. J., Baun, M. M. and Megel, M. (1999). Companion animals alleviating distress in children. *Anthrozoos, 12*(3), 142–48.

Hart, R. (1979). *Children's Experience of Place*. New York: Irvington Publishers.

Hergovich, A., Monshi, B., Semmler, G. and Zieglmayer, V. (2002). The effects of the presence of a dog in the classroom. *Anthrozoos, 15*(1), 37–50.

Hillman, M., Adams, J. and Whitelegg, J. (1990). *One False Move: A Study of Children's Independent Mobility*. London: Policy Studies Institute.

Howie, T. R. (1974). Indoor or outdoor education? *Journal of Environmental Education, 6*(2), 32–6.

Kahn, P. H. (2002). Children's affiliations with nature: structure, development, and the problem of environmental generational amnesia. In P. H. Kahn and S. R. Kellert (eds.), *Children and Nature: Psychological, Sociocultural, and Evolutionary Investigations* (pp. 93–116). Cambridge, MA: The MIT Press.

Kaplan, R. (1977). *Summer Outdoor Programs: Their Participants and Their Effects*. (No. General Technical Report NE-30); USDA Forest Service.

Kaplan, R. (1984). Wilderness perception and psychological benefits: an analysis of a continuing program. *Leisure Sciences, 6*, 271–90.

Kaplan, S. (1995). The restorative benefits of nature: toward an integrative framework. *Journal of Environmental Psychology, 15*, 169–82.

Kaplan, S. R. and Talbot, J. F. (1983). Psychological benefits of wilderness experience. In I. Altman and J. F. Wohlwill (eds.), *Behavior and the Natural Environment* (pp. 163–204). New York, NY: Plenum Press.

Katcher, A. H. W. and Gregory G. (2000). The centaur's lessons: therapeutic education through care of animals and nature study. In A. Fine (ed.), *Handbook on Animal-assisted Therapy: Theoretical Foundations and Guidelines for Practice*. San Diego: Academic Press, 153–77.

Kellert, S. R. (2002). Experiencing nature: affective, cognitive, and evaluative development in children. In P. H. Kahn and S. R. Kellert (eds.), *Children and Nature: Psychological, Sociocultural, and Evolutionary Investigations* (pp. 117–52). Cambridge, MA: The MIT Press.

Kellert, S. R. and Derr, V. (1998). *A National Study of Outdoor Wilderness Experience*. Washington, DC: Island Press.

Kidd, A. H. and Kidd, R. M. (1987). Reactions of infants and toddlers to live and toy animals. *Psychological Reports, 61*, 455–64.

Kirkby, M. (1989). Nature as refuge in children's environments. *Children's Environments Quarterly, 6*, 1–12.

Kuo, F. E. and Faber Taylor, A. (2004). A potential natural treatment for AD/HD? Evidence from a national study. *American Journal of Public Health, 94* (9), 1580–6.

Lieberman, G. and Hoody, L. (1998). *Closing the achievement gap: using the environment as an integrating context.* Paper presented at the State Environment and Education Round Table.

Limond, J. A., Bradshaw, J. W. S. and Cormack, K. F. M. (1997). Behavior of children with learning disabilities interacting with a therapy dog. *Anthrozoos, 19*, 84–9.

Melson, G. F., Peet, S. and Sparks, C. (1991). Children's attachment to their pets: links to socio-emotional development. *Children's Environments Quarterly, 8*, 55–65.

Moore, R. (1989). Plants as play props. *Children's Environment Quarterly, 6*(1), 3–6.

Moore, R. C. (1986). *Childhood's Domain: Play and Place in Child Development.* Dover, NH: Croom Helm Ltd.

Nabhan, G. P. and Trimble, S. (1994). *The Geography of Childhood: Why Children Need Wild Places.* Boston, MA: Beacon Press.

Nathanson, D. E. and de Faria, S. (1993). Cognitive improvement of children in water with and without dolphins. *Anthrozoos, 6*(1), 17–29.

Poresky, R. H. (1990). The young children's empathy measure: reliability, validity, and effects of companion animal bonding. *Psychological Reports, 66*, 931–6.

Poresky, R. H. (1996). Companion animals and other factors affecting young childrens' development. *Anthrozoos, 9*(4), 159–68.

Poresky, R. H., Hendrix, C., Mosier J. E. and Samuelson, M. L. (2001). Childrens' pets and adults' self-concepts. *The Journal of Psychology, 122* (5), 463–9.

Pyle, R. M. (2002). Eden in a vacant lot: special places, species, and kids in the neighborhood of life. In P. H. Kahn and S. R. Kellert (eds.), *Children and Nature: Psychological, Sociocultural, and Evolutionary Investigations* (pp. 305–28). Cambridge, MA: The MIT Press.

Ratanapojnard, S. (2001). *Community oriented biodiversity environmental education: its effects on knowledge, values, and behavior among rural fifth- and sixth-grade students in northeastern Thailand.* Unpublished doctoral dissertation, School of Forestry and Environmental Studies, Yale University.

Redefer, L. G. J. (1989). Brief report: pet-facilitated therapy with autistic children. *Journal of Autism and Developmental Disorders, 19*, 461–7.

Ricard, M. A. L. (1992). The reaction of 9 to 10 month-old infants to an unfamiliar animal. *Journal of Genetic Psychology*, *154*(1), 5–16.

Rivkin, M. (2000). Outdoor experiences for young children. *ERIC Digest, EDO RC-00-7*(ERIC Clearing House on Rural Education and Small Schools).

Rosenfeld, A. and Wise, N. (2001). *The Over-scheduled Child: Avoiding the Hyperparenting Trap*. New York, NY: St. Martin's Press.

Rost, D. H. and Hartmann, A. (1994). Children and their pets. *Anthrozoos*, *7*(4), 242–54.

Sebba, R. (1991). The landscapes of childhood: the reflections of childhood's environment in adult memories and in children's attitudes. *Environment and Behavior*, *23*, 395–422.

Sobel, D. (1993). *Children's Special Places: Exploring the Role of Forts, Dens, and Bush Houses in Middle Childhood*. Tucson, AZ: Zephr Press.

Spencer, C. and Woolley, H. (2000). Children and the city: a summary of recent environmental psychology research. *Child: Care, Health, and Development*, *26*(3), 181–98.

Titman, W. (1994). *Special Places, Special People: The Hidden Curriculum of School Grounds*. Surrey, UK:WWF UK/Learning Through Landscapes.

Triebenbacher, S. L. (1998). Pets as transitional objects: their role in children's emotional development. *Psychological Reports*, *82*, 191–200.

Valentine, G. and McKendrick, J. (1997). Children's outdoor play: exploring parental concerns about children's safety and the changing nature of childhood. *Geoforum*, *28*, 219–35.

Vidovic, V. V., Stetic, V. V. and Bratko, D. (1999). Pet ownership, type of pet and socio-emotional development of school children. *Anthrozoos*, *12*(4), 211–17.

Wells, N. (2000). At-home with nature: effects of 'greenness' on children's cognitive functioning. *Environment and Behavior*, *32*(6), 775–95.

Wells, N. and Evans, G. (2003). Nearby nature: a buffer of life stress among rural children. *Environment and Behavior*, *35*(3), 311–30.

Wilson, E. O. (1984). *Biophilia*. Cambridge, MA: Harvard University Press.

Marketta Kyttä

In this chapter I present a hypothetical model of a child-friendly environment, based on the covariation of opportunities for independent mobility and the actualization of affordances. I have named this model a 'Bullerby-model', according to the ideal circumstances where children enjoy sufficient possibilities to move around independently in the environment and to perceive the environment as a rich source of affordances.

'Bullerby' can be literally translated as a noisy village. It is used by the famous Swedish writer Astrid Lindgren[1] in her children's novels where she describes the life of a group of children living in a Swedish village. I chose this label for the ideal situation of a child-friendly environment because 'Bullerby' offers children possibilities to take part in all everyday activities of a village and it provides children with important roles and responsibilities in the community. With the 'Bullerby' label I don't want to claim that a rural village setting can be the only candidate for a child-friendly environment. Any 'normal' everyday environment that does not exclude children can be child-friendly.

The presented model is a theoretical tool for assessing the child friendliness of various settings. 'Bullerby' – type of environments can have many different appearances, in both rural, suburban, and urban settings. I have used this interpretative model to assist in comparing data from four Finnish and five Belarussian neighbourhoods of various levels of urbanization (Kyttä, 2003, 2004). Further empirical testing can validate the model for other countries and different settings.

Children's independent mobility and the actualized affordances of the environment – an intriguing relationship

Over a decade ago Wohlwill and Heft (1987) claimed that research should concern the ways children achieve control over their environment through object manipulation and environmental exploration. Until then

141

the freedom of children to explore the environment and to create an individual relationship with it had mainly been taken for granted. The situation has changed in the present world (Gaster, 1992). The possibilities for children to move around independently in the neighbourhood has decreased in many countries. Spatial mobility restrictions apply mostly to children in developed countries, whereas the free play of children in developing countries is restricted by other factors, such as child labour (Punch, 2000).

The presented model focuses simultaneously on children's independent mobility and the actualization of affordances in different types of children's environments. According to Moore, 'Access to and diversity [of resources] emerge as the most important themes in child-environment policy' (1986: 234). Opportunities to move freely and a variety of activity settings appear also as indicators of environmental quality as defined by children themselves (Chawla, 2002). In this chapter, access and diversity are indexed, respectively, by the degree of independent mobility and by the number of actualized affordances within that area of mobility.

As part of the search for criteria of child-friendly environments, my aim in this chapter is to examine how the interrelationship between independent mobility is related to the actualization of affordances in different environmental contexts. I approach the question by creating and applying a hypothetical model of four different types of environments, namely *Bullerby*, *Wasteland*, *Cell* and *Glasshouse*.

Independent mobility in different environments

In research on children's independent mobility at least three types of definitions and operationalizations have been applied. In the earliest studies, mobility was analyzed by measuring the territorial range of children. Territorial range means the geographical distance from children's home to places where children are allowed to wander when playing and socializing (Van Vliet, 1983). Later on, independent mobility was operationalized as 'a license' to move around independently in the environment. The degree of a mobility licence refers to sets of rules defined by parents concerning, for example, permission to cross roads or to ride a bicycle independently (Hillman *et al.*, 1990; O'Brien *et al.*, 2000; Kyttä, 1997). This approach was complemented by studies on the degree of licences or prohibitions, to go to certain places like the homes of peers or shops (Prezza *et al.*, 2001; Woolley *et al.*, 1999). Studies using the third type of definitions have striven to measure the level of children's actual mobility within a certain period of time. This can be done, for example, by using mobility diaries (Kyttä, 1997; Tillberg, 2001).

Children's freedom to move around independently has diminished during the last decades in many countries, for example in Britain (Hillman et al., 1990; O'Brien et al., 2000), in Australia (Tranter, 1993; Tandy, 1999), in the USA (Gaster, 1992), and in Finland (Syvänen, 1991). Mobility restrictions also affect children's journeys from home to school. In Italy, for instance, 71 per cent of seven to twelve-year-olds are always accompanied by adults on journeys to and from school (Prezza et al., 2001). Mobility restrictions affect younger children and girls most often (Hillman and Adams, 1992; Prezza et al., 2001). Also the size and the density of a city are connected to the opportunities for independent mobility. A consistent result of many studies is that children who live in rural or lower-density environments enjoy more freedom to move around than do children in high-density city environments (Heurlin-Norinder, 1996; Jones, 2000; Kyttä, 1997; Nilheim, 1999; van der Spek and Noyon, 1997; O'Brien et al., 2000). On the other hand, some studies on territorial range (Matthews et al., 2000) and on actual mobility (Tillberg, 2001) have not found support for the suggestion that rural children have more independence than urban children. The neighbourhood may also have an impact on children's independent mobility. The quality of traffic management, for example the enhancement of safety by creating traffic-separated areas, is connected to children's mobility (Björklid, 2002b). Prezza et al. (2001) found that the most independent children living in Rome, were those who lived in apartment buildings with courtyards, near the parks, and in new neighbourhoods. Peers can also stimulate a child to move around independently (Berg and Medrich, 1980) and the community as a whole, if the responsibility of children's supervision is collective (Hillman et al., 1990).

Studies carried out in different countries indicate that the freedom of Scandinavian children to move around independently is higher than that of children in many other countries (Kyttä, 1997; Björklid, 2002a). The other extreme, children with relatively limited freedom, can be found in Australia (Tranter, 1993), Italy (Giuliani et al., 1997; Prezza et al., 2001), and Portugal (Arez and Neto, 1999). Mobility restrictions in such countries are mostly due to increases in the volumes of traffic (Hillman et al., 1990), parents' conceptions of social dangers (Blakely, 1994; Valentine, 1995, 1997), and the unruliness of children (Holloway and Valentine, 2000). There are also practical reasons, such as convenience, weather conditions (Gartenleben et al., 2001) or school imposed restrictions (Granville *et al.*, 2002) which appear as reasons for parents to drive children to school instead of walking. In the European context, the perception of social dangers is higher in middle European countries than in Scandinavian countries (Johansson, 2002). Children themselves seem to fear people more than traffic (Giuliani *et al.*, 1997).

Children should not be seen as passively obeying the mobility restrictions of their parents. They can become skilful negotiators to increase their freedom for moving around (Valentine, 1997). This is a reason why actual mobility and the degree of a mobility licence should be distinguished. The distinction between the field of promoted action and the field of free action in the next section is one attempt to resolve this issue.

Children's levels of independent mobility influence their physical, social, cognitive, and emotional development. Hüttenmoser (1995) was able to show a decline in the motor and social development of five-year-olds who were not able to play independently outdoors, in the streets and in yards. Other studies have emphasized the importance of spontaneous outdoor play for children's motor development and physical health (Armstrong, 1993; Davis and Jones, 1996). Prezza *et al.* (2001) found that children who were more spatially independent played more often with their peers, both indoors and outdoors. Mobility restrictions can also affect the development of emotional bonds between children and the natural environment (Kong, 2000; Bixler *et al.*, 2002), and the development of children's sense of responsibility for the environment (Palmberg and Kuru, 2000). Matthews *et al.* (2000), who studied rural children in the UK found that social places were more important to these children than were natural places. One reason for this was that the children's access to the natural environment was restricted by parental fears and by the fencing-off of private land. Nevertheless, Korpela *et al.* (2002) found no association between mobility licences and the type of the favourite place or its distance from home. Finally, some studies have analyzed the effects of mobility restrictions on the development of independence and identity formation, but empirical research on this topic has so far been scarce (Kegerreis, 1993; Noschis, 1992).

Few previous studies have focused on the connection between independent mobility and the ability to recognize and use environmental possibilities and activities. Hüttenmoser and Degen-Zimmermann (1995) found that five-year-olds who played independently in the neighbourhood were referring to a more diverse and rich set of activities and play than were children of the same age who only played in playgrounds. A number of studies have, however, indicated that actual mobility promotes the acquiring, processing, and structuring of environmental knowledge (Biel, 1982; Blades, 1989; Rissotto and Tonucci, 2002; Rissotto and Giuliani, this volume).

Besides the impact of mobility restrictions on children's development, even broader influences on society can be found. The decline in children's independent mobility increases the time that parents have to use for chauffeuring (Tillberg, 2001), and thus diminishes their free time. Children's mobility restrictions may exacerbate the parents' workload, especially that of mothers (Gershuny, 1993). In many countries, traffic jams connected to travel to and from school have created serious problems (Bradshaw, 1999). A decline in children's independent mobility can be seen as a whole as a constraint for pro-environmental travel-mode choices (Johansson, 2002).

Actualization of affordances

'Affordance' is a central construct of ecological perceptual psychology. It is generally defined as the physical opportunities and dangers which the organism perceives while acting in a specific setting (Gibson, 1979/1986; Heft, 1997; Clark and Uzzell, this volume). Objects afford grasping, twisting, throwing, surfaces afford running, climbing etc. The concept has the potential to be extended to comprise even emotional, social, and cultural opportunities that the individual perceives in the environment. As it comprises features of both the environment and of the individual, it is located at the interface between the setting and the person (Gibson, 1979).

The environment has to provide something that the individual can perceive as offering the potential for activity, but the perception emerges only when the different characteristics of the individual, such as his or her physical dimensions and abilities, social needs, and personal intentions, are matched with the environmental features. It is possible to see affordances in terms of varying stages or levels rather than as either/or phenomena (Greeno, 1994). The first level comprises the potential affordances of the environment, which are specified relative to some individual and in principle available to be perceived. The set of potential affordances of the environment is infinite. In contrast actualized affordances (Heft, 1989) are that subset of the former that the individual perceives, utilizes, or shapes (Kyttä, 2002, 2003). Actualized affordances are revealed through actions of the individual.

We can further differentiate among actualized affordances in terms of those that can be considered actively actualized affordances, namely

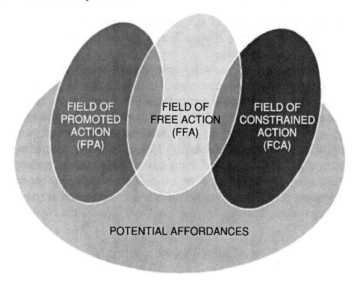

Figure 9.1. A schema of the environment as potential affordances, the actualization of which is regulated by the fields of promoted, free, and constrained action.

used and shaped affordances, and those that are actualized passively, i.e., perceived affordances. Within the process of actualization, affordances are first perceived, then possibly used or shaped. In the last case the selection of potential affordances for other actors is also modified (Kyttä, 2003).

The schema in Figure 9.1 presents the ecological environment, i.e., the perceivable, meaningful environment, as consisting of potential affordances. The potential affordances are divided into three subsets which reflect the rules that structure the actualization of affordances. Inspired by Reed (1993, 1996), I refer to the first subset as the field of promoted action (FPA). Loveland (1991) held that culturally defined and socially approved affordances constitute a subset of all potential affordances. The field of promoted action regulates which affordances can be used as well as the time, place, and manner in which they can be used in a socially approved way.

It is possible not only to promote the actualization of affordances actively, but also to restrict the process actively (Ihanainen, 1991). I refer to this subset of potential affordances as the field of constrained action (FCA). The FCA, just like the FPA, controls the perception, utilization, and shaping of affordances. Parents can restrict their children's actualization of affordances, for example, by directly restricting their behaviour, by diverting their attention to other targets, or by verbally explaining to them the reasons why they cannot actualize a specific affordance. The actualization of affordances can also be limited through the design of objects and spaces so that not all users are able to actualize the potential affordances (Costall, 1995). The environment can be unfriendly in general or to specific user-groups, like people with disabilities.

In accordance with Reed (1993), the third subset will be referred to as the field of free action (FFA), which, according to my interpretation, consists of affordances that the individual has independently perceived, utilized, or shaped. Even if children primarily learn to perceive things that they have been actively encouraged to perceive, i.e., to explore the FPA, there always exist affordances that children discover independently, often to the surprise of their parents. The quality and quantity of the individual's independently actualized affordances vary according to their bodily qualities, such as size, and according to the development of his or her perceptual, motoric, and social skills. In addition, the personality traits and personal preferences of the individual may have an effect on the independent discovery of affordances.

The fields of promoted and constrained action overlap the field of free action (FFA). The actualization of some affordances in the field of free action are socially promoted and others socially constrained. In the latter case, the affordances can still become actualized in 'unsociable' ways, either deliberately or not. The fields of promoted, free, and constrained action also extend into the set of potential affordances. This relates to the fact that as affordances are being shaped (either in a socially approved way or otherwise) the shaping of the set of potential affordances makes it available to other operators as well. When the environment changes as a result of the shaping of the affordances or as a result of urban planning, the set of potential affordances of the environment may expand.

The three fields are closely related to the activities of children. At different stages of their development, children variably remain inside, in between, or outside of these fields – in fact, they often engage in playful activities that move from one field to another. Children may also strive to enlarge the scope of the field of free action. For example, Moore (1986) noticed that children often prefer places outside the control of their parents.

I presume that the degree of independent mobility of children is related to the extent of all three fields of action. Naturally there are a number of other sociocultural factors that define the fields and their extent. Various indicators of independent mobility emphasize these fields in slightly different ways. The territorial range applies to all three fields, the degree of a mobility licence mainly pertains to the extensiveness of the FPA and FCA, and actual mobility primarily applies to the FFA. Because independent mobility influences the extent of these fields, the possibilities for independent mobility can be presumed to be linked with the actualization of affordances.

The variation of environments as a function of independent mobility and actualized affordances

To examine the connection between the actualization of affordances and the possibilities for independent mobility, and their significance for the quality of the child-friendliness of the environment, I have developed a model in Figure 9.2. The model is built on the idea that the covariation of independent mobility and the actualization of affordances define four qualitatively different types of children's environments. The names of the hypothetical environmental types are: *Bullerby* (the ideal environment), *Wasteland*, *Cell* and *Glasshouse*. The varying environmental situations of the model are interpreted on the basis of the fields of promoted, free, and constrained action (see Figure 9.1).

A child-friendly environment is primarily represented by the Bullerby type of environment, where the abundance of mobility freedom and the actualized affordances create a positive cycle: the more children can move around in the environment, the more affordances will be revealed. The actualization of affordances motivates further exploration and mobility. The opposite, i.e., a negative cycle, can also take place. In the latter case children are living in circumstances that I term Cell, without opportunities to form a personal relationship with the environment. In Wasteland, the possibilities for independent mobility reveal only the dullness of the environment. Finally, a child growing up in Glasshouse is perhaps aware of environmental affordances, but his or her view of affordances can be distorted. It will be either unrealistically positive or idealized, or dominated by negative affordances. In the latter case, the environment is seen as a nest of dangers. The media and other sources of second-hand information give children the impression that the environment is full of ample affordances, but due to mobility restrictions children do not have independent access to those affordances.

Gibson's ecological approach to perception emphasizes the significance of action and exploration to perception. Therefore, the types of

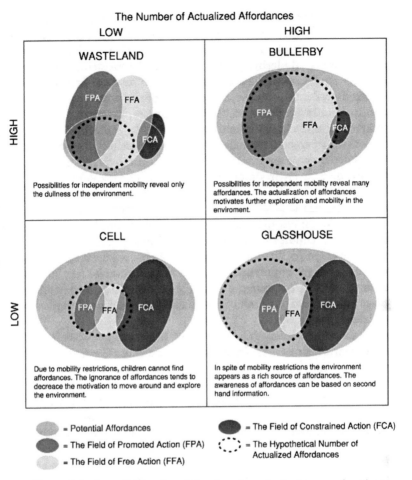

Figure 9.2. A model for describing four hypothetical types of environments that emerge from the covariation of children's independent mobility and the number of actualized affordances.

environments in the model that represent a linear connection between mobility and affordances, i.e. Bullerby and Cell, will probably be the most widely spread types in the four-fold model. Extensive mobility licences will propably correlate with an ample supply of affordances, whereas restricted mobility licences will result in a small number of perceived affordances. However, the two other environment-types, Wasteland and Glasshouse, also have to be taken into account.

The opportunities for the actualization of affordances vary in these four environments. Theoretically, they should be most extensive in the Bullerby and Glasshouse types and least extensive in Wasteland and Cell environments. Bullerby, which is the ideal representation of a child-friendly setting, should have more extensive fields of promoted and free action than the Glasshouse, but the number of possible actualized affordances should be the same. The situation is, however, different in the number of actively actualized affordances. In Bullerby the affordances are not only perceived but also utilized and possibly shaped. An example of a Bullerby-type environment could be a rural village or an urban area or any diverse environment that children can explore. In the Glasshouse a large number of affordances remain passively perceived as the limited size of the fields of promoted and free action make the actualization of affordances difficult. A present day example of such an environment for children could be an old European urban milieu full of things that are fascinating, but impossible for children to independently utilize. The environment is diverse and attractive, but it cannot be accessed freely. An extreme example of this kind of environment is a place riddled with landmines where children are forced to play in a very restricted area.

There are essential differences also between the Wasteland and the Cell environment types. In Wasteland, the extensive fields of promoted and free action do not result in a large number of actualized affordances, because the environment is empty of things to discover; its affordances are few and/or nondiverse. Living environments that are too dull, such as sleepy suburbs, can be of this type, like in a case where the territorial range of children does not extend to the greenery surrounding the suburb (Kyttä, 2002). In the Cell environment the restricted fields of free and promoted action makes it impossible for children to explore the affordances of the environment. Thus the potential affordances are not even perceived, let alone used or shaped. This kind of environment can be any setting, where children are locked inside and they cannot receive, for instance, second-hand information about the enticing affordances of the outdoor environment.

One must bear in mind that the model of the four types of environments that I have introduced is always influenced, to a certain degree by the individual experiences and the way of life of children in their contexts. The same physical environment might appear as a Bullerby-type environment to one child and as a Cell-type environment to another. The physical, social, and cultural environments form an inseparable entity, the adaptation to which is partly dependent on a child's individual characteristics (see Bronfenbrenner, 1992).

Discussion

In this chapter I have examined the theoretical interrelationship between the degree of children's independent mobility and the actualization of affordances in the context of environmental child-friendliness. In the following discussion I will briefly refer to some of my empirical findings in Finland and Belarus (Kyttä, 2004).

In accordance with the emphasis of functional activity in Gibson's ecological perceptual psychology, where 'we must perceive in order to move, but we must also move in order to perceive' (Gibson, 1979: 223), I proposed that the two extremes of the model, the positive and negative types of child-friendly environments, the Bullerby and the Cell, would figure prominently in the empirical data. This proved to be true as 68 per cent of the children's combined scores in mobility licence and affordance scales represented these environment-types (Kyttä, 2004).

The Bullerby-type environment involves a positive cyclical interrelationship between mobility licences and the actualization of affordances. In the Bullerby context children are able to interact effectively with their environment and utilize opportunities within the environment to perform independently at a level appropriate to their physical and cognitive capabilities. Also Trancik and Evans (1995) have explained the construction of environmental competence in a similar fashion. Bullerby can also function as a zone of proximal development (Vygotsky, 1986). This means that children are presented with a series of graduated zones of challenge which are slightly above their current levels of functioning. More extensive fields of free and promoted action guarantee more graduated zones of challenge. The Finnish communities primarily offered the Bullerby-type of environments, regardless of the degree of urbanization. In both the Finnish and Belarussian data, the percentage of Bullerby-type environments decreased as the degree of urbanization increased (Kyttä, 2004).

The Cell-type of environment includes a negative cycle in which the granting of few mobility licences makes it impossible to actualize affordances. Little knowledge of affordances tends to result in decreased interest in mobility in the environment. The Cell was the most common type of environment in the Belarussian city, suburb, and contaminated area. In the Finnish data, this type was only found in the city. The Wasteland- and Glasshouse-type environments also figured prominently in the Belarussian data. Wasteland environments were also encountered in the Finnish city. A sleepy suburb can be an example of a Wasteland environment, but according to these data, even urban areas or rural villages can in some cases be experienced in this way (Kyttä, 2004).

The Glasshouse-type of environment was the least prominent in the empirical study (Kyttä, 2004). In spite of mobility restrictions, children's environments may appear as a rich source of affordances. The data seem to suggest that the Glasshouse-type of environment becomes more common as the degree of urbanization increases. It is also possible that this type of environment becomes more common in the future, if children's mobility licences continue to decrease in number and their knowledge of the environment is more often based on second-hand information rather than on independent exploration of the setting. For example, information of affordances of the environment from the media may maintain the notion that the environment is a rich source of affordances.

The four-fold model in Figure 9.2 comprised two dimensions. The model could be further developed by adding a third dimension that accommodates, for instance, personally preferred affordances by the child (Kyttä, 2003). As a first step in the expansion of the model, the negative affordances can be added (Miller et al., 1998). Such an advanced model could shed some light on the motivational basis of the activity in the environment and on the attainment of person-environment fit.

Mobility licences and actual mobility, even at best, insufficiently reflect the fields of promoted, free, and constrained action. There are various other factors that regulate the extensiveness of these fields. For example, the social processes through which children are kept out of certain spaces and environments define these fields (Matthews et al., 2000; O'Brien et al., 2000). Sociocultural factors may also become apparent as we look at the so-called polymorphic or monomorphic spaces in the environment. Monomorphic spaces are strongly classified spaces that are dominated by one single use that excludes the possibility of other uses. This is the case with gardens, which are too 'precious' for children to run about in. Polymorphic places are weakly classified and they can sustain alternative uses by children even in the presence of the dominant use, for example barns and sport fields where access by children is not seen as problematic (Jones, 2000). The actualization of versatile affordances is naturally more likely in polymorphic spaces. In the hypothetical model presented in this article, the Wasteland environment represents a monomorphic space in which even mobility licences do not facilitate the actualization of affordances due to the nonversatility of the affordances.

According to Bronfenbrenner (1989, 1993), the characteristics of an environment should be studied on various levels. The level of microsystems includes the home, school, day-care centre, and other multidimensional conditions of the environmental context. Mesosystems are collections of more than one microsystem, such as a child's daily environmenal dyad, consisting of the day-care centre and home. Exosystems refer to systems that affect the individual although he or she is not necessarily involved in it. For example, a child's life is affected by happenings at the parents' workplace, or even by decisions made by social services. Macrosystems are, according to Bronfenbrenner, the prevalent models that in each culture affect the micro, meso, and exosystems.

The affordances of micro- and mesosystems are priceless for children. I found that Finnish children discovered most of the affordances that they were asked about in the interviews, in the gardens and elsewhere in the immediate surroundings. Children in Belarus, however, relied on affordances that they found at home or in the courtyards (Kyttä, 2002). The lack of affordances on the mesolevel was probably due to the restrictions on mobility and/or due to the shortcomings of the immediate surroundings. Chawla (2002) also emphasised the importance of the immediate surrondings as a source of possibilities for action.

My model for the assessment of child-friendly environments mainly concentrates on Bronfenbrenner's micro and mesoenvironments, but it also partly targets the exo and macroenvironments. Horelli's chapter in this volume refers to the meso-environmental prerequisites of child-friendly environments.

An interesting question is whether it is possible to influence the number and quality of actualized affordances for children and the child-friendliness of the setting by means of planning. Children may themselves try to shape the affordances by participating in the planning process. There is evidence that this might increase the fit between the existing affordances of the environment and their own affordance preferences (Horelli, 1998; Kyttä et al., 2004).

To sum up, a close relationship between independent mobility and the actualization of affordances seems to exist. Thus the intriguing interrelationship between independent mobility and affordances contributes to the complex task of defining environmental child friendliness and how it can be studied.

Note

1 Astrid Lindgren's homepage: *http://www.astridlindgren.se/*. English editions of 'Bullerby' books include *The Children of Bullerby, Christmas in Noisy Village* and *Springtime in Noisy Village*.

References

Arez, A. and Neto, C. (1999). The study of independent mobility and perception of the physical environment in rural and urban children. Paper presented at IPA Congress, Lisbon, Portugal.

Armstrong, N. (1993). Independent mobility and children's physical development. In M. Hillman (ed.), *Children's Transport and the Quality of Life* (pp. 35–43). London: Policy Studies Institute.

Berg, M. and Medrich, E. (1980). Children in four neighbourhoods: the physical environment and its effect on play and play patterns. *Environment and Behavior, 12*(3), 320–48.

Biel, A. (1982). Children's spatial representation of their neighbourhood: a step towards a general spatial competence. *Journal of Environmental Psychology, 2* (3) 193–200.

Bixler, R. D. Floyd, M. F., and Hammitt, W. E. (2002). Environmental socialization. Quantitative tests of the childhood play hypothesis. *Environment and Behavior, 34*(6), 795–818.

Björklid, P. (2002a). Trafikmiljöstress i föräldrarperspektiv. Forskningsgruppen för miljöpsykologi och pedagogik. Lärarhögskolan i Stockholm.

Björklid, P. (2002b). Parental restrictions and children's independent mobility. Paper presented at IAPS 17, A Coruna, 23–27 July 2002.

Blades, M. (1989). Children's ability to learn about the environment from direct experience and from spatial representations. *Children's Environments Quarterly, 6*(2/3), 4–14.

Blakely K. S. (1994). Parents' conceptions of social dangers to children in the urban environment. *Children's Environments, 11*(1), 16–25.

Bradshaw, R. (1999). Research into levels of activity relating to school travel initiatives. Transport Studies Group, University of Westminster.

Bronfenbrenner, U. (1992). Ecological systems theory. In R. Vasta (ed.), *Six Theories Of Child Development: Revised Formulations and Current Issues* (pp. 187–249). London and Philadelphia: Jessica Kingsley.

Chawla, L. (2002). *Growing Up in an Urbanising World.* London: Earthscan Publications Ltd.

Costall, A. (1995). Socializing affordances. *Theory and Psychology, 5*(4), 467–81.

Davis, A. and Jones, L. J. (1996). Children in the urban environment: an issue for the new public health agenda. *Health and Place, 2*(2), 107–13.

Gaster, S. (1992). Historical changes in children's access to US cities: a critical review. *Children's Environments, 9*(2), 23–36.

Gatersleben, B., Leach, R. and Uzzell, D. (2001). Travel to school: results of a survey among junior and secondary school children and their parents in Ash. Unpublished internal report, University of Surrey, Guildford, UK.

Gershuny, J. (1993). Escorting children: impact on parental lifestyle. In M. Hillman (ed.), *Children's Transport and the Quality of Life.* London: Policy Studies Institute.

Gibson, J. J. (1979/1986). *The Ecological Approach to Visual Perception.* Hillsdale: Lawrence Erlbaum Associates.

Giuliani, V., Alparone, F. and Mayer, S. (1997). Children's appropriation of urban spaces. Paper presented at the Urban Childhood Conference, 9–12 June, Trondheim, Norway.

Granville, S., Laird, A., Barber, M. and Rait, F. (2002). Why do parents drive their children to school? Transport Research Series. Scottish Executive Central Research Unit.

Greeno, J. G. (1994). Gibson's affordances. *Psychological Review*, *101*(2), 336–42.

Heft, H. (1989). Affordances and the body: an intentional analysis of Gibson's ecological approach to visual perception. *Journal for the Theory of Social Behaviour*, *19*(1), 1–30.

Heft, H. (1997). The relevance of Gibson's ecological approach to perception for environment-behavior studies. In G. T. Moore and R. W. Marans (eds.), *Advances in Environment, Behavior and Design*, vol. IV. New York: Plenum Press.

Heurlin-Norinder, M. (1996). *Children, environment and independent mobility.* Paper presented at IAPS 14, Stockholm, Sweden.

Hillman, M. and Adams, J. (1992). Children's freedom and safety. *Children's Environments*, *9*(2), 10–22.

Hillman, M., Adams, J. and Whitelegg, J. (1990). *One false move . . . a study of children's independent mobility.* Publications of the Policy Studies Institute. London.

Holloway, S. L. and Valentine, G. (2000). Children's geographies and the new social studies of childhood. In S. L. Holloway and G. Valentine (eds.), *Children's Geographies. Playing, Living, Learning*. London: Routledge.

Horelli, L. (1998). Creating childfriendly environments – case studies on children's participation in three European countries. *Childhood*, *5*(2), 225–39.

Hüttenmoser, M. (1995). Children and their living surroundings: empirical investigations into the significance of living surroundings for the everyday life and development of children. *Children's Environments*, *12*(4), 403–13.

Hüttenmoser, M. and Degen-Zimmermann (1995). Lebensräume für kinder (living space for children). National research programme, cities and transport no. 70. Zürich: Marie Meierhofer-Institut für das Kind.

Ihanainen, P. 1991, Koulun ja opetuksen uudistaminen: kohti Gibsonilaista diskurssia. [The renewal of schooling and teaching: towards a Gibsonian discourse]. Licenciate work, University of Jyväskylä, Department of Education.

Johansson, M. (2002). Social dangers as constraints for pro-environmental travel modes – the perception of parents in England and Sweden. Paper presented at the 17th conference of the International Association for People-Environment Studies, 23–27 July, 2002, A Coruña, Spain.

Jones, O. (2000). Melting geography. Purity, disorder, childhood and space. In S. L. Holloway and G. Valentine (eds.), *Children's Geographies. Playing, Living, Learning* (pp. 29–47). London: Routledge.

Kong, L. (2000). Nature's dangers, nature's pleasures. Urban children and the natural world. In S. L. Holloway and G. Valentine (eds.), *Children's Geographies. Playing, Living, Learning* (pp. 257–71). London: Routledge.

Kegerreis, S. (1993). Independent mobility and children's mental and emotional development. In M. Hillman (ed.), *Children's Transport and the Quality of Life* (pp. 28–34). London: Policy Studies Institute.

Korpela, K., Kyttä, M. and Hartig, T. (2002). Children's favorite places. Restorative experience, self-regulation, and children's place preferences. *Journal of Environmental Psychology*, 22, 387–98.

Kyttä, M. (1997). Children's independent mobility in urban, small town, and rural environments. In R. Camstra (ed.), *Growing Up in a Changing Urban Landscape* (pp. 41–52). Assen: Van Gorcum.

Kyttä, M. (2002). The affordances of children's environments. *Journal of Environmental Psychology*, 22, 109–23.

Kyttä, M. (2003). Children in outdoor contexts. Affordances and independent mobility in the assessment of environmental child friendliness. Publication A 28, Centre for Urban and Regional Studies, Helsinki University of Technology.

Kyttä, M. (2004). The extent of children's independent mobility and the number of actualized affordances as criteria of a child-friendly environment. In press, *Journal of Environmental Psychology*.

Kyttä, M., Kaaja, M. and Horelli, L. (2004). An Internet-based design game as a mediator of children's environmental visions. *Environment and Behavior*, 36 (1), 127–51.

O'Brien, M., Jones, D. and Sloan, D. (2000). Children's independent spatial mobility in the urban public realm. *Childhood*, 7(3), 257–77.

Loveland, K. A. (1991). Social affordances and interaction II: autism and the affordances of the human environment. *Ecological Psychology*, 3(2), 99–119.

Matthews, H., Limb, M. and Taylor, M. (2000). The street as thirdspace. In S. L. Holloway and G. Valentine (eds.), *Children's geographies. Playing, Living, Learning* (pp. 63–79). London: Routledge.

Matthews, H., Taylor, M., Sherwood, K., Tucker, F. and Limb, M. (2000). Growing-up in the countryside: children and the rural idyll. *Journal of Rural Studies*, 16, 141–53.

Miller, P. C., Shim, J. E. and Holden, G. W. (1998). Immediate contextual influences on maternal behavior: environmental affordances and demands. *Journal of Environmental Psychology*, 18, 387–98.

Moore, R. (1986). *Childhood's Domain. Play and Place in Child Development*. London: Croom Helm.

Nilheim, J. (1999). Kan ni gå ut och leka? Barns utomhusmiljö i Stockholms nybyggda innerstad. [Can you go out and play?] Publication no. 99–93, Royal Institute of Technology. Stockholm.

Noschis, K. (1992). Child development theory and planning for neighbourhood play. *Children's Environments*, 9(2), 3–9.

Palmberg, I. and Kuru, J. (2000). Outdoor activities as a basis for environmental responsibility. *Journal of Environmental Education*, 31(4), 32–6.

Prezza, M., Stefania, P., Morabito, C., Cinzia, S., Alparone, F. R. and Guiliani, M. V. (2001). The influence of psychosocial and urban factors on children's independent mobility and relationship to peer frequentation. *Journal of Community and Applied Social Psychology*, 11(6), 435–50.

Punch, S. (2000). Children's stategies for creating playspaces: negotiating independence in rural Bolivia. In S. L. Holloway and G. Valentine (eds.), *Children's Geographies. Playing, Living, Learning* (pp. 48–62). London: Routledge.

Pyle, R. M. (2002). Eden in a vacant lot: special places, species, and kids in the neighborhood of life. In P. H. Kahn and S. R. Kellert (eds.), *Children and Nature. Psychological, Sociocultural, and Evolutionary Investigations* (pp. 305–28). Cambridge, MA: The MIT Press.

Reed, E. S. (1993). The intention to use a specific affordance: a conceptual framework for psychology. In R. H. Wozniak and K. W. Fischer (eds.), *Development in Context. Acting and Thinking in Specific Environments* (pp. 45–76). Hillsdale: Lawrence Erlbaum Associates.

Reed, E. S. (1996). Selves, values, cultures. In E. S. Reed, E. Turiel and T. Brown (eds.), *Values and Knowledge* (pp. 1–15). Mahwah, New Jersey: Lawrence Erlbaum Associates.

Rissotto, A. and Tonucci, F. (2002). Freedom of movement and environmental knowledge in elementary school children. *Journal of Environmental Psychology*, 22(1), 65–77.

van der Spek, M. and Noyon, R. (1997). Children's freedom of movement in the streets. In Camstra (ed.), *Growing Up in a Changing Urban Landscape* (pp. 24–40). Assen: Van Gorcum.

Syvänen, M. (1991). Lasten elintilan kaventuminen. [The decreasing life space of children]. In P. Santalahti (ed.), *Auto, terveys ja ympäristö* (pp. 167–77). Helsinki: Gaudeamus.

Tandy, C. A. (1999). Children's diminishing play space: a study of intergenerational change in children's use of their neighbourhoods. *Australian Geographical Studies*, 37(2), 154–64.

Tillberg, K. (2001). Barnfamiljens dagliga fritidsresor I bilsamhället – ett tidspussel med geografiska och könsmässiga variationer. Geografiska regionstudier, nr 43, Uppsala Universitetet.

Trancik, A. M. and Evans, G. W. (1995). Spaces fit for children: competency in the design of daycare center environments. *Children's Environments*, 12(3), 311–19.

Tranter, P. (1993). Children's mobility in canberra: confinement or independence? Monograph Series No. 7, Department of Geography and Oceanography. University College, Australian Defence Force Academy, Canberra.

Valentine, G. (1995). Stranger-danger: the impact of parental fears on children's use of space. Paper presented at the International Conference, Building Identities. Amsterdam, The Netherlands.

Valentine, G. (1997). 'Oh yes I can.' 'Oh no you can't': children and parents' understandings of kids' competence to negotiate public space safely. *Antipode*, 29: 65–89.

van Vliet, W. (1983). Exploring the fourth environment. An examination of the home range of city and suburban teenagers. *Environment and Behavior*, 15 (5), 567–88.

Vygotsky, L. S. (1986). *Thought and Language*. Cambridge, MA: The MIT Press.

Wohlwill, J. F. and Heft, H. (1987). The physical environment and the development of the child. In D. Stokols and I. Altman (eds.), *Handbook of Environmental Psychology* (pp. 281–328). New York: John Wiley and Sons.

Woolley, H., Spencer, C., Dunn, J., and Rowley, G., (1999). The child as citizen: experiences of British town and city centres. *Journal of Urban Design*, 4(3), 255–82.

Part III

Adolescents' worlds?

10 On the other side of the tracks: the psychogeographies and everyday lives of rural teenagers in the UK

Hugh Matthews and Faith Tucker

Introduction

The notion of a rural idyll stubbornly persists as a common conception of the British countryside – especially so, when family life and young people are thought about. For many onlookers, rural places are conceived as safe, risk-free, community-rich spaces where parents can bring up their children in trouble-free ways, away from the turmoil and social tumours that comprise the canker of urban living today. A much-repeated mantra amongst those moving from towns to take up residency in rural villages is that these are better, socially healthier places in which to grow up (Valentine, 1997a). Jones (1997, 2000) suggests that the evocation of a bucolic Arcadia is engrained within the cultural fabric of British (especially English) society. He draws attention to a substantial body of literature, whose re-reading by successive generations portrays the countryside as a haven of 'primitive innocence', the last refuge of a state of humanity defined by a 'wholesome naturalness' that enables children to develop in pure, unblemished, almost perfect ways (Matthews *et al.*, 2000a: 141). By setting apart the 'authenticity' of Nature from the artifice of the town, the countryside becomes a place of the sublime and thus of enriching spirituality; bleak, possibly, but always awesome and humanizing. These values have become degraded over time into a hand-me-down romantic attitude (lower case 'r'). The observations of Shoard (1980) typify this view. She describes five conditions that make rural places enriching spaces for children's play: a) the number of environmental props that are freely available (e.g. grass, slopes, trees etc.); (b) freedom of movement; (c) the availability of play spaces away from the home; (d) animals and wildlife that provide a source of fun; (e) the unknown – that is, the surprises that are around every rustic corner. The countryside in these (re)presentations is typically that of well-organized, pastoral, Middle England and not that of remote, desolate

wild Britain, whose essence equates instead with degradation, deprivation and dehumanization (Ward, 1990). Subsequent commodification
of the Romantic ideal reinforces a view that the rural package is an entity
that is worth buying into, especially for those who have the well-being of
children in mind (Bunce, 1994).

This chapter is divided into two parts. First, we critically consider the
countryside as a place for growing up as a young teenager. In so doing we
mobilize the notion of 'psychogeography', a term particularly associated
with the situationist Guy Debord (1970, 1998). Psychogeography draws
attention to the 'specific effects of the geographical environment, con-
sciously organised or not, on the emotions and behaviour of individuals'
(Knabb, 1981: 45). Originally conceived to accommodate the emotional
or psychic aspects of the urban experience, we extend its application to
(re)consider 'everyday life' within rural spaces. The construct of 'everyday life' is itself closely linked with another figure associated with the
situationist, Henri Lefebvre (1991a, 1991b). Lefebvre was to distinguish
three types of space: the 'perceived space' of everyday social life, the
'conceived space' of planners and speculators and a sphere of 'lived
space'. Brooker (2002: 97), drawing upon Shields (1999), defines the
latter as a symbolic (re)imagining 'of [urban] space that reconfigures
the banality of the first'. In the context of this chapter we utilize these
constructs to provide new productive meanings that challenge the
representation of a rural idyll for rural youth.

Second, we consider the countryside as a fluid space that is differen-
tially experienced and constantly reinterpreted according to social constructs such as gender and age. We have argued elsewhere that there is
neither one rural childhood nor one group of rural children. In this
chapter we extend this theme by examining the 'al fresco' rural geographies of young teenage girls, partly to highlight the gender-based
prejudices that many adults (parents) bring with them as they move into
the countryside (Valentine, 1997a) and partly, to disentangle the significance of outdoor places as social sites of contestation, transition, and
rites of passage.

We have already suggested that in any (re)interpretation of the rural it
is important to identify 'which countryside'. In this case, we draw upon
and (re)consider a series of empirical studies carried out between 1998
and 2001 with teenagers aged thirteen to fifteen years resident in south
Northamptonshire, an being among the most accessible and most affluent of English counties.[1] Yet, amidst this affluence there are pockets of
relative deprivation – defined by high rates of unemployment, a large
proportion of single parent families, low social class, poor levels of
educational attainment and a high proportion of public sector housing

– from which we also drew our participants (for a full discussion of these populations and a review of the ways in which each young person was recruited see Matthews *et al.*, 2000a; Tucker and Matthews, 2001; Tucker, 2003). In every case the nature of the project was fully explained to all prospective participants – letters of consent from parents/guardians confirmed their willingness to get involved and there was no coercion to take part. It was carefully explained to each volunteer that they had the right to withdraw at any time. Each member of the research team was registered as an outreach youth worker. A multi-method approach defined every study – typically, semi-structured interviews, in-depth discussion groups and child-taken photographs and videos. In order to get as close as possible to the everyday worlds of these young people their narratives are incorporated into the text wherever possible.[2]

Rural psychogeographies – the narratives of teenagers

In their seminal ecological study of the Midwest and its children, Barker and Wright (1955: 55) discuss how certain aspects of an environment exert a 'coercive influence' on perception and activity. For example, they noted that when Midwestern (USA) children see an open level surface free from obstruction, they remember these places not for their designated purpose (for example, the Courthouse lawn, the football field) but as potential sites for vigorous activity, such as 'running and romping'. From this perspective the configurational setting of an environment is overwritten by sets of ecological affordances relevant to particular groups in time and space (Gibson, 1979). To some extent these ideas resonate with those of psychogeography, which draws attention to the emotional or psychic aspects of concrete space. Both approaches encourage reflections on how the physical make-up of a (rural) setting may impact on the ways in which young people encounter (conceived space), make sense of (perceived space) and live out (lived space) their everyday lives (see also the chapters by Clark and Uzzell and by Heft and Chawla, this volume).

There is already a considerable literature that suggests that the ways in which children and young people experience and interpret space is likely to be very different to those of adults (for reviews see Matthews and Limb, 1999; Aitken, 2001; Holloway and Valentine, 2000) For many adults, among the perceived benefits of a rural upbringing is that children can grow up and develop in settings that enable a close association with nature (Little and Austin, 1996; Valentine, 1997a). Without doubt, many studies have shown that younger children value the outdoors (Matthews, 1992; Valentine, 1997b; Ward, 1990) and there are many accounts that draw attention to the virtues of meeting and playing in 'natural spaces' (Hart, 1979; Moore, 1986; Kong *et al.*, 1999; Kong, 2000; Percy-Smith, 1999). However, within our studies we found teenagers rarely commented upon the intrinsic worth of natural settings. The notion of running freely across fields and through woods and exploring distant forests and hills may be a romantic ideal for adults (Aitken, 1994) but is a view which teenagers rarely shared. Indeed, rather ironically, opportunities to do so are also very limited as many of these spaces have been 'fenced-off' by adults as private land. For, as Davis and Ridge (1997) have pointed out, in many rural areas there is very little land that is not in private ownership, either farmland or, with an increasing number of affluent incomers, personal property. Somewhat paradoxically, too, without access to farmland, most rural villages possess very little public land and what little there is, is often fiercely defended by adults (Davis and Ridge, 1997). Within rural Northamptonshire, teenagers repeatedly bemoaned how vigilant adults routinely curtailed their attempts to access 'open spaces'.

We can't go there [a field on the edge of a new housing development]. . .There's a big sign saying KEEP OUT, TRESPASSERS PROSECUTED. We went there once and this guy comes out and starts giving us some verbal. . .it's not worth it. . .we didn't really want to go there in any case. . . (Boy, aged 13)

I was walking along with me mates down by the little stream and this old geezer starts shouting at us 'GET OFF MY LAND'. . . Stupid old fool, who does he think he is! It's just a path by a house. . . (Girl, aged 14)

There's a man who lives near the park. He shouts if people play in the trees because 'it's council property', but there's nothing else to do in this boring old park so we just do it anyway. . . (Girl, aged 13)

Sometimes we hang out at the park. . . but people tell us off for making too much noise. But it's not as if they own the place. . . (Girl, aged 13)

Jones (1997) considers the extent to which the countryside as an idyll for children is simply a (mis)representation by adults or whether it is an idealization constructed by adults to justify their own transactions. From his review, despite prevailing notions of a romantic ideal, Jones reveals a 'jumbled landscape' of otherness where, through the actions of adults themselves, children frequently comprise a group apart. Valentine (1997a: 137), too, considers how the 'imagining of a countryside as an ideal place in which to grow up' is both constructed and contradicted by rural parents. She found that whilst parents perceived the countryside as a place which offered opportunities for a stress-free upbringing away from the dangers and spatial constraints of the city, at the same time, many parents went on to contest this view by recognizing the vulnerability of their children to stranger-danger, traffic and 'rural demons, such as

New Age Travellers and gypsies' (p. 147). Within our studies we frequently found that teenagers were commonly restricted in where and when they were allowed to go by strong parental constraints, fuelled by fears and anxieties.

Over there's out of bounds [pointing to the edge of the village] and so is the woods and Jessie Pits (Girl A, aged 13). Yeah, so is Fir Tree Lane, where the gypsies are, is no go. . .me mum is always saying I must not go down there. . . (Girl B, aged 13).

Once its dark I'm not allowed to go out, unless it's to a friend's house. . .stranger-danger and all that. . . (Girl, aged 15).

I get loads of grief if they find out that I've been hanging about by the brick yard and pits. . .you know, blah, blah, blah, 'it's not safe', blah, blah, blah, 'you don't know who will be there' . . . 'bad sorts hang out there'. . . Fair enough when I was younger. . .load of cobblers now. . .(Boy, aged 15).

I cycle around here and there, the main part of the village really, but I'm not allowed to go further than that. . .me Nan's always nagging about the traffic and how I should watch out. . .I'm thirteen and I know what I am doing. . .look at this stunt. . .one wheel. . .here goes. . . (Boy, aged 13).

In our studies we found that for a significant proportion of teenagers their lived experience of the countryside often contradicted the social construction of the idyll. The routine practices of daily existence within a rural place for many young people are not filled with infinite prospects. Instead, their psychic eventuality is more likely to be a shared sense of ennui, boredom and languor. Typical complaints revolved around the lack of things to do and the paucity of settings to hang out, especially away from the adult gaze. Although claims such as these have a universal resonance for teenagers (Corrigan, 1979; James, 1986; James and Prout, 1992) given the declining service structure of rural places, poor public transport provision and the expense of private alternatives, rural teenagers typically reside within opportunity-poor environments. Problems are further exacerbated if a family lacks a car or if another family member is using their only car for another purpose, such as access to work during the school holidays. As Davis and Ridge (1997) have noted, there appears to be an age when living in the countryside can seem particularly restrictive and inhibitive.

These experiences, when taken together, define situations and events that in turn stimulate various shared mentalities or common psychogeographies amongst teenagers (Christensen, 2003). In our studies, this is represented by a cacophony of negative emotions and feelings. We often found that when talking (thinking) about their localities teenagers provided accounts full of frustration and restlessness.

[What's it like here?] Boring. It's pretty quiet. . .you need transport to get out of the village. . . there's not a lot of buses. There's about three buses a day. . .We often go out on a Friday or Saturday night and we phone up a taxi. . .it's eight pounds from here to Milton Keynes but if you get a black cab . . . it would cost you a tenner. Too expensive. . .There's no jobs like going in the village. You have to be over 16 and we're just coming up to 16 and we got restrictions. You need transport to get out of the village to get a job. . . (Girl, aged 15).

There's. . . nothing to do. . .in the winter it just gets so boring. . . . It's pathetic. Sometimes there's like discos at the rugger club and that's quite good. It's only like once a month. . .Apart from that . . .there's nothing else to do. It's somewhere to go. It's better than staying in the house anyway. . . (Girl, aged 15).

Nothing ever happens here. . .it's gross, really bad. . .so we try to make things happen by meeting together. . .but then we get moved on. . . (Boy, aged 15).

There's nothing to do here, and it's not as if you can get a bus to anywhere else. There aren't many buses, and those that there are don't go where we want. And you can't get a bus anywhere at night. . . (Girl, aged 15).

What's this place like? There's nowhere to go and nothing to do. . . (Boy, aged 13).

Among the considered benefits of living within small, discrete, relatively remote, rural places are that they facilitate a sense of belonging and community. Many studies (for example, Lewis and Sherwood, 1994; Lewis, 1989; Valentine, 1997c; Jones, 2000) have shown how rural adults – especially incomers – rely upon these constructs to authenticate their experience of the rustic. Yet, for many teenagers symbolic imagining of this kind has little meaning for them. Rather, when surmising about their localities strong feelings of angst and anger were commonplace. Several reasons trigger such disaffection. First, in the absence of dedicated meeting places, teenagers will often congregate together in the village core or in other venues where their presence is highly visible. In so doing, they transgress the sensibilities of those adults who define the public realm as an extension of their own private domain (Matthews, 2003) and who seek to admonish and castigate all those who enter within. Teenagers frequently recalled how they were asked to move on when simply hanging around together. Second, in most places, parish life and its affairs are carried out in the absence of young people. Accordingly, teenagers frequently lament that no one listens to their needs and in any decision-making their views are either ignored or tokenized. Feelings of powerlessness, exclusion, and frustration were commonplace.

We got promised loads of things would happen in the field in summer holidays. There's nothing up there now [Who made these promises?] We were down the primary school and we were all going in the pool. We weren't supposed to but we

were. And she came down, there's two of them and we were thinking, oh we'd
better make a move. And they stopped and they were asking questions like you
are now. . .going on about what we do, how we do it and everything and they
started saying that they'd be in the village and they were going to do archery and
everything. [Where were they from?] I can't remember now. That was about two
years ago. . . .(Girl, aged 15).

We have an adults council in our village for people who decide what's going to go
on in the village and I don't think they have ever had a children's say in it. . . .
(Girl, aged 13).

The council spent a lot of money, like half a million pounds, on doing up the
place. They've re-done the pavements and put in new benches and stuff. They
never ask us [young people] what we'd like. Half a million pounds – that was just
a waste of money. With that money they could have built a leisure centre or a
community centre or something. They could have built something that everyone
could use, you know, something for families. . . (Girl, aged 13).

Sentiments such as these highlight the 'profound emptiness' of rural
places for many teenagers and the falseness of the consolation of the
myth of the idyll. For them, the concrete dimensions of rurality define an
emotional landscape (or psychogeography) of 'othering', 'otherness',
and 'marginality'. Space is thus simultaneously objective and subjective,
material and metaphysical, a medium and a construct of everyday life.
The ideas of Genette (1982) are of interest here. Drawing upon the
anthropological work of Levi-Strauss (1966) he proposed a distinction
between two social beings, that of the 'engineer' and the 'bricoleur'.
'While the engineer uses the appropriate tools and designated parts for
the job, the bricoleur makes do, putting together the left-over, extracted
and borrowed pieces at hand so as to compose a new whole' (Brooker,
2002: 22). We interpret the ways of (rural) adults as those of the
engineer, persons always in-charge, manipulating the mythic and the real
for their own gains and benefits. On the other hand, (rural) teenagers are
the bricoleurs, living with and within the oddments and cast-offs of adult
endeavour and working with these scraps to carve out their own social
and cultural bricolage. As Soja (1996) surmises, social reality then is not
just coincidentally spatial, its essence is moulded by and in physical
space. These ideas are developed further in the second part of this the
chapter.

The 'bricolage' of rural teenaged girls

To date, few studies have considered how girls make use of outdoor
environments, especially beyond urban settings (Skelton, 2000; Tucker
and Matthews, 2001; Tucker, 2003). 'It is as if female use of outdoor

space comprises behaviour that is morally taboo; at best something that is of little significance and so justifiably ignored, or at worst something which only concerns an exceptional minority who are written off as troublesome 'others" (Matthews *et al.*, 2000b: 68). Yet, through our studies (Matthews *et al.*, 1998; Matthews, 2003) we have shown that 'the street' – a metaphor for all outdoor spaces within the public domain – is an important liminal setting or site of passage for many young girls, particularly as they attempt to move away from the restrictions and dependency of their childhood roots and move towards the envisaged independence of adulthood. As such streets are places infused with cultural identity, tension, and significance. In this part of the chapter we focus on the experiences of teenage girls growing up in rural Northamptonshire and consider how gender and age impact upon the ways they make sense of their everyday outdoor worlds.

Bourdieu's (1992) reflections on the concept of 'habitus' offer a useful starting point for our discussion. Habitus refers to 'a durable, transposable system of definitions' that are gained by 'conscious and unconscious practices' as children move through different social institutions from home, to school and on to the various worlds of adulthood. The habitus is thus a stable but infinitely variable cultural system, dependent on the moralities of age- and gender-based expectations, amongst other things. In this context, Jones (1999) notes how in popular constructions of ideal country childhoods, where wholesome children's activities are associated with nature, rumbustiousness, and physical activity, the only way for girls to be 'boylike' – the development of feminine identities is for other settings. Indeed, a number of girls reported that when they were much younger it was expected of them to spend their leisure time climbing trees and building dens.

Some of the boys in my year at school have dens, you know, tree houses. I used to have a den when I was little. It's not the sort of thing that I'd do now though. . . (Girl, aged 15).

When I was younger. . .when we first came to [name of village] my sister and me used to have a great time just running about. . .climbing trees, playing hide and seek in the woods. . .I can't do that now, I'm too old. . . (Girl, aged 14).

Recently, Matthews (2003) has considered how the concept of habitus is useful for considering how adults view teenagers' outdoor behaviour. He has shown that during the process of growing up, children develop a strong sense of 'knowing their place' – that is, they acquire a clear understanding of what behaviour is morally acceptable in particular settings. Keeping teenagers 'invisible' and their presence only within the background is implicit to the ways in which adults manage the habitus of the street. We have shown earlier in this chapter that when hanging around together in public places, adults will view teenagers as 'out-of-place' and consider them to be a destabilizing presence to the social order. Furthermore, as streets are masculine spaces the presence of young girls is seen to be especially discrepant.

Say we was hanging around. . .we gets all sort of looks. . .as if we shouldn't be there . . .I've even heard them mutter things like 'slags'. . .and 'tarts'. . . (Girl, aged 15).

We were having a smoke, chilling out a little. . . you know. . .and this old dear comes out and says it not safe for us to be out in the dark and we should go home at once . . .can you credit it. . .it was 6 o'clock. . . (Girl, aged 14).

However, it is not just the actions of adults that 'engineer' teenage girls' use of outdoor spaces, but also their interactions with older teenagers and/or groups of boys. As a rule of thumb we found that older groups have ascendancy over younger groups, and groups of boys hold sway over groups of girls. Here, the significance of living in a rural place matters enormously. With a lack of formal leisure spaces in many villages, inevitably groups of young people find themselves in regular competition for the social ownership of particular settings (Davis and Ridge, 1997). In this process, a dominant, older group may exclude others, creating what Percy-Smith and Matthews (2001) have described as local 'tyrannical geographies'.

Loads of [older] teenagers hang out by the bus shelter up by the shop. And on the other side of the road by the statue - they also sit there on the bench. . . They're about fourteen to seventeen [years old]. . . They can be like really horrible to you, say things and stuff. [Do you ever hang out with your friends around there?] I never go there if I can avoid it. I'd never hang out there. . . (Girl, aged 13).

A lot of older people hang out by that bench and if you walk along there at night or something, then you can get like abuse from them and things. It's not a very safe place at all. I just don't go there if I can help it. . . (Girl, aged 14).

As in many urban settings, rural spaces are frequently gendered, often to the disadvantage of young girls. For example, the number and range of places where girls are able to hang out by themselves is often very limited, especially in the closed confines of a village. In their narratives, many locations were described by young girls as 'boys' places' – sites where boys would congregate to play football, smoke, and chat. These places were typically those given over to more formal leisure uses, such as recreation grounds, playing fields, and parks. Rather than finding ways to share these spaces, many girls described how they avoided using them when boys were present.

The rec. [recreation ground] is much more for boys than girls. Boys play football and basketball there. . . And when they're playing football they take up all the space. . . (Girl, aged 13).

Quite a lot of gangs of boys hang around outside the primary school. They just go there to smoke and drink 'cos it's quite a quiet area. So quite a lot of girls stay away from here, 'cos like especially in the evening it's quite scary to come around here. . . (Girl B, aged 15).

Some of the older boys made ramps down the bottom of the road. And they used to hang around there (Girl A, aged 13). They'd skateboard there. But now they go to the tree houses, which I think is quite good as they stay out of our way (Girl B, aged 13).

There's this group of lads right. . .who just act smart. . .drinking, smoking. . . mucking around. . .we don't go near them (Girl, aged 13).

Indeed, 'girls' (only) places' were not identified. Where boys had imposed their superordinancy, many girls felt compelled to stay outside of these 'boundaries'. With a lack of alternatives – that is, open, accessible, recreational spaces – girls typically responded either by keeping on the move – that is, choosing to 'walk around the village' rather than staying in one place – or retreating to the private confines of their homes.

We don't tend to hang out in one place. I'll call for my friend and we'll walk around the village for a bit, sometimes calling on our other friend as well. . . (Girl, aged 15).

The girls don't really have a hang out place like the boys do, they just go to each other's houses. . . (Girl, aged 13).

Given the difficulties of hanging out together in single sex groups, among the strategies commonly employed by teenage girls was to meet only in mixed groups. Parents also welcomed this response.

I usually hang out with boys and girls. My mum thinks it's safer if there's boys there when I'm out in the evenings. I'm allowed out later if she knows that some of them will walk me home. . . (Girl, aged 15).

There's about twenty of us that hang around in the village. We just chat, have a smoke, have a drink. People from fifteen up to twenty one. And most of the boys have got a car, so it's quite good as they can drive us places. . . (Girl, aged 15).

There's a little wall by the newsagents. People [boys and girls] go there and just stand and sit on the wall and things like that. And it's just a place that everyone knows so you can just come and see your friends. And you get lots of people just riding their bikes down here and the steps and everything. And a lot of people come here after school as well, 'cos it's just a place to, where you know you're going to find your friends walking past here. . . (Girl, aged 14).

Among the places that young girls most liked to meet up with friends were leisure centres, cafes, shops and other commercial indoor environments. Their regular usage of such places, despite frequent requests from adults for them to move on, signifies not so much an act of defiance on their part but a response to the limited options that are available to them elsewhere in their villages. Commercial spaces of this sort, too, provide secure, delimited, overseen settings where young girls can mix and socialise with their peers in safety, away from the unpredictability of the rural outdoors.

They [leisure centre staff] say 'well you're either swimming or you just get away from the leisure centre'. And you then find lots of people hanging around the back. . . (Girl A, aged 13) Yeah, they don't usually come around the back, but if they do they just say 'can you leave', but there's nowhere else for us to go. . . (Girl B, aged 14).

We actually haven't had any trouble with them [supermarket staff], if you're in the café having a drink. But if you are wandering around. . . . the [supermarket] staff come up to you. . . 'are you buying anything?'. . .and if you say 'no, we're just meeting a friend' they go, 'can you go and wait outside'. . .(Girl, aged 13).

There was a strong temporal dimension to when girls were out and about. In general, we found that girls were expected to be back home before similarly aged boys. Also, compared to teenage girls living in nearby towns, rural girls had to be home at an earlier time – a consequence of residency in poorly lit, thinly populated places.

Me mum says that I must be home by 8.30 at the latest. . .otherwise all hell is let loose. . .she says that you never know what might happen when it's dark. . . . (Girl, aged 14).

I am waiting for a new curfew, it's going to be in my birthday card, I bet it's going to be something like 10 o'clock. . .Boys get longer curfews. . . there's a load of year seven boys out later than me, little year eights and they're out at like half past ten and I'm in my bedroom . . . . (Girl, aged 13).

From these observations, rural spaces take on a fluid, paradoxical meaning for teenage girls. For whilst many parents are keen to invoke rhetorical eulogisms that play up the empowering, liberating and enriching worth of rural living, in practice, the very act of residency in a rural place closes down what young girls are able to do. Thus, for example, we found that female teenagers were often peripheralized, marginalized and subordinated within their communities much more so than similarly aged boys. Given this scenario, we suggest that the everyday life of young girls can be symbolized by a 'lived space' that is characterized on the one hand by 'displacement' and on the other by 'resistance'. Identity formation then is played out amidst these dialectic tensions and spatial dilemmas.

Conclusion

In this chapter we have considered what it is like to be a young teenager growing-up in a part of the English countryside today. In so doing, we have looked critically at the imagining of the rural as idyll and the ways in which children are central to this configuration. Implicit within these constructions are notions that 'pastoral' equates with a state of purity, innocence, and stability, where childhoods are happy and carefree. These ideals are grounded on adultist anticipations and the legacy of Romantic sensibilities. However, in common with a growing number of other studies, our investigations have shown that far from being pastoral paradises many rural villages are desolate places for young people, characterized more often by spatialities that exclude, marginalize, and persecute. Drawing upon the notions of psychogeography we have attempted to separate fantasy from reality and to consider how residency in such places, which are generally bereft of opportunities and where young people are always within the adult gaze, impacts upon teenagers' interpretations of their rural childhoods. Typically, what emerge in their narratives are feelings of frustration, alienation and anger that play up the negative psychic and emotional aspects of the rural experience. We suggest that within these milieux children carve out their own embodied geographies in the manner of cultural bricoleurs, working imaginatively but mostly with the scraps of adult endeavour.

Also, we have considered how young teenage girls interact with and within their rural confines. Skelton (2000: 80) has noted how girls' use of public space has often been conceptualized as 'being the 'wrong' age, being the 'wrong' gender and being in the 'wrong' place'. We suggest that the public sphere of 'the street' is a significant embodied space for teenage girls, a place – which although constructed as impure by some adults – offers important settings in which to meet with 'others' and socialize. However, the prospect of the street is not boundless, instead those places where young girls can safely go is culturally determined. For them, the presence of older gangs and groups of boys is both restricting and enabling. In this sense, their 'lived space' is played out amidst the opposing strains of adult expectations and the heterogeneity of their own relationships, both of which are given additional sharpness and clarity by the spatiality of the rural domain. It would seem that whilst the notion of rural/childhood idyll may be the way in which adults valorize rural living, its essence for many young teenagers is defined instead in terms of confrontation, contradiction and frustration.

Notes

1 For reviews of 'other rurals', especially from the perspective of young people see Vanderbeck and Dunkley (2003) and Panelli (2002).
2 For reasons of confidentiality, the 'voices' of the young people are anonymized. At the outset of every interview and/or discussion group assurance was given that the views to be recorded would not be attributable to any individual or to any specific location – this guarantee was provided so that the young people would be secure in knowing that they could talk openly about matters close to their everyday lives, without fear of repercussion.

References

Aitken, S. (1994). *Putting Children in their Place*. Washington, DC: Association of American Geographers.

Aitken, S. C. (2001). *Geographies of Young People: The Morally Contested Spaces of Identity*, London: Routledge.

Barker, R. and Wright, H. (1955). *Midwest and its Children*. New York: Row, Peterson and Company.

Bourdieu, P. with Wacquant, L. (1992). *An Invitation to Reflexive Sociology*. Cambridge: Polity Press.

Brooker, P. (2002). *A Glossary of Cultural Theory*. London: Arnold.

Bunce, M. (1994). *The Countryside Ideal: Anglo-American Images of Landscape*. London: Routledge.

Christensen, P. (2003). Place, space and knowledge: children in the village and the city. In P. Christensen and M. O'Brien (eds.), *Children in the City* (pp. 13–28). London: RoutledgeFalmer.

Corrigan, P. (1979). *Schooling the Smash Street Kids*. London: MacMillan.

Davis, J. and Ridge, T. (1997). *Same Scenery, Different Lifestyle: Rural Children on Low Income*. London: The Children's Society.

Debord, G. (1970). *Society and the Spectacle*. Detroit: Black and Red.

Debord, G. (1998). *Comments on the Society of the Spectacle*. London: Verso.

Genette, G. (1982). *Figures of Literary Discourse*. Oxford: Blackwell.

Gibson, J. (1979). *The Ecological Approach to Visual Perception*. Boston: Houghton-Mifflin.

Hart, R. (1979). *Children's Experience of Place*. New York: Irvington Publishers.

Holloway, S. and Valentine, G. (eds.) (2000). *Children's Geographies: Playing, Living, Learning*. London: Routledge.

James, A. (1986). Learning to belong: the boundaries of adolescence. In A. Cohen (ed.), *Symbolising Boundaries: Identity and Diversity in British Cultures* (pp. 155–70). Manchester University Press.

James, A. and Prout, A. (1992). *Constructing and Reconstructing Childhood*. London: Falmer Press.

Jones, O. (1997), Little figures, big shadows: country childhood stories. In P. Cloke and J. Little (eds.), *Contested Countryside Cultures* (pp. 158–79). London: Routledge.

Jones, O. (1999). Tomboy tales: the rural, nature and the gender of childhood, *Gender, Place and Culture, 6,* 117–36.

Jones, O. (2000). Melting geography: purity, disorder, childhood and space. In Holloway and Valentine (eds.), *Children's Geographies: Playing, Living, Learning* (pp. 29–47). London: Routledge.

Knabb, K. (ed.) (1981). *Situationist International Anthology.* Berkeley: Bureau of Public Secrets.

Kong, L. (2000). Nature's dangers, nature's pleasures: urban children and the natural world. In Holloway and Valentine (eds.), (pp.257–71).

Kong, L., Yuen, B., Sodhi, N. and Briffett, C. (1999). The construction and experience of nature: perspectives of urban youths. *Tijdschrift voor Economische en Sociale Geografie, 90,* 3–16.

Lefebvre, H. (1991a). *Critique of Everyday Life,* vol. 1. London: Verso.

Lefebvre, H. (1991b). *The Production of Space.* Oxford: Blackwell.

Levi-Strauss, C. (1966). *The Savage Mind.* London: Weidenfeld and Nicolson.

Lewis, G. (1989). Counterurbanisation and social change in the rural south Midlands. *East Midlands Geographer, 11,* 3–12.

Lewis, G. and Sherwood, K. (1994). *Rural mobility and housing,* working papers 7–10, Department of Geography, University of Leicester.

Little, J. and Austin, P. (1996). Women and the rural idyll. *Journal of Rural Studies, 12,* 101–11.

Matthews, H. (1992). *Making Sense of Place: Children's Understanding of Large-scale Environments.* London: Harvester-Wheatsheaf.

Matthews, H. (2003). The street as a liminal space: the barbed spaces of childhood. In P. Christensen and M. O'Brien (eds.), *Children in the City* (pp. 126–42). London: RoutledgeFalmer.

Matthews, H. and Limb, M. (1999). Defining an agenda for the geography of children. *Progress in Human Geography, 23,* 59–88.

Matthews, H., Limb, M. and Percy-Smith, B. (1998). Changing worlds: the microgeographies of young teenagers. *Tijdschrift voor Economische en Sociale Geografie, 89,* 193–202.

Matthews, H., Taylor, M., Sherwood, K., Tucker, F. and Limb, M. (2000a). Growing-up in the countryside: children and the rural idyll. *Journal of Rural Studies, 16,* 141–53.

Matthews, H., Limb, M. and Taylor, M. (2000b). The street as third-space: class, gender and public space. In Holloway and Valentine (eds.), *Children's Geographies: Playing, Living, Learning* (pp. 63–79). London: Routledge.

Moore, R. (1986). *Children's Domain: Play and Play Space in Child Development.* London: Croom Helm.

Panelli, R. (ed.) (2002). Young rural lives: strategies beyond diversity, Special Issue. *Journal of Rural Studies, 18,* 113–223.

Percy-Smith, B. (1999). Multiple childhood geographies: giving voice to young people's experience of place. Unpublished PhD thesis, Centre for Children and Youth, University College Northampton.

Percy-Smith, B. and Matthews, H. (2001). Tyrannical spaces: young people, bullying and urban neighbourhoods. *Local Environment*, *6*, 49–63.

Shields, R. (1999). *Lefebvre: Love and Struggle, Spatial Dialectics*. London: Routledge.

Shoard, M. (1980). *The Theft of the Countryside*. London: Temple-Smith.

Skelton, T. (2000). 'Nothing to do, nowhere to go?' Teenage girls and 'public' space in Rhondda Valleys, South Wales. In Holloway and Valentine (eds.), *Children's Geographies: Playing, Living, Learning* (pp. 80–99). London: Routledge.

Soja, E. (1996). *Thirdspace: Journeys to Los Angeles and Other Real-and-Imagined Places*. Oxford: Blackwell.

Tucker, F. (2003). Sameness or difference? Exploring girls' use of recreational spaces. *Children's Geographies*, *1*, 111–24.

Tucker, F. and Matthews, H. (2001). 'They don't like girls hanging around there': conflicts over recreational space in rural Northamptonshire. *Area*, *33*, 161–8.

Valentine, G. (1997a). A safe place to grow up? Parenting, perceptions of children's safety and the rural idyll. *Journal of Rural Studies*, *13*, 137–48.

Valentine, G. (1997b), 'Oh yes I can'. 'Oh no you can't'. Children and parents' understanding of kids' competence to negotiate public space safely. *Antipode*, *29*, 65–89.

Valentine, G. (1997c). 'My son's a bit dizzy'. 'My wife's a bit soft': gender, children and cultures of parenting. *Gender, Place and Culture*, *4*, 37–62.

Vanderbeck, R. and Dunkley, C. (2003). Young people's narratives of rural-urban difference. *Children's Geographies*, *1*, 241–60.

Ward, C. (1990). *The Child in the Country*. London: Bedford Square Press.

11 The socio-environmental affordances of adolescents' environments

Charlotte Clark and David L. Uzzell

Introduction

Whilst children's environments have been comprehensively researched and reported in environmental psychology, adolescents' use and evaluation of their environments have received virtually no attention; we believe this to be the first review of its kind. This chapter attempts to provide a theoretical framework for examining and explaining the meaning and function of four salient environments for adolescents – the home, school, neighbourhood and town/city centre. Furthermore, this chapter focuses on the function of these environments for the realization of social interaction and retreat opportunities. The theoretical framework has been informed by, but also tries to move forward from, Gibson's (1979) theory of affordances and Heft's later application of Gibson's ideas to outdoor environments (Heft, 1988, 2001). The significant contribution of this study is that it articulates and makes the case for a more socially-driven concept of affordances. The chapter concludes by reporting briefly on recent research undertaken in the UK (Clark, 2001; Clark and Uzzell, 2002) which sought to measure the socio-environmental affordances of the environment and their implications for adolescent behaviour.

Environmental perception – Gibson's theory of affordances

The issue of environmental perception, and more specifically, social perception, lies at the heart of any attempt to evaluate the function of the environment. In order for an individual to be able to interact with the environment they have to be able to perceive its social meaning. Gibson's theory of perception and affordances (1966, 1979) meets this challenge and proposes that individuals discern possibilities for action in the environment by perceiving the affordances of either objects within the environment or the environment itself: 'The *affordances* of

176

the environment are what it *offers* the animal, what it *provides* or *furnishes*, either for good or ill', (Gibson, 1979: 127). Examples of affordances are a fire which affords warmth and illumination but also injury, or a table, which affords sitting at or on, two behaviours with very different goals. The same environmental features do not afford the same function for all individuals. Affordances are defined in relation to the features of the environment and to the attributes of the individual such as needs and intentions, as well as the physical characteristics of the individual.

Gibson's theory has been considered by many to be an asocial model of ecological perception, largely because the statements in his earlier work asserted that affordances could be directly perceived, and his focus is upon the physical affordances of the environment. Gibson, in fact, appreciated the importance of social and cultural meaning in environmental perception, and emphasized the affordances of the environment provided by the presence of other people, such as through social interaction. In fact, Gibson believed that the richest and most intricate affordances of the environment are those provided by other people (Costall, 1995). Thus, affordances can be either physical or social features of the environment. Gibson saw activity as taking place in a socially structured setting, where objects are experienced in relation to the community in which they have meaning. Social behaviour is embedded in and shaped by the environment in which it takes place (Gaver, 1996). Gibson recognized a role for learning in perception and believed that we learn about the social and cultural affordances of objects from other people who play a role constructing affordances and in defining, explaining and policing their use. As a consequence, individuals learn about the social and cultural meaning of objects and are then able to extract this information from the environment.

Physical affordances of the environment

Gibson's theory has principally been used by cognitive psychologists to examine the relationship between the physical properties of the environment and an individual observer's actions (Gibson and Walk, 1960; Gibson et al., 1987). While Gibson's ideas are typically associated with perception and thus in environmental design and architectural terms, form, Heft (1988) suggests that Gibson's conceptualization of the environment is more informative in terms of environmental function. As a consequence, Heft (1988) developed a taxonomy based on the analysis of three books (Barker and Wright, 1951; Hart, 1979; Moore, 1986) which were considered to provide the most detailed accounts of children's outdoor activities and describe the functionally significant properties of children's environments. Heft's taxonomy is primarily physical (e.g., 'climbable feature'; 'shelter'; 'graspable/detached object') and encompasses physical features which are associated with different types of children's play. Heft noted that the affordances of the environment were neither the same for all children nor were they age specific; whilst a younger child might shelter under a tree, an older child might use the same tree for climbing. Heft believed that these 'new affordances' emerged as the child developed, as their needs changed, or as they gained increasing experience with the environment. Thus, Heft believed that children were able to utilize the affordances of their environments to promote their development (see Heft and Chawla, this volume).

Heft's taxonomy, notwithstanding Gibson's later views, concentrates on the physical rather than the social or cultural affordances and meaning of the environment. Heft does not appear to consider the affordances provided by other people in the environment and almost completely ignores social perception in favour of a more cognitively based consideration of the physical features of the environment which relates to only one type of behaviour: children's play. Furthermore, no role is ascribed to the social context in which the physical features reside, and thus environments are conceptualized as being unaffected by temporal processes. This is not to say that Heft does not see a role for social meaning in the environment (Heft, 2001), it is just that no attempt has been made to integrate social context into his taxonomy.

At the centre of Gibson's theory lies a transactional belief about people-environment reciprocity; the observer and the environment have an active, reciprocal, mutually supportive, complementary, and equal relationship. The transactional perspective regards situations as being composed of actors who are engaged in psychological processes in social and physical contexts (Altman and Rogoff, 1987). Like the Gibsonian approach, the transactional paradigm as well as the concept of affordances assumes the individual and the environment coexist and jointly contribute to the meaning and nature of the situation. The individual and the environment are intricately bound together and neither can be understood without the inclusion of the other. Although Heft's perspective might seem to be sympathetic to a transactionalist position, it falls short by virtue of the fact that a transactional perspective assumes that actors' psychological processes are situated within both a physical and social context; Heft's physical affordance paradigm considers only physical contexts. This review seeks to reassess Gibson's theory of affordances and its application in explaining the functional significance of adolescent settings from a truly transactional conceptualization of the environment.

Environmental affordances

It is axiomatic within environmental psychology that environmental context plays a critical role in influencing social attitudes and behaviour (Moser and Uzzell, 2003). The environment comprises both physical and social attributes. The physical aspects of the environment are the 'building blocks' of the functional affordances of people's settings such as the surfaces, greenery, and terrain. Likewise, the presence of other people can also be thought of in terms of 'building blocks' – social knowledge, observed behaviour, expressed attitudes, and indigenous culture. All provide affordances, out of which people understand, make sense of and then act in and upon their world.

While it may be expedient to separate the physical from the social aspects of the environment, in reality this makes little sense. As Barthes (1973) wrote in relation to the signifier and signified in signs, while they can be distinguished on the plane of analysis, on the plane of experience they are indivisible. Individuals' perceive the environment holistically and do not perceive or utilize social and physical aspects of the environment separately and in isolation from each other. It is our contention that the environment supports development through the fusion of social and physical affordances; to treat them as separate is misleading as well as theoretically and philosophically contestable. Such a dualistic conception of environments ignores the interplay between the physical and social components of the environment that support behaviour and development. To conceptualize the environment in terms of independent physical and social aspects does not enable the entirety of the action to be described.

The functional significance of adolescents' environments

In order to understand the functional significance of environments it is appropriate to compare and, if possible, quantify the affordances of different environments for different user groups. It is suggested that environmental affordances[1] will vary by both type of environment and type of user. If one environment is lacking support for a specific affordance, another environment may be able to compensate.

In terms of the functional significance of adolescents' environments and therefore the environmental affordances that are valued by adolescents, key adolescent environments need to be identified. It is argued that different environments available to adolescents, for example town centres and neighbourhoods might differ in their functional significance. A comparison of the environmental affordances of the key environments available to adolescents would provide a holistic picture of the functional significance of adolescents' environments. In recent years, developmental psychologists have agreed that eleven to twenty years is an appropriate age definition of adolescence (Durkin, 1995; Beck, 2000; Berger, 2001); this is the age range accepted in this review.

Place preference

Much research on adolescents' use of environments has focused upon their favourite settings. We can hypothesize that for an environment to become favoured it must afford the adolescent activities that are important to them and might also afford activities that other environments do not support. One way of exploring this is through place preference research. Such research has taken two main paths; the study of adult memories of favourite places in childhood, and the empirical study of currentplace preferences.

Studies of adult memories of favourite places in childhood and early adolescence (Chawla, 1990; Dovey, 1990; Francis, 1995) focus on the affective characteristics of environments and have found that favourite places are essentially those associated with being peaceful, having distance from others and being close to nature. These studies all describe an idealistic image of what early adolescents' environments should be, tend to focus on natural and rural environments and are problematic as recall may be biased.

It is therefore more reliable to examine current place preferences for adolescents than to rely upon adults' memories of their favourite places in early adolescence. Studies of current place preferences have focused upon favourite places (Korpela, 1992; Lieberg, 1997), liked places (van Andel, 1990) and valued places (Schiavo, 1987; Eubanks Owens, 1988, 1994). The underlying assumption of most of these studies is that preference for a place relates to the function and use of the place: if a place is preferred it is likely to be used, if a place is disliked then it is unlikely to be used.

In a study of the favourite places of seventeen to eighteen-year-old Finnish adolescents, Korpela (1992) found that the home, sports facilities, natural settings, and commercial places were favourite places, with the home being mentioned most frequently. Lieberg (1997) examined the favourite places of thirteen to seventeen-year-old Swedish adolescents and also found that private spaces such as the home or a friend's home were named as favourite more often than public places. Other favourite places included outdoor spaces near the home, the shopping mall and green areas. Both Korpela and Lieberg's studies suggest that shopping malls are highly favoured places for adolescents (see also Anthony, 1985; Lewis, 1989; Hopkins, 1991; Matthews, Taylor, Percy-Smith and Limb, 2000; Vanderbeck and Johnson, 2000).

van Andel (1990) made a link between place preferences and reasons for preference. He compared the place preference of children and adolescents (aged six to thirteen years) across three Dutch neighbourhoods and found that the types of places liked (i.e., playgrounds and green areas) were similar across neighbourhoods, as were the reasons given for preference. These areas were preferred for three reasons: the place was good for a specific type of activity, e.g., football; the place included certain environmental features, e.g., open space; the place offered the company of other children. Thus, liking a place was associated with the social and physical affordances of the place.

Eubanks Owens (1988) found that American adolescents, aged fourteen to eighteen years valued outdoor places where they could enjoy natural and developed parks and undeveloped agricultural land for four reasons: visual quality, e.g., the beauty and impressiveness of the place; primary intent, e.g., the primary activities/behaviours associated with the place; supportive intent, e.g., the extent to which the place provides safety, accessibility, and a sense of belonging; unconscious intent, e.g., the extent to which place provides for activities that involve putting things in perspective. Although Eubanks Owens does not explicitly use the word affordance, her analysis essentially involves matching the needs of adolescents with the amount of support available in the environment for those specific needs. Indeed, more frequently valued places supported a greater range of behaviours than the less frequently valued places, suggesting that environments can be valued for the range of behaviours they support rather than for specific behaviours per se.

In a similar study with Australian adolescents from a suburb of Melbourne, aged thirteen to eighteen years, Eubanks Owens (1994) found that adolescents valued parks, commercial areas, and the home, indicating, perhaps not surprisingly, that place preference is strongly influenced by place availability. Eubanks Owens' results reflect the affective emphases of the environmental autobiographies studies and the functional findings of current place preference studies. Studies of place preference illustrate the adolescent's preference for the home, areas near the home (the neighbourhood), commercial areas and green spaces. This suggests that the home, neighbourhood, and town centre environments should be considered as key adolescents' environments.

Environments for development

Although place preference studies are important such research tends to be descriptive and lacks a theoretical framework. Consequently, this review reflects the shift in recent years by focusing on how the use of the environment can support the developmental needs of adolescents (Coleman, 1979; Noack and Silbereisen, 1988; Schiavo, 1988; Lieberg, 1995, 1997). The 'development as action in context theory' (Silbereisen and Eyferth, 1986) proposes that adolescents are active players in their future development and that development occurs through goal-directed action. If there is a discrepancy between desired development and actual development, adolescents can either attempt to change internal conditions or the external contexts (i.e., the environment itself) in order to achieve their developmental goals.

There are two types of contextual changes that adolescents can make when trying to achieve their developmental needs; they can either *select* an environment or environments that will support the pursuit of their goal/s or they can try to *shape* an environment so that it will support the pursuit of their goal/s. These ideas are sympathetic to both Gibson and Heft's conceptualization of the role of the environment in learning. In deciding whether a particular environment will support their goals, an adolescent will have to make an evaluation about the function of the environment. The idea of shaping environments so that they will support their goals suggests that as adolescents perceive new affordances in the environment, so the environment will afford them something that they did not perceive before.

Although psychologists often treat the environment as a neutral and a value-free backdrop to human activity, it is clear from these studies that the environment is *used* functionally to support and realize self development. Noack and Silbereisen (1988) used the 'development as action in context theory' to examine how adolescents used contexts to promote their development. They contrasted the use of the home with public environments over two years by adolescents (from age thirteen) in different states of partnership development. Three types of adolescents were identified: *novices* – had no partner and no aspiration for a partner; *searchers* – had no partner but would like a partner; *fulfilled* – had a partner. 'Novices' tended to spend their leisure time in the home; 'searchers' tended to leave the home environment and increasingly use public environments; and 'fulfilled' adolescents consistently preferred public places. Noack and Silbereisen concluded that seeking out public leisure settings was a strategy employed by adolescents to achieve their goal of finding a partner.

As one moves through time and space, so the development opportunities and affordances of different types of environments change. Coleman (1979) and Schiavo (1988) provide examples of the temporal properties of affordances. Coleman believed that there were three main developmental needs in adolescence: to establish relationships with the opposite sex; to be accepted by one's peers; and to gain independence from one's parents. He argued that adolescents are concerned with gender roles and relationships with the opposite sex and this reaches a peak at about thirteen years of age. Subsequently, the adolescent becomes concerned about peer relationships, peaking at about fifteen years of age, and then with gaining independence from their parents at about sixteen years of age. Coleman believed that adolescents focus on heterosexual relationships in organized activity settings, peer-relationships in casual leisure settings, and independence in commercial leisure settings. Hendry, Shucksmith, Love and Glendinning (1993) found that adolescents make the transition from organized to casual to commercial leisure settings at around eleven to twelve years and use of casual leisure settings such as the neighbourhood started to decline at around sixteen years of age.

Schiavo (1988) compared use of the neighbourhood for three age groups, pre-adolescents (mean age = 9.5 years), young adolescents (mean age = 12.8 years) and older adolescents (mean age = 16.8 years). He found that the neighbourhood was evaluated less positively and utilized less frequently by the older adolescents than the younger and pre-adolescents. The number of adolescents who did not spend any of their leisure time in the neighbourhood increased with age and the older adolescents reported fewer social relationships in the neighbourhood than the pre-and young adolescents. Although Schiavo did not measure the developmental needs of the adolescents per se, he interpreted these findings in terms of the different age groups having different developmental needs. Schiavo postulated that older adolescents have a developmental need to move beyond the pre- and early-adolescent environment of the neighbourhood and concluded that, 'The independence-striving needs of older adolescents may not be satisfied within the local neighbourhood regardless of its facilities or design' (Schiavo, 1988: 9). These studies suggest that if an environment cannot fulfil an adolescent's needs then an alternative environment will be sought (see also Matthews and Tucker, this volume).

The developmental need for social interaction and retreat

Lieberg (1995, 1997) examined the relationship between developmental needs and Swedish adolescents' use of their local environment. He conducted a three-year study of adolescents aged between thirteen to seventeen from the same Swedish neighbourhood and examined not only what activities the adolescents engaged in, but also where these activities took place and with whom. Lieberg drew upon Goffman's (1963) work on behaviour in public places to account for adolescents' use of the neighbourhood and city centre[2] environments. The city centre acts as a front stage where adolescents can show themselves off to a passing audience and try out different behaviours; the neighbourhood acts as a backstage where adolescents can retreat when they have had enough of being on show in the city centre.

Lieberg concluded that there are two principal ways in which adolescents' appropriate space,[3] which he termed places of interaction and places of retreat. Places of interaction have two purposes: first, they enable the adolescent to withdraw from the adult world and to be with their peers, and second, they enable the adolescent to encounter the adult world through social involvement, for example, in city centres. Places of retreat are used for avoiding other teenagers and peers. These two types of environmental use reflect the developmental needs of adolescents. Lieberg found that the neighbourhood offered good opportunities for places of retreat but not for social interaction; conversely, the city centre afforded social interaction but not retreat. Lieberg was unable to offer, however, any explanation of differences between the two settings that resulted in them supporting different behaviours.

Environmental use and developmental needs are intricately bound together and Lieberg suggests that social interaction and retreat are the main developmental needs in adolescence. The use of public spaces (e.g., city centres and neighbourhoods) for social interaction and retreat provide important learning experiences for adolescents. Social competence develops through the use of public spaces and this competence is a vital training for adult life. The anonymity afforded by public environments also allows the adolescent to learn about being amongst strangers, and it is in this public context that lifestyles and collective and personal identities can be developed.

Psychoanalytic and social psychologists see the peer group as an important support system in adolescence (Newman and Newman, 1976; Palmonari, Pombeni and Kirchler, 1990). Psychoanalytic psychologists regard adolescence as a stage of development where identity is formed and emotional ties with parents are severed; social psychologists consider socialization and role acquisition as key developmental changes in adolescence. Given the support gained from the peer group in these processes it is no surprise that adolescents seek out and use environments which afford social interaction.

Spencer and Woolley (2000) believe that there are two important psychological consequences of the environment supporting development: identity formation and well-being. In terms of identity, social and environmental psychologists have proposed a strong link between the physical environment and an individual's identity (Proshansky, Fabian and Kaminoff, 1983; Proshansky and Fabian, 1987; Lalli, 1992; Twigger-Ross and Uzzell, 1996; Speller, 2000; Moser and Uzzell, 2003). Wallenius (1999) illustrated a relationship between a supportive environment and psychological well-being for adults and it is probable that a similar relationship exists for adolescents. A sense of belonging in the neighbourhood has been found to predict loneliness for early adolescents (twelve to fourteen years) and also to predict subjective quality of life and loneliness for pre-adolescents (ten to eleven years). For mid-adolescents (fifteen to seventeen years), a sense of belonging in the school predicted loneliness (Pretty et al., 1996; Chiuper et al., 2003). Thus, different environments may be important at different developmental stages.

The Mall as a social setting

Social interaction is a strong motivator in adolescents' use of shopping malls, (Anthony, 1985; Lewis, 1989; Hopkins, 1991; Matthews, Taylor, Percy-Smith and Limb, 2000; Vanderbeck and Johnson, 2000). For example, Anthony (1985) found that adolescents spent most of their time in the central places of the shopping mall as this afforded them greater opportunities to interact with other people, the principal reason for using this kind of place. Some researchers (Anthony, 1985; Lewis, 1989; Matthews et al., 2000) have described the shopping mall as a third ground between the home and school, and suggest that it may act as an antidote to the regulation that occurs in the adolescent's home and school environments, affording freedom and limited self expression.

Studies of shopping malls in the UK confirm that these retail settings are an important social environment for adolescents (Uzzell, 1995; Vanderbeck and Johnson, 2000). More importantly, the shopping mall was an important social environment for all age groups. Woolley, Spencer, Dunn and Rowley (1999) found that adolescents (aged ten to twelve years) valued town and city centres as they afforded social interaction and a 'social buzz'. The town centre afforded the adolescents places to meet people, be with friends, be with the opposite sex and to be part of a crowd.

The leisure environment as a social setting

The importance of social interaction in adolescents' use of the environment has also been highlighted in a unique study by Cotterell (1991). Cotterell examined how adolescents, aged between thirteen to nineteen years of age, utilized the Expo 88 exhibition in Brisbane. Although the exhibition was not an everyday adolescent setting, Cotterell found that the visits and favourite places of adolescents were concentrated around large scale places that were associated with being entertained, fun and having social contact. Cotterell interpreted these places as 'adolescent territories' in the sense that adolescents assembled in these places in large numbers and they also made frequent return visits to these places. He suggested that adolescents established territories in this new environment based upon their conceptions of how a place should function, which was derived from their experiences elsewhere. Concentrations of adolescents in particular areas of the exhibition could be understood in terms of the fit between the leisure needs and interests of adolescents and the stimulus characteristics of the settings.

Social interaction in the school, home, and neighbourhood

As previously discussed, Schiavo (1988) found that the neighbourhood supported social interaction for younger adolescents (mean age = 12.8 years) but not for older adolescents (mean age = 16.8 years), suggesting that the neighbourhood is an important environment for social interaction for younger adolescents only.

The school is also an important setting for social interaction (Eubanks Owens, 1988; Blatchford, 1998). Blatchford conducted a longitudinal study into break-time activities for adolescents aged eleven and sixteen. At eleven years of age break-time was used for active games, such as football and also talking with friends, walking around, hanging around and sitting down. By sixteen years, break-time was used more for hanging around and socializing. There was also a gender difference in use, with males using the school more actively than females at both eleven and sixteen.

Schiavo (1987) asked children and adolescents aged eight to eighteen to photograph and discuss places in the home that had special meaning for them. He found that over half of the places photographed were used with friends; the bedroom was an especially important environment that afforded entertaining friends and social interaction. Females shared more of their special places in the home with friends and had more friends visit their home than males.

Social interaction is a key developmental need in adolescence;relationships with peers lie at the heart of adolescents' social interaction and the need for social interaction motivates adolescents' use of the environment (Matthews and Tucker, this volume). Previous studies suggests that many environments support social interaction for adolescents and this raises interesting questions about the similarities and differences in the affordances of different settings for social interaction and motivations for use.

Environments for retreat

The importance of using environments for retreat has been demonstrated by research in environmental psychology on restoration and restorative environments (Kaplan and Kaplan, 1982, 1989; Ulrich, 1983; Korpela, 1992). Restorative environments are settings that are sought to enable the individual to be alone, to organize their thoughts and feelings, to reduce stress and to get away from the constraints of everyday life.

Korpela's theory of environmental self-regulation (Korpela, 1989, 1992; Korpela and Hartig, 1996) postulates that individuals' use the environment to regulate pleasant and unpleasant feelings and to maintain a coherent self-concept and a favourable level of self-esteem.The self-regulation theory draws upon Kaplan and Kaplan's attention restoration theory (1989) and states that individuals seek out environments for self-regulation when social pressures become too much for the individual and there is a need to maintain the self. Korpela believed that favourite places play a special role in self-regulation, both for adults and adolescents. He hypothesized that adolescence was a critical time when self-regulation activities would be significant as the self is being developed; self-concept development is a central aspect of adolescence (Erikson, 1968; Rosenberg, 1979; Coleman and Hendry, 1990). Furthermore, the predominance of relationships with peers and the opposite sex during adolescence, which can be stressful, is likely to result in the need for self-regulation.

Korpela (1989) found that Finnish adolescents used their favourite places for self-regulation, including privacy, togetherness, clearing one's mind, relaxation, freedom of expression, pleasure, control, belonging, and familiarity. In a further study, Korpela (1992) examined the positive and negative situational and emotional experiences that preceded adolescents seeking out their favourite places, which included threatening or negative experiences, positive or supportive experiences, a physically stressful period and conflicts or arguments with other people.

Restoration in the home, town centre and neighbourhood

Schiavo (1987) found that as well as being an important setting for social interaction, the home is also an important environment for retreat behaviours. Two-thirds of the places photographed by adolescents in the home were used for retreat behaviours when they were alone. The bedroom was used for solitary activities such as being alone, relaxing and being in a place they could control. Females used more places around the home for solitary activities than males, who tended to confine solitary activities to one or two places.

Clark and Uzzell (2002) found that the home environment afforded adolescents retreat involving close friends and feelings of personal security, while Sebba and Churchman (1986) found that both children (aged five to thirteen years) and adolescents (aged thirteen to eighteen years) regarded having control as a main function of the home environment. Adolescents also saw the home as a place for self-expression, whereas the children placed more emphasis upon the home as a place where they could feel secure.

Despite conceptualizations of natural settings as being the primary source of retreat (Kaplan and Kaplan, 2003; Bryant, 1985) there is evidence that the town/city centre, the neighbourhood, and the school are also used to support retreat behaviours for adolescents (Clark and Uzzell, 2002). Similarly, Woolley et al. (1999) found that as well as being used for its 'social buzz', the town centre paradoxically was also an important setting for quiet reflection.

A new measure of socio-environmental affordances

Although adolescents' environmental use is often driven by the desire either for social interaction or retreat, the relationship between these behaviours and specific environments is, however, unclear. While Heft's taxonomy describes the functionally significant properties of children's environments, no such measure of the social properties of the environment has been developed that allows researchers as well as environmental designers to understand, plan, and support socio-environmental affordances of the home, neighbourhood, school, and town centre environments for two key developmental needs in adolescence: the need for social interaction and the need for retreat.

In order to quantify the affordances of different settings, a sample of 411 adolescents, from Guildford in the United Kingdom, aged 11–15 (249 females, 162 males) rated the neighbourhood and town centre environments on their use of these environments for 40 different socio-environmental affordances. The initial list of forty affordances was then reduced to twenty-eight using Principal Components Analysis. Subsequently, six single gender focus groups were held with groups of adolescents in Years 9, 10 and 11 (thirteen to sixteen years of age) who identified six additional affordances that might have a particular relevance to the home and school environments. Thus thirty-four affordances of the environment were derived for use in a scale to measure adolescents' evaluation of the socio-environmental affordances of the home, school, neighbourhood and the town centre (see Table 11.1).

The socio-environmental affordances scale was then employed in a study of 539 adolescents, aged 11–16 (323 females, 216 males). The principal findings of the study were that the neighbourhood, school and town centre all supported both social interaction and retreat behaviours. The town centre provided significantly more places for interaction than the neighbourhood and school but there was no significant difference in how often the environments were used for interaction. The

Table 11.1. *Thirty-four socio-environmental affordances*

Avoid people	Be in your own space
Be active	Be noisy
Be alone	Be on your own to think
Be entertained	Be peaceful
Be free from the expectations of your family	Be with close friends
Be free from the expectations of your friends	Be with similar people
Be free from the pressures of your friends	Be yourself
Be free from the pressures of your parents	Enjoy yourself
Be free to enjoy yourself	Feel secure
Be happy	Get away from your friends
Be in a place where I feel I belong	Get away from your parents
Be in an area that belongs to teenagers	Get away from your peers
Be in an area that is mainly used by teenagers	Hang around
Be in control of the environment	Have freedom of expression
	Have privacy with your best friend/s
	Have space to be upset in
	Meet up with friends
	Meet new people
	Relax
	Try out new behaviours

neighbourhood provided significantly more places for retreat than the school and town centre and the town centre was used less often than the neighbourhood and school. The finding that both the town centre and neighbourhood afford interaction and retreat contrasts with Lieberg's finding that the town centre was associated with social interaction and the neighbourhood with retreat. The home environment did not support interaction behaviours; it provided instead affordances for two different types of retreat – retreat involving close friends and retreat involving security-seeking (Clark, 2001; Clark and Uzzell, 2002).

Conclusion

The environment is used functionally to support and realize development. Knowledge about adolescents' use of the environment to support their developmental need for social interaction and retreat, and the consequences of this type of environmental use for learning, identity formation and psychological well-being, serve to legitimize adolescents' use of the environment. The degree to which the environment is used changes as adolescents' roles, relationships and activities in the environment change. Therefore, the environment can be seen to have a developmental dimension. As people develop their cognitive, affective and behavioural capacities so too should the environment be designed to facilitate, support and encourage this. Thus each of the environments we have discussed – the home, the school, the neighbourhood and the city centre – should be created and structured so that they too have a developmental dimension which complements the individual's development. Furthermore, the most stimulating environments are likely to be those which provide the greatest range of affordances.

The advantage of a socio-environmental affordance theory is that it can be applied to examine any environment for any user group. Once taxonomies are developed comparisons can be made between environments and user-groups. This information results in a greater understanding of the functional significance of the environment and would potentially inform design, planning and management for all user-groups, e.g., identify situations where there is conflict in an environment between user groups. Considering that most environments are shared between user groups it would seem pertinent to further examine functional significance using the theory of socio-environmental affordances, with a view to informing the design and management of environments.

Previous research has not, however, made quantifiable comparisons between the function of different environments and more importantly has failed to compare the function of the key environments available to adolescents, in order to obtain a holistic picture of adolescents' environments. This research has systematically sought to derive a set of socio-environmental affordances that are specifiable and measurable.

The theoretical reassessment of Gibson's theory of affordances and the subsequence development of a methodology to examine the socio-environmental affordances of adolescents' key environments enables the environmental support for developmental needs to be compared across environments. This is a significant development for this field as it is the first quantifiable comparison of the function of key adolescents' environments. By conceptualizing environments in terms of mutual physical and social affordances, social context and social behaviours are incorporated into the taxonomy. This approach provides rich data concerning the function of adolescents' environments and moves the field of research on from the descriptive studies of one or two environments which have dominated.

Recent years have seen increasing conflict between adults and adolescents concerning their use of environments. Adolescents have stereotypically been associated with using public places in the neighborhood and town centre for activities such as hanging around, petty vandalism, under-age drinking and taking drugs (Brown, 1995; Valentine, 1996; Lupton, 1999).

Whilst measures such as surveillance, restricting access and curfews have been implemented to prevent adolescents from congregating in public places, adolescents also face an increasing risk of being designed out of environments (Hall, 1994; Uzzell, 1995; Malone and Hasluck, 1998; Eubanks Owens, 1999). Contrary to the trend amongst architects and planners who are increasingly being asked to discourage the use of public spaces by adolescents, Eubanks Owens believes that this is detrimental to the social and emotional development of adolescents and proposes that places for hanging out and gathering in groups should in fact be 'designed into' environments. Whilst this proposal should be applauded, it illustrates the need for accurate knowledge about how adolescents use and evaluate different environments. It is only through such knowledge that adolescents will be regarded as legitimate users of public space and considered in the design, planning and management of public spaces.

Notes

1 From this point, we take the term environmental affordance to have an equally strong social dimension; the affordances provided for adolescents may be

direct (from the physical environment) or indirect (mediated by the social presence or behaviour of others).

2 Lieberg uses the terms city centre and town centre interchangeably.

3 Appropriation is concerned with making a place one's own at an individual and group level (Korosec-Serfaty, 1976, as cited in Uzzell, 1995). Appropriation can be defined as a particular affective relation to a place or an object, which in turn may become part of the identity of the individual (Barbey, 1976).

References

Altman, I. and Rogoff, B. (1987). World views in psychology: trait, interactional, organismic and transactional perspectives. In D. Stokols and I. Altman (eds.), *Handbook of Environmental Psychology, Volume 1.* Florida: Krieger Publishing Company.

Anthony, K. H. (1985). The shopping mall: A teenage hangout. *Adolescence, 20,* 307–12.

Barbey, G. (1976). L'appropriation des espaces du logement: tentative de cadrage théorique. In P. Korosec-Serfaty (ed.), *Actes de la 3ème Conférence Internationale de Psychologie de l'Espace Construit* (pp. 215–18). Strasbourg: Université de Strasbourg Press.

Barker, R. G. and Wright, H. F. (1951). *One Boy's Day: A Specimen Record of Behavior.* New York: Harper.

Barthes, R. (1973). *Mythologies.* St Albans: Granada.

Beck, L. E. (2000). *Child Development.* Boston: Allyn and Bacon.

Berger, K. S. (2001). *The Developing Person Through the Lifespan,* 5th Edition. New York: Worth Publishers.

Blatchford, P. (1998). *Social Life in Schools.* London: Falmer Press.

Brown, S. (1995). Crime and safety in whose 'community'?: Age, everyday life and problems for youth policy. *Youth & Policy, 48,* 27–48.

Bryant, B. K. (1985). The neighbourhood walk: sources of support in middle childhood. *Monographs of the Society for Research in Child Development,* Serial No 210, *50*(3).

Chawla, L. (1990). Ecstatic places. *Children's Environments Quarterly, 7*(4), 18–23.

Chipuer, H. M., Bramston, P. and Pretty, G. (2003). Determinants of subjective quality of life among rural adolescents: a developmental perspective. *Social Indicators Research, 61,* 79–95.

Clark, C. (2001). *The Affordances of Adolescents' Environments.* Unpublished PhD Thesis, Guildford: University of Surrey, UK.

Clark, C. and Uzzell, D. L. (2002). The affordances of the home, neighbourhood, school and town centre for adolescents. *Journal of Environmental Psychology, 22*(1/2), 95–108.

Coleman, J. C. (1979). *The School Years.* London: Methuen.

Coleman, J. C. and Hendry, L. B. (1990). *The Nature of Adolescence,* 2nd Edition. London: Routledge.

Costall, A. (1995). Socializing affordances. *Theory & Psychology, 5*(4), 467–81.

Cotterell, J. (1991). The emergence of adolescent territories in a large urban leisure environment. *Journal of Environmental Psychology*, *11*, 25–41.

Dovey, K. (1990). Refuge and imagination: places of peace in childhood. *Children's Environments Quarterly*, *7*(4), 13–17.

Durkin, K. (1995). *Developmental Social Psychology*. Oxford: Blackwell Publishers.

Erikson, E. (1968). *Identity: Youth and Crisis*. New York: Norton.

Eubanks Owens, P. (1988). Natural landscapes, gathering places and prospect refuges: characteristics of outdoor places valued by teens. *Children's Environments Quarterly*, *5*, 17–24.

Eubanks Owens, P. (1994). Valued outdoor places: a study of teen places in Sunshine, Australia. In R. M. Feldman, G. Hardie and D. G. Saile (eds.), *Power by Design* (pp. 62–6). Chicago: The Environmental Design Research Association.

Eubanks Owens, P. (1999). No teens allowed: the exclusion of adolescents from public spaces. *Bulletin of People-Environment Studies*, *14*, 21–4.

Francis, M. (1995). Childhood's garden: memory and meaning of gardens. *Children's Environments*, *12*(2), 183–91.

Gaver, W. W. (1996). Affordances for interaction: the social is material for design. *Ecological Psychology*, *8*(2), 111–29.

Gibson, E. J. and Walk, R. D. (1960). The 'visual cliff'. *Scientific American*, *202*, 64–71.

Gibson, E. J., Riccio, G., Schumuckler, M. A., Stoffregen, T. A., Rosenberg, D. and Tamorina, J. (1987). Detection of the traversability of surfaces by crawling and walking infants. *Journal of Experimental Psychology: Human Perception and Performance*, *13*, 533–44.

Gibson, J. J. (1966). *The Senses Considered as Perceptual Systems*. Boston: Houghton Mifflin.

Gibson, J. J. (1979). *The Ecological Approach to Visual Perception*. Boston: Houghton Mifflin.

Goffman, E. (1963). *Behavior in Public Places*. New York: Free Press.

Hall, L. (1994). Teenagers in suburbia: a case study in a California suburb. In R. M. Feldman, G. Hardie and D. G. Saile (eds.), *Power by Design*. Chicago: The Environmental Design Research Association.

Hart, R. (1979). *Children's Experience of Place*. New York: Irvington Publishers Inc.

Heft, H. (1988). Affordances of children's environments: a functional approach to environmental description. *Children's Environments Quarterly*, *5*(3), 29–37.

Heft, H. (2001). *Ecological Psychology in Context: James Gibson, Roger Barker and the Legacy of William James's Radical Empiricism*. New York: Lawrence Erlbaum Associates.

Hendry, L. B., Shucksmith, J., Love, M. J. G. and Glendinning, A. (1993). *Young People's Leisure and Lifestyles*. London: Routledge.

Hopkins, J. S. P. (1991). West Edmonton Mall as a centre for social interaction. *The Canadian Geographer*, *35*(3), 268–79.

Kaplan, S. and Kaplan, R. (1982). *Cognition & the Environment: Functioning In An Uncertain World*. New York: Praeger.

Kaplan, R. and Kaplan, S. (1989). *The Experience of Nature: A Psychological Perspective*. New York: Cambridge University Press.

Kaplan, S. and Kaplan, R. (2003). Health, supportive environments, and the reasonable person model. *American Journal of Public Health*, *93*(9), 1484–89.

Korpela, K. (1989). Place identity as a produce of environmental self-regulation. *Journal of Environmental Psychology*, *9*(3), 241–56.

Korpela, K. (1992). Adolescents' favourite places and environmental self-regulation. *Journal of Environmental Psychology*, *12*(3), 249–58.

Korpela, K. and Hartig, T. (1996). Restorative qualities of favourite places. *Journal of Environmental Psychology*, *16*(3), 221–33.

Lalli, M. (1992). Urban-related identity: theory, measurement and empirical findings. *Journal of Environmental Psychology*, *12*(4), 285–303.

Lewis, G. H. (1989). Rats and bunnies: core kids in an American mall. *Adolescence*, *24*, 881–9.

Lieberg, M. (1995). Teenagers and public space. *Communication Research*, *22*(6), 720–44.

Lieberg, M. (1997). Youth in their local environment. In R. Camstra (ed.), *Growing up in a Changing Urban Landscape*. Assen, Netherlands: van Gorum and Co.

Lupton, D. (1999). Dangerous places and the unpredictable stranger: constructions of fear of crime. *The Australian & New Zealand Journal of Criminology*, *32*(1), 1–15.

Malone, K. and Hasluck, L. (1998). Geographies of exclusion: young people's perceptions and use of public space. *Family Matters*, *49*, 20–6.

Matthews, H., Taylor, M., Percy-Smith, B. and Limb, M. (2000). The unacceptable flaneur – the shopping mall as a teenage hangout. *Childhood – A Global Journal of Child Research*, *7*(3), 279–94.

Moore, R. C. (1986). *Childhood's Domain: Play and Place in Child Development*. London: Croom Helm.

Moser, G. and Uzzell, D. L. (2003) Environmental psychology. In T. Millon and M. J. Lerner (eds.), *Comprehensive Handbook of Psychology, Volume V: Personality and Social Psychology* (pp. 419–45). New York: John Wiley and Sons.

Newman, B. and Newman, P. (1976). Early adolescence and its conflict: group-identity versus alienation. *Adolescence*, *11*, 261–74.

Noack, P. and Silbereisen, R. K. (1988). Adolescent development and choice of leisure settings. *Children's Environments Quarterly*, *5*, 25–33.

Palmonari, A., Pombeni, M. L. and Kirchler, E. (1990). Adolescents and their peer groups: a study on the significance of peers, social categorisation processes and coping with developmental tasks. *Social Behaviour*, *5*, 33–48.

Pretty, G. M. H., Conroy, C., Dugay, J., Fowler, K. and Williams, D. (1996). Sense of community and its relevance to adolescents of all ages. *Journal of Community Psychology*, *24*(4), 365–79.

Proshansky, H. M., Fabian, A. K. and Kaminoff, R. (1983). Place identity: physical world socialisation of the self. *Journal of Environmental Psychology*, *3*(1), 57–83.

Proshansky, H. M. and Fabian, A. K. (1987). The development of place identity in the child. In C. S. Weinstein and T. S. David (eds.), *Spaces for Children: The Built Environment and Child Development*. New York: Plenum Press.

Rosenberg, M. (1979). *Conceiving the Self*. Florida: Robert E. Krieger Publishing Company.

Schiavo, R. S. (1987). Home use and evaluation by suburban youth: gender differences. *Children's Environments Quarterly*, 4(4), 8–12.

Schiavo, R. S. (1988). Age differences in the assessment and use of a suburban neighbourhood among children and adolescents. *Children's Environments Quarterly*, 5, 4–9.

Sebba, R. and Churchman, A. (1986). The uniqueness of the home. *Architecture & Comportment: Architecture & Behaviour*, 3(1), 7–24.

Silbereisen, R. K. and Eyferth, K. (1986). Development as action in context. In R. K. Silbereisen, K. Eyferth and G. Rudinger (eds.), *Development as Action in Context: Problem Behaviour and Normal Youth Development*. New York: Springer.

Speller, G. M. (2000). *A community in transition: a longitudinal study of place attachment and identity processes in the context of an enforced relocation*. Unpublished PhD thesis. Guildford: University of Surrey, UK.

Spencer, C. and Woolley, H. (2000). Children and the city: a summary of recent environmental psychology research. *Child: Care, Health and Development*, 26 (3), 181–97.

Twigger-Ross, C. L. and Uzzell, D. L. (1996). Place and identity processes. *Journal of Environmental Psychology*, 16, 205–20.

Ulrich, R. S. (1983). Aesthetic and affective response to the natural environment. *Human Behaviour & Environment: Advances in Theory and Research*, 6, 85–125.

Uzzell, D. L. (1995). The myth of the indoor city. *Journal of Environmental Psychology*, 15(4), 299–310.

Valentine, G. (1996). Children should be seen and not heard: the production and transgression of adults' public space. *Urban Geography*, 17(3), 205–20.

Vanderbeck, R. M. and Johnson, J. H. (2000). 'That's the only place where you can hang out': urban young people and the space of the mall. *Urban Geography*, 21(1), 5–25.

van Andel, J. (1990). Places children like, dislike and fear. *Children's Environments Quarterly*, 7(4), 24–31.

Wallenius, M. (1999). Personal projects in everyday places: perceived supportiveness of the environment and psychological well-being. *Journal of Environmental Psychology*, 19, 131–43.

Woolley, H., Spencer, C. P., Dunn, J. and Rowley, G. (1999). The child as citizen. *Journal of Urban Design*, 4, 255–82.

Part IV

Children and the design process

12 Children as agents in sustainable development: the ecology of competence

Harry Heft and Louise Chawla

The great challenge of the twenty-first century may well be achieving sustainable development – which is 'development that meets the needs of the present without compromising the ability of future generations to meet their needs' (WCED, 1987: 8). Children stand at the heart of this definition in two respects. First, concern for future generations, which takes form in each new cohort of children, motivates development of this kind. Second, if practices consistent with sustainable development are to be carried forward through time, then children must be the bridge conveying their value and ways. For these reasons, many municipal governments and agencies that work with children are currently experimenting with approaches to integrate children into environmental planning.

What is lacking in these efforts, however, is a coherent theoretical framework for investigating the question that these practical initiatives raise: what experiences prepare children to value and care for their local environment and join in community decision-making? Although there have been many surveys of young people's environmental attitudes and knowledge, much less is known about environmental learning as children engage with their localities, or about how children learn to take collaborative action on behalf of the places where they live (Rickinson, 2001). Drawing on ideas in ecological psychology, we propose a framework for research on this topic. We submit that one impediment to advances on this front resides in dominant assumptions about the nature of perceiving and cognition. After offering some thoughts on this subject, we explore how the ecological approach of James and Eleanor Gibson forms a particularly appropriate theoretical foundation for research on children's developing environmental awareness and competence. At the centre of their view is the claim that perceiving and acting are basic and intertwined processes of knowing, and that through action, individuals *simultaneously* discover properties of the environment and possibilities for their own emerging environmental competencies. Further, we suggest that the work of Roger Barker and his colleagues on behaviour settings provides a fruitful way to evaluate whether communities support children's environmental learning and participation.

Sustainability and community participation

In practice, 'children's participation' and 'sustainable development' are contested terms. Some advocates intend participation to be 'systems maintaining' whereas others believe that it should be 'systems transforming' (Pearse and Stiefel, 1979). Those who seek to maintain existing systems see participatory processes as occasions to disseminate information and mobilize co-operation with predetermined policies. Those who advocate systems-transforming participation seek to transfer significant decision-making to the people whose lives will be most affected (see Horelli, this volume). This division is similar to the distinction drawn by Orr (1992) between two competing visions of sustainable development. One, which he terms 'technological sustainability', is based on a belief that sustainable relations with the environment will be engineered by experts in technology and economics, and for that reason, other citizens only need to be receptive to these expert decisions. According to another view, which Orr terms 'ecological sustainability', the public at large needs to be active and well-informed so that people can critically review expert recommendations and contribute their own initiatives.

This chapter advocates systems transforming participation and ecological sustainability. It is based on the principle that people who share localities are particularly well qualified to evaluate the impact of decisions on themselves and their surroundings, and that this 'local expert knowledge' extends to children. Although adults may be best qualified to identify invisible toxins or disease vectors that threaten children, children can identify physical and social features of their communities that make these places alienating and forbidding, or places where young people feel that they can thrive.

We also define participation to include both formal and informal dimensions. For children, these dimensions are interdependent. Informal participation involves freedom to move about and explore natural and built environments, to gather with others, and to observe and try out roles in public places. Through children's participation in their locality in this informal sense, they come to understand issues discussed in the formal arena of environmental planning, such as traffic flow, green space, watersheds, crime or 'eyes on the street'. These issues become grounded in local realities for them, and they gain experience that they can later contribute to formal processes of community decision-making.

Defining participation broadly to include both formal and informal processes of engagement also accommodates young children, who primarily know their communities through informal channels of everyday life. Typically, formal mechanisms of participatory planning involve young people from middle childhood through adolescence, even though younger children often have thoughtful views as well (see Sutton and Kemp, this volume). One advantage of applying ecological psychology to the evaluation of participation is that it flexibly covers this informal as well as formal domain.

The relevance of ecological psychology

Ecological psychology offers a strong theoretical basis for evaluating children's participation, in both the formal and informal sense, for at least three reasons: it focuses on children's agency; it provides a rich description of the environmental context for action and development; and it places children and the environment together in a common realm.

As self-evident as the latter assertion may seem to many, it is not the position held by the dominant epistemologies in the psychological and social sciences. The standard view is that the world and individuals' awareness of it inhabit separate realms – a physical and a mental realm, respectively – and that what most individuals know immediately is their own experience of the world, typically in the form of a mental representation, rather than the world itself. Most theorists who hold this *representationalist* view operate as if the relationship between the mental representation and the world itself is unproblematic. But as Hume (1748/1955) persuasively demonstrated in the eighteenth century, the logical consequence of this viewpoint, *at best*, is an attitude of scepticism about what one holds to be true about the world. Even more problematic is another conclusion based on this representationalist view, which has gained wide currency in recent decades: namely, *all* that can be known about the world is limited to one's own mental experience of it. In either case, individuals are left adrift in their own separate subjective realms, which exist apart from a common world.

We submit that views that take awareness of the environment to be a mental construction are not compatible with an interest in environmental activism. They put the 'real' world that can motivate shared concern and action *always* out of reach in so many separate minds. They emphasize the uniqueness of individual experience – or experience socialized by gender, class, or ethnic group – to the neglect of common experiences. The basic assumption driving the concept of sustainability is that a shared environment exists independently of individuals' experience of it, with real qualities and real limits that shape human lives and that human beings can discover. And yet it is precisely that presupposition that social constructivist theories, at bottom, call into question.

The ecological psychology of the Gibsons' assumes that to be animate – to be a living organism – means to have agency that functions in the service of maintaining an awareness of the environment (E. Gibson and Pick, 2000; Gibson, 1966, 1979). Action, from manipulating an object in one's hands to moving through the landscape, is a means of staying in touch with the environment's significant properties. From a psychological point of view, a species' evolutionary history includes the selection of perceiving-acting systems that serve the function of detecting those aspects of its econiche that matter from a functional standpoint. The econiche and the animal are reciprocal facets of a shared functional system, and as such, awareness of psychologically significant properties occurs *within* the animal-environment relationship. That is, mind and world, at a psychological level of analysis, are not two separate realms, mediated somehow by a mental representation. Instead they constitute a common, *relational* domain, and their relationship rather than being mediated is *direct*.

To say that perceiving is direct is to make the claim that what an individual perceives is specified by the stimulus information available in its surroundings. To take the case of vision, properties of objects are carried as structures in reflected light, and these structures serve as potential information about those objects and their qualities (Gibson, 1979). That is, information specific to features of the environment is available to be perceived. Moreover, potential information available to a particular perceiver is also available to other perceivers who are also present. This array of available stimulus information constitutes a potential common ground for all perceivers.

But to say that different individuals have access to the same array of stimulus information is not to suggest that each individual necessarily perceives the same features of the world. The world is a plenum of structures and qualities, and at any particular time, different perceivers may be attuned to different features of it. But *what* each individual experiences *is* a feature of the world, not a mental fabrication of it. This viewpoint has significant consequences for collective action concerning ecological sustainability, for it holds out the possibility that with appropriate experiences, people can become aware of the same features of the common world. That is, it leaves room for perceptual learning that converges toward a common ground.

Another distinctive contribution of the Gibsons' ecological approach is the concept of *affordances:* relational and functionally significant

Figure 12.1. Shelter building inside the forest at the Orana School, Canberra (photo courtesy of Karen Malone).

properties of the environment (see Clark and Uzzell, this volume). This term marks a significant conceptual advance in epistemology because it views the meaning of environmental features as a property of the *relationship* between the environment and the individual, rather than being a quality that individuals impose on the world through a mental construction. To illustrate, the tree branches in Figure 12.1 afford for these children the activity of building a shelter because of specific properties of the branches taken with respect to the competencies of the children and the goals of the task. For example, only those branches that are long enough that when rested on a tree create a suitably sized shelter *relative* to the children's body size, and only those branches that are light enough *relative* to the children's capacity to carry them, can be used for this construction. Put another way, from the perspective of these children, branches with these properties afford building a shelter – that is, these environmental features are functionally meaningful, and their meaning is specified relative to properties of the object, the task, and the children considered collectively.[1]

This example also serves to illustrate the relationship between perceiving and acting discussed previously, and allows us to distinguish between exploratory and performatory activities (Reed, 1996a). The branches' affordances were, no doubt, discovered and tested through *exploratory* activities, and in the construction of the shelter – a *performatory* action – these environmental features were realized.

A common criticism of the ecological approach is that it focuses on the material aspects of the environment while neglecting the social and cultural. This criticism is groundless, however (Heft, 2001; Reed, 1996a). The children's shelter building, for example, was intensely social. It was a social project for social ends, and in carrying out this task, individuals perceived both social and non-social features of their environment. The importance of the larger social and cultural context is further demonstrated by the research project that included these observations of the children. Malone and Tranter (2003) compared students' use of five school yards. Three sites had a rich array of natural resources, but children engaged in exploring their environment at one site only – the Steiner school illustrated here, where teachers' educational philosophy encouraged activities of this kind.

In fact, considerable evidence indicates that humans even in infancy are particularly responsive to information from social sources (E. Gibson and Pick, 2000). From a very early age children become participants in the reciprocal exchange of information with others. Further, around six months of age children begin to exhibit attention to a feature of the environment that another individual is attending to. This emergence of *joint attention* during the second half of the first year becomes the basis for all subsequent instruction and learning. Discovery is rarely, if ever, an individual achievement, but rather it is built on involvement with others who direct the individual's attention to concrete features, and later in life, abstract features, of everyday existence (either intentionally or incidentally). Childhood, and indeed much of our lives beyond childhood, can be accurately described as a set of apprenticeships with someone more experienced in a particular domain. This point is vital for education for sustainable development.

Ecological psychology and sustainability

These features of the ecological approach are compatible with the goals of sustainable development and children's participation in a number of ways. The Gibsons' ecological psychology is squarely anchored in the natural domain, eschewing a matter-mind dichotomy and placing humans in a world in which they have co-evolved with other living things. This evolutionary perspective implies human beings' dependence on the intrinsic qualities of the world, its resources, and its limits.

Further, with its emphasis on agency, and on perceiving-acting, the ecological approach recognizes that animals alter their environments to varying degrees, from burrowing by earthworms and nest building by birds to the construction of cities by humans. In the process, organisms need to preserve the resources that are the conditions for their on-going existence and well-being. The movement for sustainable development, too, grows out of this recognition.

Ecological psychology's emphasis on agency also accords with the goals of 'systems transforming' participation, which seeks to engage people in actively learning about, monitoring and managing their surroundings rather than passively accepting existing conditions. According to both ecological psychology and this view of participation, people more fully realize their capabilities – more fully *flourish* in a human sense – when they have these opportunities.

The ecological perspective, with its emphasis on animal-environment reciprocity and the role that information plays in guiding actions, is also consistent with reports from around the world on the sustainable management of natural resources: namely, that ecosystems are most successfully maintained when the people who directly depend upon these habitats for their livelihoods have a strong voice in decision-making (UNDP *et al.*, 2000). On this level people live close to the realities of natural environments, such as grasslands or forests, and here they see how their lives depend on this ecosystem and how their actions affect it. The same rule applies to maintaining the livability of urban areas (Badshah, 1996).

Finally, ecological psychology's emphasis on agency and efforts toward perceiving meaningful features of the environment coincides with children's strong motivation to move about, explore, and shape their environment. Consequently, ecological psychology helps us maintain in the foreground of our consideration the significance of children's informal as well as formal participation in their communities. Children want to know what water is by splashing in it, and what earth is by digging and moulding it. They want to know their surrounding society by being in the middle of the places where action unfolds. They want to do these things with friends. Through children's integration into environmental planning, they gain opportunities to use and expand this base of knowledge and they learn directly how participatory democracy is achieved. Through first hand experiences, children (as well as adults) most fully learn about the natural and social features of the environment and about their own competencies in these settings (Reed, 1996b). Reviews of environmental autobiographies reveal that people attribute lasting significance to memories of convivial city streets and alluring natural areas where they enjoyed discoveries of this kind in childhood and adolescence (Cooper-Marcus, 1992). Special childhood places of this kind are the most frequent reason that environmental educators and activists give for their dedication to protecting the environment (Tanner, 1998).

Environmental qualities that promote competence

With this commentary about ecological psychology and its relationship to environmental sustainability as a backdrop, we proceed to consider conditions that support the development of children's environmental competencies. We propose that the following four conditions are particularly significant: (1) affordances that promote discovery and responsive person-environment relationships; (2) access and mobility to engage affordances; (3) guided participation that supports perceptual learning and action; and (4) opportunities for meaningful participation in community settings.

Affordances that promote discovery and responsive
person-environment relationships

Agency is a hallmark of human functioning, and from the earliest days of life, purposive actions are embedded in a dynamic, reciprocal transaction between the individual and the environment. From infancy on, what most influences continuing engagement is *immediate* and *contingent* information produced by self-directed action. This relationship was clearly demonstrated by Rovee-Collier (1986) who compared infants as young as two months under two sets of conditions. In one condition, the infant's ankle was connected by a cord to a mobile suspended over the crib; and as a result, the infant produced movements of the mobile which were contingent on her kicking. In the non-contingent condition, the cord was detached from the ankle. The experimenter observed that when the movement of the mobile was contingent on the infant's actions, the rate of kicking increased. However, when the mobile was moved by the experimenter rather than the infant, the rate of kicking declined rapidly. What was different between these two conditions? By linking the action to the object, the infant could learn to *control an event in the world,* and in so doing, learn something about *her own capabilities.* In this condition, she was motivated to continue her engagement.

These kinds of effects have been demonstrated often during the first year of life, even with infants as young as two to four weeks old (Van der Meer, van der Weel, and Lee, 1996). Furthermore, similar work demonstrates that with on-going exploration, infants fine tune their actions in relation to contingent environmental events in order to control outcomes more effectively (Goldfield, Kay, and Warren, 1993; Thelen and Smith, 1994). This reciprocity of self-produced action and environmental events lies at the heart of the development of competence, or self-efficacy. Noting similar research, Fuglesang and Chandler (1997) argue that responsive early childhood programs and parent training to increase interactive experiences of this kind are important precursors to children's readiness for more formal types of participation.

Environmental features vary in the degree to which they provide these effects (Heft, 1988). Many resist alteration – such as hard surfaces that can't be shaped, sheer walls that can't be climbed, or streets with fast traffic where there is no time or space for children. Although both natural and constructed features can be malleable, natural areas are often particularly rich in the effects they offer. Soft earth invites digging, moulding, and drawing. Branches afford climbing, swinging, and bouncing. Water's fluid responsiveness is one of the reasons for this element's universal appeal.

This relationship between goal-directed actions and contingent environmental events can also be found in research with adolescents and adults. Although stated in different terms, the literatures on self-efficacy (Bandura, 1997, 2001), learned optimism (Seligman and Csikszentmihalyi, 2000), and life satisfaction (Ryan and Deci, 2001) demonstrate that the experience of efficacy promotes subsequent purposive, goal-directed action. As Bandura (1997) noted, people can be inspired with a sense of agency by various means, including verbal encouragement and seeing influential role models succeed, but nothing is as motivating as 'mastery experiences' of one's own capability.

This is an important principle to apply in designing participatory projects with children. Because many goals of community participation depend on numerous actors and success may be uncertain or long delayed, it is important to build in a sequence of more easily achievable, proximal goals. For example, while children are involved in petitioning their local government to dedicate a vacant lot for a community garden for all ages, they can taste initial success by creating a garden in their school grounds. Not only is the garden itself a visible accomplishment, but it forms a setting for numerous 'micro-achievements' during planting, harvesting, and sharing food.

In short, we propose that children can most effectively contribute to sustainable development when they first build up a history of engagement with responsive environmental features that produce positive outcomes. By positive outcomes we mean those that match the child's unfolding intentions (see section below) *and* that provide information to the child about her own developing competencies. People develop a resilient sense of efficacy by overcoming obstacles, but they are more likely to persevere if they have a previous history of successes behind them.

Access and mobility to engage affordances

It is not sufficient for there to be a rich array of affordances in children's surroundings. Access to engage with them is equally important. In our rapidly urbanizing world, a number of barriers impede access: the hazards of traffic, crime, and pollution; parents' fears of strangers; and children's fears of bullies (see, for example, Chawla, 2002; Risotto and Tonucci, 2002; Kytta, 2002, 2004, and Rissotto and Giuliani, this volume). Another factor is the increasing privatization of space (McKendrick, Bradford and Fielder, 2000). A shopping centre, for example, is a much more restrictive setting than a traditional street market.

As Kyttä has shown in her chapter in this volume, the best communities for children provide for 'positive interactive cycles'. Children have independent mobility to explore their surroundings, and if they find responsive affordances around them, they become motivated to explore further and to discover more. In the process, it may be added, they are building a growing repertoire of environmental competencies.

Guided participation that supports perceptual learning and action

From the perspective of the ecological approach, perceiving is a process of extracting or selecting information present in the surroundings. In this on-going process of selection and discovery, children are not solitary learners. Adults and other more experienced children often directly collaborate with a 'novice child' in play or in carrying out some joint task. In more indirect ways, others create environments that put behavioural possibilities within a child's reach. For example, parents may put their one-year-old in a walker or provide child-sized tools for their five-year-old. Children's play, exploration and work, in other words, are typically *scaffolded* activities. Possibilities for action are established by the convergence of the individual's existing skills, the tools and artifacts available in the setting, and the presence of others who can help to extend the range of actions. This *field of promoted action* (Reed, 1996a), with its roots in Vygotsky's (1978) zone of proximal development, clearly illustrates that when considering everyday environments, any distinction drawn between the so-called physical and the social is apt to be artificial.

People learn most effectively when they engage in an activity under the guidance of others who are more knowledgeable (Mayer, 2004). In a variety of ways, *the principal function played by the more experienced individual is to direct the learner's attention to relevant features of the task.* Sometimes the guide literally points or verbally singles out some feature for the child's attention (as when a parent points to shriveled leaves on a plant and explains that they indicate that the plant needs water). At other times, the guide may simply position an object so that a critical feature can be discovered (as when an older sister turns over a leaf to show an insect clinging to its underside). Quite commonly, what the more experienced person knows is tacit and not readily articulated in words. Still, what this person can do is create conditions that facilitate the learner's discovery. These are the conditions of apprenticeship, taken in the broadest sense of that term; and it typifies the social contexts for learning that are so characteristic of humans (Rogoff, 1990, 2003). They are also the conditions that encourage perceptual learning, which involves becoming sensitized or selectively attuned to particular information out of the larger field of potential information. In the process, individuals with similar learning experiences become attuned to the same information. Because perceptual learning is a life-long process, the possibility always remains open that individuals holding divergent views can find some common ground, or if not that, at least become aware of what the other party identifies as most crucial.

Thomashow (2002) argues that these kinds of field experiences are critical for environmental learning that can mobilize common action. One reason why people have difficulty understanding global environmental change and the urgency of addressing problems is that many of the components of an ecosystem's functioning unfold in dimensions of time and space that easily escape people's notice, or show seasonal patterns that are out of sight and out of synchrony with the pace of increasingly mechanized societies. Yet for those who have learned how to see them, the messages carried by migrating birds, shifting weathers, and flowing waters tell the story of an interdependent world.

Although representations of the environment in books and on television and computer screens can contribute to this process of learning to see, they can never replace the role of direct experience. As Reed (1996b) has argued, *primary* or first-hand experience of the world exposes a person to inexhaustible possibilities for learning. A person outdoors encounters a dynamic, dense, multisensory flow of diversely structured information. In contrast, in *secondary* experience, when others tell about the world second-hand through a text or an image, this information is radically reduced – literally, in most cases, two-dimensional.

What is more, it is in the world of full-bodied experience where people form personal relationships and place attachments, draw motivation to protect the people and places they care for, and gain competencies to do so.

Opportunities for meaningful participation in community settings

Thus far, we have been mostly emphasizing children's engaging with individual features of the environment, or affordances. Affordances, however, are constituents of *places*, and to understand and evaluate children's role in their communities, it is necessary to look at these more encompassing social contexts. The richest analysis of places in the psychological literature is Roger Barker's treatment of behaviour settings. Behaviour settings are those places where individuals gather and engage in particular activities. Indeed, behavioural settings *are constituted by* the joint actions of individuals as well as the affordances that support those actions (Barker, 1968; Schoggen, 1989).[2] Behaviour settings create opportunities for individuals to participate in the social life of the community, and from a psychological perspective, they provide some of its most vital ecological resources.

Like affordances, behaviour settings are real entities in the environment, rather than mental constructions. They can be located geographically and temporally (e.g., a meeting of a community ecological association occurs at a specifiable time and place), and their distinctive properties can be perceived. Thus behaviour settings, like affordances, are perceptually *meaningful* features of the environment (Heft, 1989, 2001). As is true of affordances, some behaviour settings are more responsive than others to an individual's actions, and hence offer richer opportunities to develop competencies.

The degree of competence that a person feels in a behaviour setting is likely to depend on her level of *involvement and responsibility* in contributing to a group's goals. Barker (1968) distinguished among different levels of 'penetration' that an individual could inhabit in a setting, from a very peripheral level involving primarily observation and little influence over a setting's functions, to central levels with considerable power to influence activities (Table 12.1). Comparisons of large and small schools (Barker and Gump, 1964) and different communities (Barker and Schoggen, 1973) have shown how the availability of responsible positions affect children's opportunities to experience leadership and play a variety of roles.

Barker's idea of levels of penetration can be useful for the design and evaluation of participatory programs for children.[3] Given limited

Table 12.1. *Zones of penetration in a behaviour setting*

1 Onlooker – Takes no active role in the setting. Has no power. Example: a submissive child sidelined by more aggressive children who dominate a program activity.
2 Audience – Have a recognizable place, but very little power. Example: audience members when children produce a play to dramatize a community issue.
3 Members – Have potential rather than immediate power. Example: classmates who are eligible to elect a representative to a school council.
4 Active Functionary – Have power over a part of the setting. Example: cast member in a play; a member of a team which is monitoring pollution in a local river.
5 Joint Leaders – Have immediate authority over the entire setting, but this power is shared. Example: a play's creators and directors; the children elected by their peers to represent them at a council meeting.
6 Single Leader – Has immediate and sole authority over the operations of the setting (not characteristic of a participatory program).

Adapted from Barker (1968).

funding by children's organizations, considerations about the development of children's competence suggest that resources can be best invested either in enhancing existing behaviour settings or creating new settings where as many children as possible can serve in positions of influence. For example, a child-run radio program or newspaper creates a large number of ongoing roles for children to serve as reporters, researchers, informants, performers, editors, and technicians who collectively cover issues of interest and concern for all children in their region (see Figure 12.2). Participatory research that involves young people in documenting their environments and determining priorities for change also creates numerous roles for researchers, informants, and spokespeople at public meetings (McIvor, 2001; Chawla and Malone, 2003). This recommendation does not mean that there is no role for other approaches, such as a few child representatives in events planned by adults, or children's councils or parliaments in which only a few elected officers take responsible roles. If the goal, however, is to prepare as many children as possible for competent citizenship, then these limited approaches are inadequate by themselves.

Conclusion

This chapter began with the claim that sustainable development is perhaps the most pressing challenge of our new century, and then

Figure 12.2. Young people operating a community radio station El Salvador.

proceeded with a discussion of a psychological theory. How do we justify addressing this very real environmental problem with this theoretical response? Put simply, the very possibility of sustainable development depends on nurturing a generation of children who recognize the connection between human action and environmental sustainability and, most critically, who can *imagine themselves as being participants* in achieving this end. When setting out, then, to provide experiences for children that might foster these ends, one necessarily steps into the arena of theory because of how we think about the development of a sense of agency and competence is unavoidably theory-driven.

In our view the empirically-grounded theoretical approach that offers the most promise for tackling this vital problem is ecological psychology. From this perspective, all animate beings are viewed as agents in the environment who, through their actions, simultaneously learn about the environment and about their own competencies in effecting change. The development of perceiving, thinking, and acting, so conceived, transpires within an on-going, dynamic individual-environment relationship where experience of the environment is direct. As a consequence, the prospects for individuals' *collectively* knowing a common environment can be realized, and so too hopes for co-ordinated efforts toward achieving a shared end. With this view of person-environment reciprocity at its core, ecological psychology forms a fertile ground for planning and evaluating environmental experiences that can best promote children's developing competencies in a shared, interdependent world.

Notes

1 This example raises the question of whether an affordance is solely specified relative to an individual, or whether it can be specified relative to a group of individuals. We do not view these possibilities as mutually exclusive, and indeed some research is underway to investigate joint affordances (Marsh, Baron and Richardson, 2002).
2 Barker (1968) does not employ the concept of affordances, which in fact was not formally proposed by Gibson until the late 1970s. In a proposed synthesis of Gibson's and Barker's ecological psychology, Heft (2001) argued that the concept of affordances can be readily assimilated into, and in fact enriches, Barker's ecological approach.
3 For a more detailed discussion of evaluating participation from this perspective, see Chawla and Heft (2002).
4 For analysis of the relationship between availability of responsible positions in a setting and individuals' participation and experiences in those settings, see Barker and Gump (1964).

References

Badshah, A. (1996). *Our Urban Future*. London: Zed Books.
Bandura, A. (1997). *Self-Efficacy*. New York: W. H. Freeman.

Bandura, A. (2001). Social cognitive theory: an agentic perspective. In S. T. Fiske, D. L. Schachter and C. Zahn-Waxler (eds.), *Annual Review of Psychology, 52*, 1–26. Palo Alto, CA: Annual Reviews.

Barker, R. (1968). *Ecological Psychology.* Stanford University Press.

Barker, R. and Gump, P. (1964). *Big School, Small School.* Stanford University Press.

Barker, R. and Schoggen, P. (1973). *Qualities of Community Life.* San Francisco: Jossey-Bass Publishers.

Chawla, L. (2002). *Growing Up in an Urbanising World.* London/Paris: Earthscan Publications/UNESCO.

Chawla, L. and Heft, H. (2002). Children's competence and the ecology of communities: a functional approach to the evaluation of participation. *Journal of Environmental Psychology, 22*, 201–16.

Chawla, L. and Malone, K. (2003). Neighborhood quality in children's eyes. In M. O'Brien and P. Christensen (eds.), *Children in the City* (pp. 118–41). London: Falmer Press.

Cooper Marcus, Clare (1992). Environmental memories. In I. Altman and S. Low (eds.), (pp. 87–112). New York: Plenum Press.

Fuglesang, A. and Chandler, D. (1997). *Children's Participation – A Case for a Strategy of Empowerment in Early Childhood.* Oslo: Save the Children Norway.

Gibson, E. and Pick, A. D. (2000). *An Ecological Approach to Perceptual Leaning and Development.* Oxford University Press.

Gibson, J. J. (1966). *The Senses Considered as Perceptual Systems.* Boston: Houghton-Mifflin.

Gibson, J. J. (1979). *The Ecological Approach to Visual Perception.* Boston: Houghton-Mifflin.

Goldfield, E. C., Kay, B. C., and Warren, W. H. (1993). Infant bouncing: the assembly and tuning of actions systems. *Child Development, 64*, 1128–42.

Heft, H. (1988). Affordances of children's environments: a functional approach to environmental description. *Children's Environments Quarterly, 5*, 29–37.

Heft, H. (1989). Affordances and the body: an intentional analysis of Gibson's ecological approach to visual perception. *Journal for the Theory of Social Behavior, 19*, 1–30.

Heft, H. (2001). *Ecological Psychology in Context: James Gibson, Roger Barker, and the Legacy of William James's Radical Empiricism.* Mahwah, NJ: Lawrence Erlbaum Associates.

Hume, D. (1955). *An Enquiry Concerning Human Understanding and an Enquiry Concerning the Principles of Morals.* Oxford: Clarendon Press (originally published in 1748).

Kyttä, M. (2002). Affordances of children's environments in the context of cities, small towns, suburbs and rural villages in Finland and Belarus. *Journal of Environmental Psychology, 22*, 109–23.

Kyttä, M. (2004). The extent of children's independent mobility and the number of actualized affordances as criteria of a child-friendly environment. *Journal of Environmental Psychology, 24*, 179–98.

Malone, K. and Tranter, P. J. (2003). School grounds as sites for learning. *Environmental Education Research, 9*, 283–303.

Mayer, R. E. (2004). Should there be a three-strikes rule against pure discovery learning? The case for guided methods of instruction. *American Psychologist,* 59, 14–19.

Marsh, K. L., Baron, R. M. and Richardson, M. J. *The affordance structure and dynamics of duo lifting,* paper presented at the 12th International Conference on Perception & Action, Gold Coast, Australia: July, 2003.

McIvor, C. (2001). Do not look down on us: child researchers investigate informal settlements in Zimbabwe. *PLA Notes 42* (Participatory Learning and Action), London: International Institute for Environment and Development.

McKendrick, J., Bradford, M. and Fielder, A. (2000). Kid customer? Commercialization of playspace and the commodification of childhood. *Childhood, 7,* 295–314.

Orr, D. W. (1992). *Ecological Literacy.* Albany: State University of New York Press.

Pearse, A. and Stiefel, M. (eds.) (1979). *Enquiry into Participation – A Research Approach.* Geneva: UNRISD (United Nations Research Institute for Social Development).

Reed, E. S. (1996a). *Encountering the World.* Oxford University Press.

Reed, E. S. (1996b). *The Necessity of Experience.* New Haven: Yale University Press.

Rickinson, M. (2001). Learners and learning in environmental education, special issue of *Environmental Education Research,* 7(3), 207–317.

Rissoto, A. and Tonucci, F. (2002). Freedom of movement and environmental knowledge in elementary school children. *Journal of Environmental Psychology, 22,* 65–77.

Rovee-Collier, C. K. (1986). The rise and fall of infant classical conditioning research: its promise for the study of infant development. In L. P. Lipsett and C. K. Rovee-Collier (eds.), *Advances in Infancy Research, Vol. IV* (pp. 139–59). Norwood, NJ: Ablex.

Rogoff, B. (1990). *Apprenticeship in Thinking: Cognitive Development in Sociocultural Activity.* Oxford University Press.

Rogoff, B. (2003). *The Cultural Nature of Human Development.* Oxford University Press.

Ryan, R. M. and Deci, E. L. (2001). On happiness and human potentials: a review of research on hedonic and eudaimonic well-being. In S. T. Fiske, D. L. Schachter and C. Zahn-Waxler (eds.), *Annual Review of Psychology, 52,* 141–66. Palo Alto, CA: Annual Reviews.

Seligman, M. and Csikszentmihalyi, M. (2000). Positive psychology: an introduction. *American Psychologist, 55,* 5–14.

Schoggen, P. (1989). *Behavior Settings: A Revision and Extension of Roger G. Barker's Ecological Psychology.* Stanford University Press.

Tanner, T. (ed.) (1998). Special issue on significant life experience research. *Environmental Education Research 4.*

Thelen, E. and Smith, L. B. (1994). *A Dynamic Systems Approach to the Development of Cognition and Action.* Cambridge, MA: MIT Press.

Thomashow, M. (2002). *Bringing the Biosphere Home.* Cambridge, MA: MIT Press.

van der Meer, A. L. H., van der Weel, F. R. and Lee, D. N. (1996). Lifting weights in neonates: developing visual control of reaching. *Scandinavian Journal of Psychology*, *37*, 424–36.

UNDP (United Nations Development Programme), UNEP (United Nations Environment Programme), World Bank and World Resources Institute (2000). *World Resources 2000–2001: People and Ecosystems*, Washington, DC: World Resources Institute.

Vygotsky, L. (1978). *Mind in Society*. Cambridge, MA: Harvard University Press.

WCED (World Commission on Environment and Development) (1987). *Our Common Future*, Oxford University Press.

13   Children and city design: proactive process and the 'renewal' of childhood

Mark Francis and Ray Lorenzo

> I know we've come a long way. We're changing day to day. But tell me
> . . . where do the children play? – Yusuf Islam
>
> (formerly Cat Stevens)

How can designers and planners better engage children and youth and include their ideas in urban design? This chapter focuses on the culture of childhood today and the limits it places on meaningful children's participation in design and planning. We examine some of the ideas children themselves have about city form and suggest a more proactive process for city design. It is our hope that through more meaningful participation, critical aspects of childhood can be renewed, including children's access and reshaping of the built environment (Gaster, 1991; Perez and Hart, 1980).

We have previously developed a historical and critical review of children's participation in city planning and design over the last forty years (Francis and Lorenzo, 2002). We suggested that participatory efforts with children can be viewed in at least seven distinct approaches or 'realms' – advocacy, romantic, needs, learning, rights, institutionalization, and proactive (see Table 13.1). The proactive realm is seen as the most integrative and effective way to involve children and youth in design and planning. At the same time, this approach can also help create places that better satisfy the needs of all citizens including children. It can, we believe, activate a process of childhood renewal rendering local environments, and entire cities, accessible, comprehensible and friendly to children of all ages.

Changing childhood in cities

There is evidence that childhood has changed from one that is child-centered to one that is over-controlled and over-structured by adults (Postman, 1994; see Rissotto and Giuliani, this volume). This change has led to children spending less time outdoors including on streets, in

Table 13.1. *The seven realms of childrens' participation in city design and planning (Source: Francis and Lorenzo, 2002)*

1. Romantic

Approach	'Children as planners', 'Children as futurists'.
Theory	Planning 'by' children. Children define and make their own future, often without adult involvement. Much of the 'rights' movement grew out of this approach.
Objectives	Child-defined cities.
Audience	Schools, communities, architects and planners, futurists.
Key participants	Individuals: Mayer Spivak, Nanine Clay, Simon Nicholson, Ray Lorenzo. Organizations: World's Futures Society, World Wildlife Fund, Childhood City.
Research advances	Contributed important concepts and case studies.
Design advances	Provided useful ideas about what cities would be like if planned entirely by children. Developed innovative methods and proposed children's participation as a global issue.
Limitations	Relied on children to envision and make their own communities, future environments, etc. Did not typically involve adults in process.
Status	Still practiced by those seeking more child-generated ideas of the future. Visioning has become the standard first step in official participatory process such as Agenda 21.

2. Advocacy

Approach	'Planners for children'.
Theory	Planning 'for' children with needs advocated by adult planners.
Objectives	Represent the interests of children by advocating their needs as adult professionals.
Audience	Citizen group; public planning bodies making decisions and plans that effect childrens' lives.
Key participants	Individuals: Paul Hogan, Jeff Bishop, Karl Linn, Randy Hester. Organizations: Planners Network, Association of Community Design Centers, Congress for New Urbanism, some private and public firms.
Research advances	Developed politically sophisticated methods and theories of participation.
Status	Largely replaced by other realms

3. Needs

Approach	'Social science for children'.
Theory	Research-based approach that addresses children's needs.
Objectives	Define the spatial needs of children and incorporate them into design.
Audience	Largely academic, but has expanded to include design and policy makers.
Participants	Individuals: Kevin Lynch, Roger Hart, Clare Cooper Marcus, Florence Ladd, Robin Moore, Joost van Andel, Patsy Owens, Louise Chawla, Gary Moore.

Table 13.1. (*cont.*)

	Organizations: Environmental Design Research Association; American Horticultural Society; Urban Parks Institute.
Research advances	Contributed key findings and principles about what makes good environments for children.
Limitations	Sometimes did not recognize the importance of children's participation in advancing knowledge.
Status	Still an energetic part of environmental design research.

4. Learning

Approach	'Children as learners'.
Theory	Participation through environmental education and learning.
Objectives	Learning outcomes of participation is as important as physical changes; architects teach children about architecture.
Audience	Teachers; environmental educators
participants	Individuals: Doreen Nelson, Elaine Adams, Sharon Stine, Wendy Titman.
	Organizations: Landscapes for Learning; American Institute of Architects.
Research advances	Has contributed important methods
Design Advances	Increased use of natural environment and vegetation in outdoor places for children.
Limitations	Designers and decision makers do not always utilize research knowledge; children are frequently not directly involved in social science research.
Status	A specialized but active part of child participation projects.

5. Rights

Approach	'Children as citizens'.
Theory	Children have rights that need to be protected.
Objectives	Mandate children's participation in planning and city decision making.
Audience	City official; international organizations.
Participants	Roger Hart, David Satterthwaite, Sheri Bartlett, Robin Moore
	Organizations: IPA; UNICEF; Childwatch International; Save the Children.
Research advances	Has developed useful new methods.
Design advances	Has created child developed plans for neighbourhoods and cities.
Limitations	Tends to focus more on childrens' rights and less on their environmental needs.
Status	Popular in many countries due to United Nations mandate and support from international aid organizations.

6. Institutionalization

Approach	'Children as adults'.
Theory	Planning 'by'children but within institutional boundaries set by adults, authorities, and clients.
Objectives	Mandated/required child participation.
Audience	Typically official city plans and programs.
Participants	Individuals: city officials; child advocates
	Organizations: Children City Council, UNICEF, Childwatch International, National organizations concerned with children.
Research advances	Useful methods

Table 13.1. (*cont.*)

Design advances	Numerous case studies.
Limitations	Tends to create limited results or results counter to what children really want.
Status	Becoming more of the standard way of child participation today.

7. Proactive

Approach	'Participation with vision'.
Theory	Planning 'with' children. Combines research, participation and action to engage children and adults in planning and design. Children are active participants in process but designers/planners play an important role.
Objectives	Develop participatory plans and designs with children that incorporate their ideas and needs. Plans should be focused on strong vision of both empowering children and making substantive changes to the city environment.
Audience	Children; community organizations; design professionals
Participants	Individuals: Randy Hester, Marcia McNally, Laura Lawson Organizations: Japan/Taiwan Group; Community design centres, some private and public firms, non-profit organizations.
Design advances	Contributing useful theory and methods.
Limitations	Not always possible in every project; requires designers/planners with special training and skills.
Status	Becoming a more common form of participation.

parks and natural areas in favour of indoor, institutionalized and virtual environments.[1] The loss of childhood is especially pronounced in cities today. It also threatens the ability of design and planning to effectively improve the lives of children and youth.

The last four decades of childhood have seen both negative and positive change. Most alarming is that in 'developed' cities, children are increasingly disappearing from the urban scene. They are not using public space and when they are, it is under the watchful eye of adults, caretakers and authorities. While there are good reasons for this, such as concerns over safety and security, the cost to both child and urban life is significant (Blakely, 1994). As researchers have pointed out, these cultural, economic and technological factors have contributed to the denial of the rights and needs of children to inhabit, freely, and enjoy our cities (Alexander, 1993; Hart, 1997).

Goodman had already predicted in 1962 several of the 'inevitably modern conditions' which would, in successive years, 'render our cities unmanageable' and unliveable with respect to children. These include traffic, the distancing of the countryside and distinct natural places; the weakening of neighbourhood identity and social networks; the loss of accessible, unstructured play spaces; hidden technology, labour mobility and increasingly stressful family time schedules (Ulrich *et al.*, 1991; Taylor, 2001). Cultural changes since then include demographic patterns and the reduction of family size, parental fears, and real dangers regarding urban safety, the institutionalization of child care and recreational opportunities, the concentration of commercial distribution centres, consumer behaviour (of children and others) and the extraordinary evolution of communication technology. In addition, there has been a net diminution of the recognition by parents and adults of the importance of neighbourhoods and informal city places for growing up, learning, socializing, and acquiring 'culture' (Lynch and Carr, 1968; Lynch, 1978).

Many children today are captive in their homes and often alone. They are institutionalized, over programmed, information stuffed, TV dependent, 'zoned in' and age segregated. While they may be intellectually advanced, too many lack direct experience with the built and natural environment (Lorenzo, 1992; Postman, 1994). Children have largely lost the capacity, desire or permission to move autonomously in the urban milieu. They have become increasingly dependent on adults ('mommy cab drivers' and 'daddy coaches') and no longer possess the 'street smarts' which previous generations of children utilized to move around and grow up in cities.

Children, unable to experience autonomous contact with their peers, with their elders, with nature, with their neighbourhood and city, are too often troubled children. As a result, they too often grow into troubled adults. Roger Hart notes that this situation is not limited to the cities of the so-called 'developed world' (Bartlett *et al.*, 1999).

Around the world urban children and adolescents speak of their fears and of their desire to live in peace and safety among their neighbors. For many children this is a more pressing concern than even the need for food or health care. It is a concern, too, for those who are committed to raising strong and responsible citizens. Children who grow up in environments that provoke fear and limit social interaction are handicapped by this distortion of community life, and are unlikely to develop the understanding or skills that are fundamental to life as responsible and involved adults and citizens.

At the same time, there have been important positive advances in ways to design cities for children (Lynch, 1981). This has included an increased understanding of children's needs in public space (Stine, 1997; Altman and Zube, 1989) and the increased use of participatory process that engage them in design and planning (Driskell, 2001; Hart, 1992, 1997; Sutton and Kemp, this volume). Colin Ward, for example, has examined, in both historic and cultural terms, the place of childhood in both urban (1978) and rural environments (1988). Our view is that good

Figure 13.1. Access to the outdoors is critical for personal and social development as well as environmental competency (photo: Francis).

design and planning alone, even with direct participation of children and youth, is not enough to change the culture of childhood today. Adult attitudes need to be transformed as well to the point where children's access to and experience of cities is once again valued. This is where the proactive approach to city design is useful.

Urban design and the loss of childhood

City design is partially responsible for the decline of childhood. By the 1960s most Western cities had already been 'planned around children' and included playgrounds, and schools, and specialized places (Cranz, 1982). Before then, children were relatively free to move outside this framework. They selectively used places planned for them but also sought out and used other places such as streets and found spaces (Jacobs, 1993). Traffic was a problem, but in many United States cities children continued to move about independently and many were able to play on the street. They met together in mixed age groups and met freely on residential streets, on street corners and in vacant lots. They possessed a relatively wide range of action and a considerable knowledge of their neighbourhoods. This is not usually the case today. Children have lost a street sense and city knowledge. A decline of natural areas and habitat has created a changing relationship of children and nature (Chawla, 1995; Kahn and Kellert, 2002). Even everyday activities such as walking to school have been replaced by car pools and buses.

The changing nature of children, participation, and city design

In response to largely a top down or technocratic approach to urban planning and design, there has been a gradual emergence of more of an innovative approach towards the planning, design and management of cities. Participatory city planning and design, from the mid 1960s, introduced a new actor into urban decision-making processes, the user. Before then, children were largely ignored during the processes of urban development. City planning was no longer viewed as an exclusively political or technical process, but also a socio-cultural process. The processes of planning and design were expanded to include ongoing community conversations between individuals, groups, interests, planners and decision makers concerning alternative visions and projects for urban spaces and city life.

Figure 13.2. Gardening is one way for children to exert control over their local environment (Photo: Francis).

Figure 13.3. Children developing park design ideas in a workshop (Photo: Lorenzo).

Early on, children and youth were recognized as one of those social groups most harmed by the worsening state of our cities and, as such, researchers began to systematically study and document their essential, and often overlooked, needs in urban places. Contemporarily, architects, planners, educators and researchers, mainly in England and the USA, developed various arguments underlining the value of involving children and youth in the very processes aimed at improving the urban environment.

What began largely as an advocacy process on the part of adults to expose the needs and defend the rights of children in design and planning gradually became more of an accepted and mainstream approach to planning. Children's participation, like participation in design and planning in general, has been evolutionary, moving through several distinct stages from tokenism to more effective participation to institutionalization (Hart, 1992; Francis, 1999). Advances regarding the theory and practice of user participation in general have aided this evolution (Davidoff, 1965; Arnstein, 1969). Significant progress has been made on techniques that effectively involve children in design and planning (Moore et al., 1987; Lepore and Lorenzo, 1990, 1993). Additionally, better practices aided by empirical research and theoretical advances have rendered more convincing arguments for the value of children's participation (Chawla, 2001; Hart, 1997; Moore, 1990).

In Europe, this transformation was aided by the UN Convention on the Rights of the Child (CRC) ratified in 1989. The Convention confirmed the right of all children to a safe and healthy immediate living environment to play, socialize, and express themselves. According to the Convention, children possess the right to receive information, express their views and be listened to regarding all matters that concern their well-being. In the many nations that successively ratified the CRC, children advocates and sensitive political leaders astutely utilized this institutional basis for the passage of innovative, far reaching national and local legislation which widely promoted Child Friendly Cities (CFC) and the participation of children in their making. As a result, funding and programs such as Agenda 21 in Europe, now support participation in design and planning and are more common in all Western nations.

What do children consider a 'child-friendly city'?

While an impressive literature exists on the needs of children in cities, little has been written on the overall characteristics of a city that can be truly considered child friendly. One noteworthy attempt at defining the

Figure 13.4. Children developing their ideas at the Bologna Children's Congress (photo: Lorenzo).

Figure 13.5. Children presenting their Manifesto to Grazia Francesca-
to, then president of the World Wildlife Federation, at the Bologna
Children's Congress (photo: Lorenzo).

dimensions of child-friendly cities is the book *Cities for Children* (Bartlett
et al., 1999). This grew out of a participatory effort sponsored by
UNICEF and UNEP involving over eighty international experts from
various fields in a three-day workshop in preparation for the UN Habitat
II Conference in 1996. The authors intercross all aspects of childhood
experience with the complex nature of urban governance and policy
making. They stress the importance of process: collaboration, citizen
and children participation, learning from the documentation and ex-
change of best practice. It has, however, two shortcomings which appear
endemic and natural to most UNICEF sponsored efforts: the problems
and solutions of children in 'developed countries' are underrepresented,
as are considerations concerning the physical design of CFCs.

Few of the efforts to define 'child-friendly cities' have begun with
the views of children and youth themselves, but children gathered in
Bologna, Italy undertook one such effort in April 1994. Over 300 children from almost 100 elementary and middle schools from all over Italy
met for three days with adult facilitators, educators, planners and administrators to discuss and identify problems and 'propose solutions' to
their urban condition. All of the children were involved already in local

participatory design projects promoted by the WWF Italy. This effort was to eventually involve over 1000 schools and recreational groups from 1992–96.

The resulting document *The Children's Manifesto: How to Win Back our Cities* suggests some direction for future city design (see Table 13.2). Kids, when asked, can be quite inventive and creative about city design. Ideas proposed included increasing the number of gathering places in neighbourhoods and town centres. Providing more natural areas and elements was also a common theme. Traffic and parking were seen as barriers to their use of the outdoors and many creative ideas were provided to better manage traffic in cities. Children also wanted more say over how and where they use their free time.

Qualities of city design for children

Given the effort by both experts and children to define good cities, we now know some of the essential qualities that are critical for children and youth in city design (Owen, 1988). From our own experiences in Italy, Norway and the United States in collaborative design efforts with children, we have attempted to extrapolate the most repeatedly indicated 'characteristics' of better city places.

Accessibility

For children, especially the very young, traffic is the principal impediment to their use of city spaces. The places they design are ideally close to home (streets, piazzas small green spaces) or when further away, they need to be better connected to home and school by pedestrian or cycle paths. Traffic in residential streets can be moderated based on the model of the Dutch 'woonerf'. 'Woonerf' (Street for living) is a Dutch term for a common space created to be shared by pedestrians, bicyclists and low-speed motor vehicles. They are typically narrow streets without kerbs and sidewalks, and vehicles are slowed by placing trees, planters, parking areas, and other obstacles in the street. Motorists become the intruders and must travel at very low speeds below 16 Km/h (10 mph). This makes a street available for public use that is essentially only intended for local residents. A woonerf identification sign is placed at each street entrance. Parents, teachers and other adults should be involved in the transformation processes as children recognize that the problem is not only of a physical design nature, but is principally cultural involving parental and adult fears.

Table 13.2. *Children's manifesto 'How to Win Back Our Cities*[2] *(Source: World Wildlife Fund, 1994)*

We, the children gathered at the Children's Congress in Bologna, declare our intention to 'win back our cities'. We ask the adults and those who can decide to help us and to help those who, like us, want to change the current state of things.

We need:
- Gathering places where we can meet friends;
- To be able to interact with nature, even in cities. Which means: playing, climbing, building huts, listening, looking and understanding;
- To roam freely throughout the city without serious risk;
- To acquire the trust of others;
- To experiment with a series of different experiences: sleeping out of doors; strolling together, 'kites between the houses'; 'bridges between the windows', etc.
- To have the possibility to decide how we spend our free time; which means being trusted by adults.
- Remember that in the city, amongst others, there are children and youth, the elderly, physically challenged persons, animals, etc.

In our cities we want:
- To have at our disposition spaces entrusted by the city administrators directly to us children;
- Spaces where we can play in the immediate vicinity of our houses;
- Streets where cars must go slowly;
- To do all that is possible so that open spaces can be managed by those community members who have more free time (e.g.: the elderly);
- To have more occasions to meet new people, more neighborhood and street fairs;
- To have spaces which are not furnished with the same old playing structures, but which we can modify and change;
- To have more available sports facilities;
- To have children's theaters;
- If meeting places are lacking, children remain isolated and do not have the possibility to grow;
- To communicate with the 'others' (the sick, kids in difficult situations, foreigners, etc.);
- Frequent interchanges with groups from different realities. A meeting place, different that the usual hangout, not with the title 'The Children's Piazza'[3] but with something special like water – a safe exciting place to play;
- To be able to be alone;
- To be able to be in the company of others.

In our cities we want green spaces:
- With lots of natural elements;
- With many trees, bushes and with high grass to hide in;
- With lots of fruit trees, from which we can pick fruit;
- Without fixed, unchangeable play structures;
- With the possibility to find branches, twigs, leaves, mud and stone to build huts and hiding places;
- With large lawns to role on and dive into;
- Easily reached by public transport;
- Used frequently by lots of people;
- Safe and closed to traffic;

Table 13.2. (cont.)

- With lots of water at our disposition to play with;
- With paths with lots of slopes to ride our bikes on;
- Available in every neighborhood.

In our schools we want:

- To use courtyards to play in and to meet our friends;
- To plant gardens;
- School buildings that are easy to get to;
- A beautiful, colorful school in the middle of a garden.

To save us from the suffocating traffic, we want:

- To be able to move about safely in the city, at all hours;
- Streets with bike lanes;
- Eliminate the autos which park on the sidewalks;
- Quiet zones which are closed to traffic;
- To have more public transport;
- Places to leave our bicycles;
- Paths without steps with ramps for bicycles and wheelchairs;
- Public transport which is accessible for everyone. Smaller buses;
- Green barriers (hedges, etc.) which impede parking on the sidewalk and paths;
- Street signs that are understandable and friendly.

To decide our future, we want:

- Children's councils which make decisions;
- Regularly scheduled meetings with administrators;
- To be informed;
- To be listened to.

In conclusion, it's clear that we want to be able to contribute to decisions that affect us!!!!!

Mixed use and mixed users

Children appear to be against strictly mono-functional zoning. They do not desire special places for children only but want to be able to meet and interact with other age groups and other cultures. They want to be able to observe and 'try' functions and activities that are not limited to an adult conception of 'play'. Recreation can and should be mixed with work, commerce and culture. Their ideas fit well with current thinking about the desirability of mixed use and zoning being advanced by new urbanist architects and planners (Calthorpe, 1993).

Sociability

Children want to be able to meet with other children and youth of various ages autonomously. For younger ones, places they imagine and design are primarily open spaces. Teenagers tend to request, in addition, closed places such as music and art centres, libraries, and community

centres. Children and youth want to be involved in the management of
some places.

Small, feasible, flexible

Children do not prefer large investments to create places they like. They
often favour small scale construction that utilizes recycled and low cost
materials and includes natural or 'green' elements. They expect a role in
the construction and management of the site and are highly favourable
to places that are flexible in form, materials and uses.

Natural, environmentally healthy, growing and in movement

'Green' places are very often requested. They are 'softer', change
through time and seasons and require care. Children request the presence of 'other living creatures' and know that caring for a place and
considering carefully its design can represent opportunities for active,
effective environmental education. They recognize this not only for
themselves but also for other members of their communities. Access to
water, preferably in a natural form and in movement, is a prime request
in all projects (Moore and Wong, 1997).

Urban and place identity

Alongside the desire for nature and country, there is an equally strong
call for urban places in children's projects. Density allows for more
opportunities for encounters and more different faces and activities.
Complexity in scale, form and function in children's projects evokes
the idea of the piazza or market place, which in the Italian context are
'off limits' to children. Children know that places need to be identifiable.
Signs and signals can be designed into the physical plan. Colours,
materials, plantings, etc. are often their 'design solutions'.

Places and opportunities for participation

Most projects designed by children require continuing and permanent
participation. They are flexible and require ongoing care and involvement by children and other users. An eleven-year-old at the end of a
design project in Perugia City General Plan sums it all up:

> . . . the most important part of all the work was that I finally felt useful and proud
> of what I (we) had done. It's beautiful that 'big people' asked my collaboration in
> designing the future of our neighbourhood. I was able, with my classmates, to

express my opinions, my doubts, and my problems. I really felt 'big' [i.e. adult] and 'bravo' . . . like an apprentice architect. I don't know if our 'ship' will 'arrive in the port' but I won't lose hope and I'm sure that at least a few of the 'thousands' of proposals we (and others) developed will be built. At least we can say that we've contributed to the future of our neighbourhood.

Proactive process

Despite the great advances made in children's participation and child-friendly cities, contemporary cities remain, in most cases and for the most part, unfit for children. As children's lives have become more institutionalized so has children's participation. It requires planners and parents to rethink and modify past approaches to make children stronger advocates for their needs in planning. A new approach is required, one that is proactive and involves the ideas of children, adults and professional designers (Hester, 1999; Francis, 1999; Sutton and Kemp, this volume).

Proactive process is a fundamentally different approach to children's participation. It relies primarily on multiple points of view and multiple participants. It is typically an inclusive process that involves children, adults, planners, designers and decision makers. The process also depends on active listening and learning on the part of all participants. Differences and conflicts between children and adult ideas are made clear and directly negotiated. It also involves concepts of equity, justice and sustainability to be addressed as part of the design process. Proactive process relies on a variety of social science methods such as environmental autobiography as a way for adults to rediscover their own child-hood experiences and share them with their children. It also can include the use of interactive and digital media and the Internet as a tool in the design process. (See Table 13.3).

Proactive process assumes that the participation of children working together with other social and age groups will, eventually, contribute to the creation of liveable, ecologically sustainable, child-and adult-friendly cities. This requires a process where the acquisition and ex-change of values, knowledge, and skills is critical. It is a form of design as negotiation where children work with adult designers and planners to develop program and design ideas. We have found in our work that despite the limits placed on their development by adults today, children still possess a strong curiosity to explore and learn, and when asked, can be the catalysts to transform city design.

Roger Hart (1997) has argued for such shared decision-making with adults:

Table 13.3. *Dimensions of proactive process with children*

- Is an inclusive process that involves children, adults, planners, designers, and decision makers
- Involves learning on the part of children and adults
- Involves active listening by adults and designers
- Includes the ideas of professional designers and planners
- Involves negotiation between children and adults
- Is not romantic about wanting to return to an earlier and more primitive form of childhood
- Addresses concerns of safety and security by getting children outdoors
- Uses new and interactive media as a tool in the design process.

Figure 13.6. Proactive processes require children to work actively with adults as when presenting their ideas to the City Council (photo: Lorenzo).

I do not want children as a separate society. We are trying to prepare children to be participating members of society. There is a naive wing to the children's rights movement that talks about children's power, and the child's world as separate. This is nonsense. The movement should be about children's rights to have a voice with adults. So often in newspapers one sees pictures of children carrying out some project in the community with a headline like 'New Park Built By Children' and the adults pretend that they had nothing to do with it. It is, of course, often patently obvious that it was an adult-controlled project, thereby making a mockery out of the idea of children's participation. We need to make adults, including journalists, more honest about the different and important roles of both adults and children. All too often, the most crucial phase of problem identification does not involve children.

Renewing childhood: a call for design and research

One way to move toward a new culture of city design is to adopt a new research and design agenda, one focused on the true ideas and needs of children today. Urban designers need to experiment with creating new forms of spaces in cities for children beyond just providing traditional elements such as playgrounds and schools. Future urban design must make more of an effort to incorporate children's rights into plans and policies (Bartlett, 1999). The current movement to create healthy cities by promoting higher densities and urban forms that support biking and walking is an encouraging development in this regard (Bedard, 2000). Proactive process is one of many paths needed to restore childhood and make cities better places for all people.

Notes

1 Our purpose here is not to review fully the reasons and effects of the changing culture of childhood. The literature on 'the loss of childhood' is extensive and examined elsewhere. See, for example, Bartlett et al., 1999; Holloway and Valentine, 2000; Postman, 1994.
2 This congress, which was organized in 1994 by the World Wildlife Fund (WWF) and sponsored by the City of Bologna, saw the participation of over 300 children of elementary and intermediate school age. The children were representatives of approximately 100 schools from all over Italy involved in WWF's national campaign – 'Let's Win Back Our Cities'. Parallel to the children's workshops, numerous teachers, planners, and city administrators took part in seminars and working groups with over 400 schools involved.
3 The children are criticizing here a recent practice in some Italian municipalities to dedicate a piazza to 'children' – almost like a 'monument to the war dead' – empty spaces which are supposed to assuage the city's conscience regarding children.

References

Alexander, J. (1993). The external costs of escorting children. In M. Hillman (ed.), Children, Transport and Quality of Life (pp. 77–81). London: Policy Studies Institute.
Altman, I. and Zube, E. (eds.) (1989). Public Places and Spaces. Volume X: Human Behavior and the Environment. New York: Plenum.
Arnstein, S. (1969). The ladder of citizen participation. Journal of the American Institute of Planners, 35(4), 216–24.

Bartlett, S. (1999). How urban design can support children's rights. UNCHS, 5, 2. The United Nations Centre for Human Settlements.

Bartlett, S., Hart, R., Satterthwaite, D., de la Barra, X. and Missair, A. (1999). *Cities for Children: Children's Rights, Poverty and Urban Management.* London: Earthscan.

Bedard, M. (2000). *Healthy Landscapes: Guidelines for Therapeutic City Form.* Unpublished Master's Thesis, University of California, Davis.

Blakely, K. S. (1994). Parent's conceptions of social dangers in the urban environment. *Children's Environments Quarterly, 11*(1), 16–25.

Boulding, E. (1979). *Children's Rights and the Wheel of Life.* New Brunswick, NJ: Transaction Books.

Calthorpe, P. (1993). *The Next American Metropolis.* New York: Princeton Architectural Press.

Carr, S., Francis, M., Rivlin, L. and Stone, A. (1992). *Public Space.* New York: Cambridge University Press.

Carr, S. and Lynch, K. (1968). Where learning happens. *Daedalus, 97*, 4.

Chawla, L. R. (1986). The ecology of environmental memory. *Children's Environments, 3*(4), 34–42.

Chawla, L. R. (2001) (ed.) *Growing up in an Urbanizing World.* London: Earthscan Publications.

Cobb, E. (1976). *The Ecology of Imagination in Childhood.* New York: Columbia University Press.

Corbett J. and Corbett, M. N. (2000). *Designing Sustainable Communities: Learning from Village Homes.* Washington, DC: Island Press.

Cranz, G. (1982). *The Politics of Park Design.* Cambridge: MIT Press.

Davidoff, P. (1965). Advocacy and pluralism in planning. *Journal of the American Institute of Planners, 21*(4), 331–8.

Driskell, D. (2001). *Creating Better Cities with Children and Youth.* London: Earthscan Publications.

Fjørtoft, I. and Sageie, J. (2000). The natural environment as a playground for children: landscape description and analyses of a natural playscape. *Landscape and Urban Planning, 48*, 83–97.

Francis, M. (1988). Negotiating between children and adult design values in open space projects. *Design Studies, 9*, 67–75.

Francis, M. (1989) Control as a dimension of public space quality. In I. Altman and E. Zube (eds.), *Public Places and Spaces*, vol. x (pp. 147–72). New York: Plenum.

Francis, M. (1999). Proactive practice: visionary thought and participatory action in environmental design. *Places, 12*(1), 60–8.

Francis, M. and Lorenzo, R. (2002). Seven realms of children's participation. *Journal of Environmental Psychology, 22*, 157–69.

Gaster, S. (1991). Urban children's access to their neighborhoods: Changes over three generations. *Environment and Behavior, 23*(1), 70–85.

Goodman, P. (1962). *Growing up Absurd.* New York: Vintage.

Hart, R. (1978). *Children's Experience of Place.* New York: Irvington.

Hart, R. (1992). *Children's Participation: From Tokenism to Citizenship.* Innocenti Essay no. 4. Florence, Italy: UNICEF International Child Development Center.

Hart, R. (1997). *Children's Participation: The Theory and Practice of Involving Young Citizens in Community Development and Environmental Care*. London: Earthscan and New York: UNICEF.

Herrington, S. (1999). Playgrounds as community landscapes. *Built Environment*, 25(1), 25–34.

Hester, R. (1999). Refrain with a view. *Places*, 12(1).

Holloway, S. and Valentine, G. (eds.) (2000). *Children's Geographies: Living, Playing, Learning and Transforming Everyday Worlds*. London: Routledge.

Horelli, L. (1998). Creating child-friendly environments: case studies on children's participation in three European countries. *Childhood*, 5(2), 225–39.

Jacobs, J. (1993). *The Death and Life of Great American Cities*. New York: Modern Library.

Kahn, P. H. and Kellert, S. R. (eds.) (2002). *Children and Nature*. Cambridge: MIT Press.

Lepore, L. and Lorenzo, R. (1991). *Immaginiano il Futuro*. (Imaging the Future). Rome: World Wildlife Fund – Italy.

Lorenzo, R. (1983). Community context, future perspective and participation. *Childhood City Quarterly*.

Lorenzo, R. (1992). *Italy: Too Little Time and Space for Childhood*. Florence: UNICEF Innocenti Research Center.

Lynch, K. (1978). *Growing Up in Cities*. Cambridge: The MIT Press.

Lynch, K. (1991). *Good City Form*. Cambridge: MIT Press.

Moore, R. C. and Wong, H. H. (1997). *Natural Learning*. Berkeley: MIG Communications.

Nabhan, G. P. and Trimble, S. (1994). *The Geography of Childhood: Why Children Need Wild Places*. New York: Beacon Press.

Nicholson, S. (1971). How not to cheat children: The theory of loose parts. *Landscape Architecture*, 61, 30–34.

Owens, P. E. (1988). Natural landscapes, gathering places, and prospect refuges: characteristics of outdoor places valued by teens. *Children's Environments Quarterly*, 5(2), 17–24.

Perez, C. and Hart, R. (1980). Beyond playgrounds: children's accessibility to the landscape. In P. F. Wilkinson (ed.), *Innovations in Play Environments*. New York: St Martin's Press.

Postman, N. (1994). *The Disappearance of Childhood*. New York: Dell Books.

Rivkin, M. S. (1995). *The Great Outdoors: Restoring Children's Right to Play Outside*. Washington, DC: National Association for the Education of Children.

Sandels, S. (1995). *Children in Traffic*. London: Paul Elek.

Scott, S., Jackson, S. and Backett-Milburn, K. (1998). Swings and roundabouts: risk, anxiety and the everyday world of children. *Sociology*, 32(4), 689–705.

Spencer, C. P. (1998). Children, cities and psychological theories: developing relationships. *Journal of Environmental Psychology*, 18(4), 429–33.

Stine, S. (1997). *Landscapes for Learning*. New York: Wiley.

Taylor, A. F., Kuo, F. E. and Sullivan, W. C. (2001). Coping with ADD: the surprising connection to green play settings. *Environment and Behavior*, 33(1), 54–77.

Ulrich, R. S., Simmons, R. F., Losito, B. D., Fiorito, E., Miles, M. A. and Zelson, M. (1991). Stress recovery during exposure to natural and urban environments. *Journal of Environmental Psychology, 11*, 201–30.

UNICEF (1996). *Children's Rights and Habitat: Report of the Expert Seminar.* February 1–2, 1996. New York: United Nations Children's Fund.

UNICEF (2000). *Towards Child-Friendly Cities.* New York: United Nations Children's Fund.

Valentine, G. (1999). Oh please, Mum, oh please, Dad: negotiating children's spatial boundaries. In L. McKie, S. Browlby and S. Gregory. *Gender, Power and the Household* (pp: 137–57). New York: MacMillan.

Valentine, G. and Holloway, S. L. (2000). Transforming cyberspace: children's interventions in the new public sphere. In S. L. Holloway and G. Valentine (eds.), *Children's Geographies: Living, Playing, Learning and Transforming Everyday Worlds.* London: Routledge.

Van Vliet, W. (1983). An examination of the home range of city and suburban teenagers. *Environment and Behavior, 15*, 567–88.

Ward, C. (1978). *The Child in the City.* New York: Pantheon.

Ward, C. (1988). *The Child in the Country.* London: Robert Hale.

Watt, P. and Stenson, K. (1998). The street: it's a bit dodgy around there: safety, danger, ethnicity and young people's use of public space. In S. Watson and G. Valentine (eds.), *Cool Places: Geographies of Youth Culture* (pp. 249–65). London: Routledge.

White, M., Kasl, S., Zahner, G. E. P. and Will, J. C. (1987). Perceived crime in the neighborhood and the mental health of women and children. *Environment and Behavior, 19*(5), 588–613.

Woolley, H. J., Dunn, J., Spencer, C. P., Short, T. and Rowley, G. (2000). Children describe their experiences of the city centre: a qualitative study of the fears and concerns which may limit their full participation. *Landscape Research, 24*, 287–301.

World Wildlife Fund (1994). *Children's Manifesto: How to Win Back Our Cities.* Bologna, Italy: WWF.

14 A learning-based network approach to urban planning with young people

Liisa Horelli

Introduction: the context of planning with young people

Citizens of the Western industrialized world are increasingly living in informational network societies. Castells (1996) states that the latter are characterized by the spaces of global flows of information, finances, and technology which subjugate localities and places. This means that new challenges are posed to urban and rural policies, including planning and development. Local areas are increasingly seen as part of regions which are forced to compete with one another to become attractive spaces for desired activities. The winners of this competition are those who have the know-how to take advantage of the opportunities of globalization. One of the strategies that has been applied in the competition for economic survival is the building of regional development networks (Kostiainen, 2002). Such networks might ultimately turn into lucrative regional innovation systems that will bring forth new economic activities and consequent material gains. The actors in these *networks of competitiveness* are usually 'big players', such as enterprises, public institutions, financial agents, and universities (Cook *et al.*, 2000).

The losers in the globalization game are those who are unable to cope with the negative impact of globalization, and who lack the control over and voice in local matters. The negative effects of globalization can be felt not only in developing countries, but also in many Western nations, and especially in the everyday lives of children, young, and elderly people, and many women.

There is a need for creative economic, social and cultural responses to the challenges of the exploitative aspects of globalization. Several citizen groups, especially among the women's movement in both Europe and on other continents have striven to find new solutions as they have been tacitly mainstreaming gender and intergenerational equality in planning and development for the past twenty years (Horelli, 1998a, 2001, 2002a). Mainstreaming equality in urban planning and development can be defined as the application of a set of gender and age sensitive

238

visions, concepts, strategies, and practices in the different phases and arenas of the development and evaluation cycle (cf. Horelli, 1997). The vision embedded in the mainstreaming efforts has been the creation of human settlements that comprise supportive *networks of social cohesion.*

The UN Convention on the Rights of the Child with its focus on the three Ps – provision, protection, and participation – has legitimized the efforts to promote children's participation in many countries (cf. Chawla, 2002; Francis and Lorenzo, 2002). Since the early 1980s and 1990s children's participation in environmental planning and development has increased in countries like Finland. The Finnish Land Use and Building Act implies that even children can be recognized as 'official' participants in zoning initiatives. The Finnish Ministry of the Interior has also enhanced public participation through specific development projects among which those with children have been the most successful ones. For example, the provision of a supportive infrastructure for children's participation through the Helsinki Voice of Youth, based on the Norwegian Porsgrun-model (Familj- o ungdomsministerium 1997), has turned out to be a significant step forward in citizenship for adolescents.

The research, including my own studies into 'children as urban planners', shows that young participants can be both able critics of their environments and producers of new ideas for implementation. But their participation has not become part of an accepted child policy, nor a praxis in European planning systems (Horelli, 1998b, 2001). Bridging the gap between the competent young people (aged seven to eighteen) and the adult gatekeepers of urban planning and development remains a problem. The provision of resources and methodological supports to children, such as Internet-assisted urban planning (Horelli and Kaaja, 2002; Kyttä *et al.*, 2004), might alleviate this gap slightly, but as long as the participation of young people takes place within a traditional top-down, hierarchic planning paradigm, little progress is made (Booher and Innes, 2002).

However, the network approach, mentioned above, has given positive signs which indicate that young people can improve their position, if they are members or partners in networks of social cohesion (Horelli, 2003). Such networks provide a context and arena, in which young people are treated not in terms of their age but on the basis of their skills and knowledge. This, in turn, enhances the opportunities for collaboration in local and even regional development (Kostiainen, 2002).

The managing and improvement of everyday life in complex network societies in which people struggle with 'glocal' problems, require multi-level and multi-dimensional approaches as well as new concepts. These include the notions of place-based politics, a variety of strategies and knowledges (Harcourt and Escobar, 2002), environmental competence, and a learning-based network approach to planning.

My argument is that the gap between adolescents and the adult gatekeepers of urban planning and development can be alleviated by creating a learning-based network approach in which young people and adults take part in interdependent actor networks (Latour, 1993; Booher and Innes, 2002; Arquilla and Ronfelt, 2001). The aim of this chapter is to present a model of the network approach and to discuss its impact on the environmental competence of young people and youth work.

A transdisiplinary framework of the network approach to planning with young people

Due to the complexity of the problem, a transdisciplinary framework, including perspectives from environmental psychology, participatory planning, as well as gender and age-sensitive urban and regional studies, has been constructed. The integrative element of the framework is provided by participatory action research (Figure 14.1). Transdisciplinary here means here that the framework of different disciplines consists of some shared basic concepts and methods of research. These are discussed below.

Environmental psychology

Environmental psychology, which shares the spirit of positive psychology, is often regarded as a subdiscipline of psychology or social psychology. However, the approach to environmental psychology that has been adopted here, finds its home within an interdisciplinary environment-behaviour-design-research. The latter is influenced by the psychosocial and behavioural processes of different individuals and groups of people in diverse settings, in the varying phases of the cycle of research, policy planning, design, implementation, and evaluation (Moore, 1987; Horelli, 2002b). Planning is regarded in this framework as the provider of support to the communicative transactions that enhance the fit or congruence between the intentions of the users and their settings.

This approach also implies a transactional ecological perspective, which means that the development and behaviour of individuals, as well as the promotion of child-friendly settings can only be fully understood in the multi-dimensional and multi-level context in which they live. Bronfenbrenner's (1993) seminal model of environmental transactions and development, includes, besides direct involvement with the

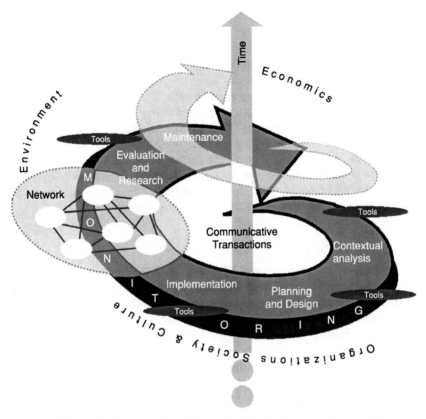

Figure 14.1. A schema of the methodological approach to participatory planning in which co-operative learning and capacity building take place through an on-going monitoring and self-evaluation system.

micro-setting, such as the home or the school, interactions within a meso-system (home-school-youth club), an exo-system (adult friendship and workplace relationships) and macro-systems (cultural and societal traditions and beliefs). Transactions are influenced by the environmental competence and the individual mobility of the individual. Environmental competence means the motivation (values, feelings), self-efficacy beliefs (Bandura, 1997), and know-how to act in an environmentally responsible way.

Another important concept within environmental psychology comes from the theory of environment-person fit which focuses on the 'goodness criteria' of environments. The criteria for child- or human-friendly environments and the consequent indicators seem to be quite constant all over the world (Chawla, 2002). The scope of the concept can be grouped into ten dimensions, but the modelling of different kinds of human-friendly environments needs further elaboration and comparative studies (UNICEF, 2002; Horelli, forthcoming; see Kyttä, this volume).

Environmental psychology struggles with the question of how to resolve the mediation of the impact between different environmental levels – the micro, meso, and macro. The networking approach might give an empirical solution to the problem as the network allows to the different levels to be transcended. It can draw actors from the macro- and the microlevels and place them in an interdependent context (Booher and Innes, 2002). The network might also transcend the Habermasian barrier between the life-world and that of the system.

Participatory and collaboratory planning

Participatory or collaboratory planning and development is another important perspective. The procedural theories of planning should be able to explain, how participation can be organized in such a way that the planning cycle becomes an arena for learning, and capacity building, for young people, experts, and decision makers (cf. Healey, 1997).

Participatory planning and development is defined here as 'a social, ethical, and political practice in which women and men, children, young and elderly people take part in varying degrees, in the overlapping phases of the planning and decision-making cycle that may bring forth outcomes congruent with the participants' needs, interests, and goals' (Horelli, 2002b). Booher and Innes (2002) have, however, claimed that only the network approach provides an authentic situation for participation and the consequent psychological growth.

Figure 14.1 shows the methodological schema that has been developed on the basis of projects with women, children, and young people. The purpose of planning is to support the communicative transactions of the participants in a specific environmental, organizational, economic, cultural, and temporal context. The various transactions taking place are supported by a multitude of enabling tools during the overlapping and iterative phases of the planning and development process – initiation, planning or design, implementation, evaluation, and maintenance. The tools are both enabling methods (consensus building instruments and other heuristics) as well as traditional research methods.

Citizen groups tend to see participatory planning and development as a form of empowerment, if it is connected to real opportunities to have an impact on the decision making. It can also be considered as a site of agency-building and environmental competence leading to positive youth development (Larson, 2000). Therefore, I have complemented the perspective of collaborative planning with the theories of co-operative learning (Johnson and Johnson, 1990) and empowerment evaluation (Fetterman, 2001). The on-going monitoring and self-evaluation provides the participants with feedback on the quality of the change process and its results. The monitoring and self-evaluation can also be organized as a 'knowledge management system' which focuses on the externalization, systematization, and exercising of local and situational knowledges (see Table 14.1; Nonaka *et al.*, 2000).

The systematic creation of environmental networks with children and young people is a special case that has not yet been covered in the literature of participation. For example, the North Karelian Youth Forum-project in Finland has shown that the network approach and its methodology can provide opportunities for bridging the gap between young people and adults.

The perspective of participatory planning provides concepts for procedural theories of planning, but it does not say much about the content or substance of planning which has to be found in other disciplines.

Table 14.1. *Systematic knowledge creation and application, enhanced by a set of enabling methods and measures in the NUFO-project. The eventual future steps are marked with an asterisk (cf. Nonaka et al., 2000)*

Originating the nodes (1)	Interacting the nodes (2)
participatory workshops	self-assessment sessions of the project team
events	role-playing events with the regional council
an interactive website	follow-up participatory workshops
collaboration with the youth councils	facilitated web-sessions, www.ponu.net
local youth/adult teams	use of the media
Exercising the nodes (4)	**Systemizing the nodes (3)**
	action research
networking with the partners	founding of the regional youth forum
working patterns of the regional youth-forum	founding of the youth-housing association
*mentoring the youth-cafe enterprises	founding of the youth-band association
*working models and patterns of the youth competence centre	*networking youth-cafes
	*founding of a regional youth competence centre

Gender and age-sensitive urban and regional studies

Gender and age-sensitive urban and regional studies provide opportunities to analyze the content and substance of environments from everyday perspectives. Taylor (1998) pointed out that current theories of content are inadequate for defining a good or healthy environment. However, the European women's movement in planning and development has been constructing, for the past twenty years, concepts and models of action for creating an infrastructure of everyday-life that allows the work and care of children and elderly people to be reconciled (The Research Group for the New Everyday Life, 1991; Horelli and Vepsä, 1994; Gilroy and Booth, 1999). These concepts can be used for defining and modelling child- and human-friendly environments and their ecological, social, economic, cultural and political dimensions (UNICEF, 2002; Horelli, forthcoming).

The gender and intergenerational mainstreaming of the EU structural policy and hence regional development in many of the European countries has provided groups, such as women and young people with opportunities to take part in the development of their localities (Horelli, 1998a). The most recent strategies for creating the conditions for supportive networks in this century have been accelerated by the so called place-based politics. Politics of place is 'place-based but not place-bound' (Harcourt and Escobar, 2002). This implies a vision of politics that includes projects that are embedded, contextualized and localized but also linked, networked, and meshworked (meaning non-hierarchical, informal networking). In fact, it is a 'politics of becoming' which presupposes the application of innovative, hybrid strategies. The impact of the networking of these groups can be seen in new local and regional structures and characteristics. The environmental outcomes, especially those of young people, can be regarded as 'eco-social', as the preferred features imply green areas, a human scale in building, safety, settings for socializing, and even socially sustainable businesses (Horelli, 2003).

An application of the network approach to planning with young people

The application of the chosen framework to planning with young people can be illustrated by the North-Karelian Youth Forum-project, which was a five-year long action research -study, conducted by the author, and funded by the Finnish Academy (Horelli, 2003).

The task of action research is to solve both a practical problem (in this case the construction of supportive networks with young people and adults) and a theoretical one (what methodology is relevant for the construction process). The methodology consists of both enabling methods, which enhanced the mobilizing and nurturing of the emerging network, and traditional data gathering (questionnaires, interviews, participatory observation, psychological tests), as well as of analytic (content analysis, network analysis) methods. The research questions include ones like, how were the network(s) mobilised and nurtured? How did the co-operative learning take place? What were the outcomes of the network? What is learning-based participatory networking and evaluation like?

The creation of the North-Karelian Youth Forum

North-Karelia (170,000 residents) is the easternmost region in Finland (and in the EU), which has a 300 km long common border with Russia. The region is sparsely populated with vast areas of forests and lakes. Currently, the formerly agrarian region has several well-functioning clusters of forestery and metal industries as well as several high-technology centres. Most municipalities provide the residents with free access to Internet services and opportunities for developing e-citizenship skills. Nevertheless, the unemployment rate is high, around 18 per cent, especially among young people. Young people are therefore moving to the more prosperous parts of the country. Although the Regional Council had been aware of the youth problem for a long time, it took nearly three years to negotiate a special project that would seek to create supportive local and regional networks for young people. In the autumn of 2001, the North-Karelian Youth Forum-project (NUFO) was granted 500000 euros from the European Social Fund and three municipalities (Joensuu, Kitee, and Lieksa). This made it possible to hire four young people to co-ordinate and manage the project for two years. They began to mobilize the network, consulted by the evaluator-researcher (the author of this article) and the steering committee. The latter included a variety of regional representatives, from the regional council, the municipalities, some schools, the Bic, several citizen organizations, as well as two young people.

The vision of the project, which was created together with the participants, became crystallized as 'A joyful North-Karelia with survival opportunities for young people'. The aim of the project was to create with adolescents and adults a supportive network that would provide arenas of empowerment, and opportunities for meeting both face to face and virtually. The objectives focus on the possibilities for work and local initiatives through subprojects, involving events, and the opportunity to have a say in regional development.

The project itself was a success story as the networking managed to bring in new groups of participants of varying age and both sexes. Over 5000 people were in some way involved with the project. Eighty per cent of them were young people, with slightly more young women than men, in the age range of fifteen to twenty-five years. The endeavour succeeded in creating small improvements in many parts of the region, such as spaces for playing music and drama, happenings, motor cycle workshops, Internet-cafes, as well as many mobilizing parties and other platforms for action. The results of the study showed that a transition from 'complainers into agents' did indeed take place.

If the Forum had not been constructed, maybe we would still complain here in Lieksa. It (NUFO) has moblised us (Maija, sixteen years)

Adolescents found that the Nufo-network was, and still is, a catalyst and a mediator between the world of adults and the opportunities for action and enjoyment.

Nufo is to me a kind of catalyst that speeds up issues. I think that it is really cool that it exists. It is a kind of foundation which helps to spur on. And, many towns still lack Nufos. I can't understand, how dispersed people who want to have a say, can do anything? If somebody gets an idea here, (s)he knows where to find support (Sirkka, eighteen years)

The platforms for action were also political spaces (Eyerman and Jamison, 1991) which enabled young people to articulate their ideas. Their voices were, however, frail and in need of constant nurturing. Nonetheless at the end of the project, the Regional Council was persuaded to put up a new structure, a Regional Youth Forum with two representatives from each of the nineteen municipalities of North Karelia. The Forum has a yearly budget of 50,000 euros to initiate development projects for and by young people. However, the Nufo-project still waits for other institutional supporters to develop structures to encourage adolescents' participation and involvement in on-going events and happenings.

Assessment of the capacity building of the network

The mobilization of the Nufo-network followed roughly the pattern, logistics, and methodology in Figure 14.1. A variety of enabling methods were applied throughout the phases of the development cycle (see Table 14.1). One of the most important techniques was the organizing of participatory workshops in schools to launch the project. Each event mobilized around 100 young people who had the opportunity to discuss their ideas and visions for improving the region with a panel of decision makers. The girls and boys who wanted to continue participation were organized into local or thematic groups, and they implemented events, happenings, and new projects. Eventually these evolved into small social movements that enhanced the creation of the political space for young people, as mentioned above.

The initiative was arranged as a collaborative learning and capacity building process. The latter refers to organizing interactions with people through shared goals, and supported activities, to create cognitive, emotional, and behavioural learning mechanisms in specific contexts (Johnson and Johnson, 1990). Gustavsen (2001:186) points out that 'working together in a development program with a broad range of actors has to deal with much more than the achievement of short- or middle term outcomes. It has to do with certain links, ties and relationships between actors, with developing competence to work across organisational boundaries and with the creation of new arenas where this work can be performed'. Therefore, the research task was to understand, not only the actors and their individual learning, but the process, dynamics, and the learning of the network.

The Japanese theorist of organizational learning, Ikujiro Nonaka, has created with his colleagues (Nonaka et al., 2000) a set of concepts and a methodology to enhance and assess the knowledge-creation process of an organization. According to Nonaka, knowledge is dynamic, since it is created in social interactions among individuals and organizations. Knowledge is also context-specific as it depends on particular time and space (Nonaka et al., 2000). The knowledge creation process can be intentionally enhanced, if specific spaces, places or platforms (BA in Japanese) for people to meet and interact are created for different types of knowledge in an organization. Tacit knowledge can emerge in places where people socialize informally, such as cafes or concerts, but sharing and externalizing tacit knowledge so that it becomes explicit knowledge requires spaces for creative interaction and brainstorming. The systemizing of knowledge and transforming it into guidelines, models or prototypes requires more stable arenas, such as research or resource centres. The last step in the elaboration of knowledge is turning knowledge into creative know-how and its application in practice. After exercising the know-how, the spiral of knowledge-creation goes on by nurturing new tacit knowledge and its externalization in turn.

The knowledge creation approach as part of the monitoring and evaluation system was applied in the implementation of the project by using the concept of the 'node'. The research question focusd on, *how the nodes for learning originated, interacted, were systemized, and exercised.* Table 14.1 shows that several types of nodes and modes of learning were generated during the project by applying various enabling methods to facilitate the mechanisms of change and learning. Some of the nodes were systemized or institutionalized by organizing the activities into associations. Nevertheless, the knowledge creation and learning only began to reach the stage of 'exercising the nodes in practice', during the life cycle of the project. The progress of the network was discussed with the managers of the project and the key partners. Table 14.1 shows the interventions implemented in the project.

Young activists in close-up

Well over one hundred boys and girls could be called activists, as they participated in the creation of several events, or they were regular members of thematic and local teams. For example, one thematic group of eight girls and boys in Lieksa succeeded in getting permission and some financial support from the municipality to build a volley ball court by the lake, which immediately became popular among all age groups. Another group in Joensuu, found spaces for rehearsing music. The young musicians founded an association, called 'Save the band-spaces', which gradually managed to get five small rooms in the attic of the municipal youth house. This led to a series of concerts and eventually a recording on CD which was marketed through the project's internet site www.ponu.net. Two girls wanted to organize an international summer camp around environmental art in North-Karelia. They came to the Nufo-office which helped them to contact the International Centre of Mobility in Finland. The girls received some funding and the camp was organized with about twenty adolescents from Italy, Hungary, and Ireland. The striking monument made by these adolescents, of painted hay poles on a field, can still be admired from the road passing the Jakokoski-village, between Joensuu and Lieksa.

The energy expressed by the activists made me consider what makes a young person an activist. I therefore developed environmental biographies with ten boys and girls. These biographies included a self-efficacy scale (Wallston, 1992), a personal network analysis and a conceptual mapping of their daily life. The young people who were interviewed worked in different fields, such as drama, writing, politics, skateboarding, ICT, and environmental protection. The results of the biographies showed that 'activism' can be of varying sorts.

We were a small group which founded this first action group that later on produced the Mopo-musical, then the Growth-project. . .and music events and others. It is a kind of 'save the world'- work. We also founded an internet café where four to five unemployed persons are working, subsidised by the municipality'. (Laura, 17 years) '. . .to be able to understand, how to influence, is important, not that I would always like to influence, but I want to have the keys to influencing, which can be used when needed. Personally I am not interested in politics. (Seppo, 19 years)

No conspicuous differences were found in the amount of involvement of girls and boys except that girls did not enter fields, such as ICT or skate-boarding. However, environmental activists, in the narrow sense of the word, were surprisingly few. Environmental protection is often seen as a special field with a great many of facts that have to be mastered, and is a field reserved for an inner circle who wish to 'reform the world'.

Irrespective of the field with which the active adolescents were involved, the activists displayed conspicuous *environmental competence*. This has been defined here as including knowledge of a particular field or substance, a high degree of self-efficacy (as measured by the Wallston scale) and mastering the tension between autonomy and dependence, which is critical in successful networking (Booher and Innes, 2002).

On the basis of the analysis of the interviews, the following factors seem to be seminal in the life-course of an activist:

- an accessible adult role-model
- motivated action or activities
- a supportive network
- emerging environmental competence
- opportunities for meaningful action in the locality.

All the activists who were interviewed had at least one accessible role-model, who was most often a parent, grandparent, a neighbour or a teacher. Another shared characteristic was that the young people had many hobbies from an early age, from which they chose the most important one to pursue. The latter usually brought forth a network of different people of all ages who supported the goal achievement of the person. These boys and girls came from small towns or agrarian villages but in spite of the modest settings, they were able to find opportunities for meaningful action.

. . .it bugs me that some of the students who are my friends, keep complaining that here is nothing (to do), and I have begun to point out that here is what ever you wish, and that this (the small town of 8000 residents) is a fantastic place to dwell, to live and to do. (Kati, seventeen years)

Nonetheless, if the municipality is very poor and has few opportunities for meaningful action, even the activists may have difficulties in finding relevant affordances (see Kyttä, this volume).

Modelling the network approach to planning with adolescents

The analysis of the process and results of the project enabled a tripartite schema of the network approach to planning to be constructed, comprising

- a learning-based network model of development,
- specific tasks of development, and
- a monitoring and self-evaluation system that is closely connected to research.

The learning-based network model of development (see Figure 14.2) differs from the spiral of planning presented in Figure 14.1 because the former ignores the specific phases of planning. The network model only includes the core idea (the idea of constructing innovative arenas of empowerment), the contextual analysis, the collective envisioning of the future, as well as a few shared principles of implementation. The latter gradually crystallize into strategies of implementation. In the case of the Nufo-project, the strategies of implementation comprised the creation of meaningful events (or buzz), participatory networking, capacity building, applying ICT, informing and marketing integrated interventions, applying art and creative methods, and on-going monitoring and self-evaluation (Horelli, 2003). The chosen set of strategies encourages the stakeholders to create and reproduce nodes and links of the network that eventually provide a supportive infrastructure in everyday life.

Gender and age-sensitive co-ordination is, according to the Finnish experience, not about enforcement but about constant negotiating and interacting with different partners. This presupposes that special attention is paid both to the time-dimension (present and future) and to the necessities and contingencies of everyday life. The matrix of these dimensions showed that four types of tasks are important in the implementation. They are daily problem solving, shaping of structures, organization of 'buzz', and nurturing of hope (see Figure 14.3). The latter is particularly important in the unpredictable glocal context of diminishing resources, such as the Finnish North Karelia.

The third part of the schema is the monitoring and self-evaluation system (Horelli, 2003). This includes tools for on-going monitoring of the operational level (weekly assessment sheets, work plans, the budget

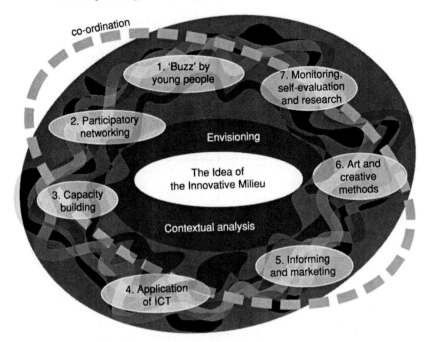

Figure 14.2. The model of learning-based network approach to development in which nodes and their links emerge through the implementation of the chosen strategies and a sensitive co-ordination.

etc.), tools for collective self-evaluation of the network as a whole (meta-phoric and analytic assessment of the nodes and links), and thematic research on various subjects and methodology.

Discussion

The case-study presented above shows that the networking-project succeeded in bridging the gap between adolescents and adults because concrete results and meaningful outcomes for young people were achieved. Also the meeting of the two groups – adolescents and adults – took place on several arenas of empowerment.

The path to activism of the young people, in this study, showed remarkable similarities with the research on adult activists, conducted by Chawla (1999). The latter found that childhood experiences with nature, meaningful social relationships and involvement with supportive

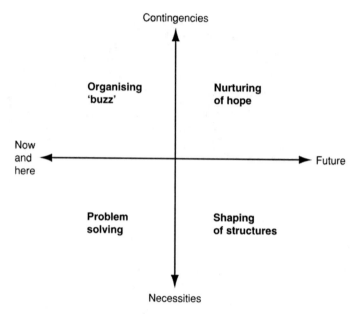

Figure 14.3. The tasks of the learning-based network approach to development are the problem solving, shaping of structures, organization of 'buzz' and the nurturing of hope.

organizations in later life are decisive and lead to effective environmental action. The Finnish activists, like the ones that Chawla interviewed in Norway and in the US, had mostly learned their skills outside the context of formal education. This observation has consequences for the pedagogy and strategies of environmental education which should recognize the importance of out-of-school experiences. It might also profit from the application of a learning-based network approach, because the implementation of education requires a broad-based alliance of educators, local officials and associations, designers, planners, developers, recreation and park directors, and the media. Chawla (1999) also pointed out that activists are leaders with special skills (or environmental competence in the Finnish study), who can mobilize others to take environmental action.

In spite of the increased environmental competence and networking skills that the Finnish activists displayed, it turned out that even the latter needed cognitive, emotional, and practical support. Young people seem to be thirsty for learning more skills about how to influence others, and they want to know what the paths to decision making are. This know-how is particularly important to those girls and boys who share the view that 'the decision makers do not really understand what is relevant in everyday life'. Therefore, the significance of projects, such as the North-Karelian Youth-forum, lies in their mediating and catalytic role.

The latter inspired to develop a new model to be applied in the Finnish youth work. Youth work has been in crisis for a long time because, due to scant resources, young people are treated as a homogeneous mass and not as girls and boys with varying interests. The new model of youth work and youth policy that emerged is based on the *fair meeting of young and adults*. The role of the municipal and regional youth work should be to function as an arena for the meeting of these two groups. Their interactive meetings will then, on the one hand, support the action and culture of adolescents themselves, and on the other hand, influence the action and culture of the decision makers. This refers to both immediate youth work, and to the mainstreaming of the young people's perspective in relation to all relevant policies. The implementation could well take place through the learning-based network approach that provides a way to enhance the expression of diversities.

The methodology of participatory planning includes many enabling tools that have emerged from the work, conducted with the involvement of children and young people in the improvement of their neighbourhoods (Horelli, 2002b; Driskell, 2002). Similarly, the tripartite schema of the network approach to planning with young people can be transferred to other contexts, for example when adult groups strive to create social cohesion. Thus, the learning-based network approach to planning and development is promising, but further work with its concepts, strategies, and methods needs to be conducted in other contexts.

References

Arquilla, J. and Ronfeldt, D. (2001). *Networks and Netwars*. Santa Monica, CA: RAND.

Bandura, A. (1997). *Self-efficacy*. New York: W. H. Freeman.

Booher, D. and Innes, J. (2002). Network power in collaborative planning. *Journal of Planning Education and Research*, *21*, 221–36.

Bronfenbrenner, U. (1993). Ecology of cognitive development: research models and fugitive findings. In R. H. Wozniak and K. W. Fischer (eds.), *Development in Context. Acting and Thinking in Specific Environments* (pp. 221–88). Hillsdale, NJ: Lawrence Erlbaum.

Castells, M. (1996). *The Rise of the Network Society*. Cambridge, MA: Blackwell.

Chawla, L. (ed.) (2002). *Growing up in an Urbanising World*. London: UNESCO and Earthscan.

Chawla, L. (1999). Life paths into effective environmental action. *The Journal of Environmental Education*, *31*, 15–26.

Cook, P., Boekholt, P., and Tödtling, F. (2000). *The Governance of Innovation in Europe. Regional Perspectives on Global Competitiveness.* London: Pinter.

Driskell, D. (ed.) (2002). *Creating Better Cities with Children and Youth, A Manual for Participation.* London: UNESCO and Earthscan.

Eyerman, R. and Jamison, A. (1991). *Social Movements. A Cognitive Approach.* Pittsburg: Pennsylvania State University Press.

Familj- o ungdomsministerium (1997). 'ra Barnetråkk till ungdomsting. Medvirkning fra barn og ungdom i kommuner – erfaringer og eksempler', Oslo: Familj- o ungdomsministerium.

Fetterman, D. (2001). *Foundations of Empowerment Evaluation.* London: Sage.

Francis, M. and Lorenzo, R. (2002). Seven realms of children's participation. *Journal of Environmental Psychology, 22,* 157–69.

Gilroy, R. and Booth, C. (1999). Building infrastructure for everyday lives. *European Planning Studies, 7,* 307–24.

Gustavsen, B. (2001). New forms of work and the legitimacy to organise, in the Report of the 8th European Assembly on New Ways to Work, pp. 184–91. Helsinki: The Finnish Ministry of Labour.

Harcourt, W. and Escobar, A. (2002). Women and the politics of place. *Development, 45,* 7–14.

Healey, P. (1997). *Collaborative Planning: Shaping Places in Fragmented Societies.* London: Macmillan.

Horelli, L. Forthcoming. Environmental human-friendliness as a contextual determinant for quality of life. *European Review of Applied Psychology.*

Horelli, L. (2003). Valittajista tekijöiksi (From complainers to agents; Adolescents on the arenas of empowerment). Espoo: Helsinki University of Technology.

Horelli, L. (2002a). European women in defence of place – with a focus on women's resource centres in Finland. *Development, 45,* 137–41.

Horelli, L. (2002b). A methodology of participatory planning. In R. Bechtel and A. Churchman (eds.), *Handbook of Environmental Psychology* (pp. 607–28). New York: John Wiley.

Horelli, L. (2001). Young people's participation, lip service or serious business. In H. Helve and C. Wallace (eds.), *Youth, Citizenship and Empowerment* (pp. 57–71). UK: Ashgate Publishing Ltd.

Horelli, L. (ed.) (1998a). Proceedings of the EuroFEM International Conference on Local and Regional Sustainable Human Development from the Gender Perspective. Hämeenlinna: EuroFEM.

Horelli, L. (1998b). Creating child-friendly environments – case studies on children's participation in three European countries. *Childhood, 5:* 225–39.

Horelli, L. (1997). Engendering evaluation of structural fund interventions. From a minuet to progressive dance. *Evaluation, 3,* 435–50.

Horelli, L. and Kaaja, M. (2002). Opportunities and constraints of Internet-assisted urban planning with young people. *Journal of Environmental Psychology, 22,* 191–200.

Horelli, L. and Prezza, M. (eds.) (2004). *Child-Friendly Environments, Approaches and Lessons.* Espoo: Helsinki University of Technology.

Horelli, L. and Vepsä, K. (1994). In search of supportive structures for everyday life. In I. Altman and A. Churchman (eds.), *Women and the Environment.*

Human Behavior and Environment, vol. XIII (pp. 201–26). New York: Plenum.

Johnson, D. W. and Johnson, R. T. (1990). Cooperative learning and achievement. In S. Sharan (ed.), *Cooperative Learning. Theory and Research* (pp. 23–37). New York: Praeger.

Kostiainen, J. (2002). Learning and the 'ba' in the development network of an urban region. *European Planning Studies, 10,* 613–31.

Kyttä, M. (2005). Environmental child-friendliness in the light of the Bullerby Model. In Christopher Spencer and Mark Blades (eds.), *Children and Their Environments*. Cambridge: Cambridge University Press.

Kyttä, M., Kaaja, M. and Horelli, L. (2004). An Internet-based design game as a mediator of children's environmental visions. *Behavior & Environment, 36,* 127–51.

Larson, R. W. (2000). Toward a psychology of positive youth development. *American Psychologist, 55,* 170–83.

Latour, B. (1993) *We Have Never Been Modern*. Cambridge, MA: Harvard University Press.

Moore, G. (1987). Environment and behavior research in North America. In D. Stokols and I. Altman (eds.), *Handbook of Environmental Psychology*, vol. II (pp.1371–410). New York: John Wiley and Sons.

Nonaka, I., Toyama, R., and Konno, N. (2000). SECI, ba and leadership: a unified model of dynamic knowledge creation. *Long Range Planning, 33,* 5–34.

The Research Group for the New Everyday Life (1991). *The New Everyday Life – Ways and Means*. Oslo: Nord.

Taylor, N. (1998). *Urban Planning Theory since 1945*. London: Sage Publications.

UNICEF (2002). Child-friendly cities project. http://www. childfriendlycities. org/

Wallston, K. A. (1992). Hocus-pocus, the focus isn't strictly on locus: Rotter's social learning theory modified for health. *Cognitive Therapy & Research, 16,* 183–99.

15 Young people's participation in constructing a socially just public sphere

Sharon Egretta Sutton and Susan P. Kemp

'Well the children because they were nice and . . . they were very idealistic, and they had some ideas that were out of the normal thinking. The adult community members . . . did provide some more practical information about the neighbourhood and that kind of thing. The practitioners were helpful in that they were, I don't know. Obviously the students were able to learn, the young kids were able to take a look at their neighbourhood and see how they might be able to improve it. And the adults would get a little taste of that idealism and maybe try to pursue something that they wouldn't have normally.' (university student)

This student's reflections on how children's idealism can nudge adults out of sedimented ways of thinking provides the central theme of this chapter. Youth not only have a right to participate in social decision making, they benefit from such inclusion and can make valuable contributions to playful, transformative thinking. Youth participation yields collective and individual benefits, and is 'part of the process and part of the answer for social inclusion' (Hill *et al.*, 2004). Yet, a powerful ontology of childhood delimits young people's opportunities for activism, framing them as adults-in-waiting (Wyness, 1999), rather than as social agents capable of bringing a uniquely valuable perspective to civic discourse (see also Francis and Lorenzo, this volume). This tendency to see youth primarily in developmental terms – as *becoming* rather than *being* – focuses attention upon their future potential in lieu of their present competence (James, Jenks, and Prout, 1998).

Popular depictions of children-as-vulnerable/adolescents-as-dangerous restrict the freedom of both groups to navigate public space (Valentine, 1996), hindering their potential contributions (see also Rissotto and Giuliani, this volume). As with other members of society who lack full citizenship, prevailing constructions of youth often frame them as dependent (Fraser and Gordon, 1994), subject to the influences of the public domain, but lacking the capacity to act productively within it. Social justice theories likewise focus upon adults (see e.g. Fraser,

2001), perpetuating dominant constructions of the public sphere as external to youth, rather than as a context they can influence. This exclusion of youth from public life denies them their rights of citizenship in the present and compromises their ability to develop into competent, engaged adults. In addition, most youth spend their developmental years in uniform environments with persons of similar age, race, class, and ability, isolated from the cultural complexities of a society of international scope.

The globalization of cities throughout the world has had a profound effect upon the lives of young people. In the United States as elsewhere, decentralized commerce and industry, uneven spatial development, and hardened class-based separations have combined with evolving social roles, increasing individualism, and the erosion of collective traditions and norms (Marcuse and van Kempen, 2000), altering the structure of family life, schooling, and work. These sociospatial changes contribute to rising socioeconomic inequality, degradation of the physical environment, and disruption of the cultural understandings and social structures that traditionally buttressed communities and their economies (Arizpe, 1992). Impoverished youth face an array of environmental challenges (Evans, 2004; Tienda and Wilson, 2003), yet their surroundings would seem to provide a compelling canvas for civic activism, beckoning them to mobilize and seek a better future. In evidence of young people's creativity stand all sorts of youth-led endeavors, from political and environmental activism to entrepreneurship and cultural and artistic expression, demonstrating that 'children are not simply cultural novices en route to adult-level mastery of cultural knowledge. They are producers of culture in their own right' (Goodnow, Miller, and Kessel, 1995: 43). Thus, we would argue that young people bring an indispensable youth voice to public life, their agency and participation is essential to social justice (see e.g., Bojer, 2000) and to the creation of culturally rich urban neighbourhoods.

In this chapter, we use a case study to derive a conceptual model for enabling young people's participation in the public sphere. We define the 'public sphere' as (1) the tangible sociospatial conditions that exist within urban neighbourhoods and (2) the social decision making processes that can maintain or transform those conditions. Throughout the chapter, we use the terms 'youth' and 'young people' interchangeably and inclusively to mean children, adolescents, and young adults who have not reached intellectual or social maturity (Simpson, 1997), or social acceptance as independent agents. However, when referring to participants in the case study, we use the term 'fifth graders' to distinguish the elementary school students from the university students. We begin the chapter by providing the background for an intensive public workshop that focused upon the case study neighbourhood. The workshop, called a *community design charrette*, brought youth and adults together to envision solutions for decades-old spatial disjunctures resulting from race and class inequities. We use a thematic analysis of interview data collected after the charrette to characterize its context and social dynamics. Based upon this analysis, we derive a conceptual model of youth-involved decision making within the public sphere.

Testing ideas within the case study charrette

The case study neighbourhood

Many historians have documented the dramatic sociospatial changes that occurred in US cities after the Second World War (Sugrue, 1996). Aided by public investments in interstate highways and single-family housing, countless businesses and middle-class white families relocated to the suburbs, draining central cities of their human, social, and economic capital. In 1954, the same year that Congress approved funding for the highways that so degraded black neighbourhoods, a landmark Supreme Court decision requiring the integration of school facilities overturned centuries of government-sanctioned racism. Programs to bus youth outside their neighbourhoods to achieve integration intersected with the opposing forces of suburbanization, further contributing to the transformation of 'America's metropolitan areas into segregated doughnuts, with blacks in the urban centre and whites in a suburban ring' (Cohen, 2004: 23).

The case study neighbourhood provides a vivid illustration of this process of slum formation and its effect upon young people's lives. In the early 1900s, the school district constructed an imposing Jacobean-style elementary school on the crest of a hill in a marginal area of the city. Built to house 500 primarily Jewish, Japanese, and European American students, by the 1960s it had become overcrowded with 800 primarily black youth whose families found themselves involuntarily segregated within what planners refer to as a *ghetto of exclusion* (Marcuse and van Kempen, 2000). Then, the state began buying homes and clearing property for a new highway. The loss of residential properties combined with a decade of highway construction, effectively isolating the school from an increasingly blighted neighbourhood. At the same time, school officials began busing youth to integrate in schools outside the neighbourhood. Enrolment dropped to 300 students and the school closed altogether in the mid 1980s.

As the school district planned a replacement facility elsewhere, residents began to envision the vacant building as a heritage museum. This vision gained momentum after several activists occupied the building over a period of years. Time passed, more housing disappeared, and the school site became completely inaccessible. Eventually, gentrification began to force many of the area's low-income residents to relocate further away from the urban core, but this highly visible symbol of racial discrimination remained on the crest of the hill, bringing to the forefront a passion to preserve its memory and place in the history of the city and nation.

Conceptual framework for the charrette

After a quarter century of dissension, a community-based agency purchased the site and began developing a plan – opposed by the activists – for restoring the building to house a small heritage museum, along with other income-producing uses. At the agency's request, we organized a community design charrette to generate ideas for reconnecting the building to its surrounding context and for extending museum activities out into the neighbourhood. Professionals in the planning and design disciplines commonly undertake such events, believing that tightly scheduled, focused brainstorming increases the potential to mobilize creative individuals and engage in out-of-the box thinking. 'The most successful charrettes bring factions of a community together to focus mental energy, heighten awareness, and develop consensus on a difficult, timely problem' (Sanoff, 2000). Certainly, the obdurate conflicts surrounding the abandoned school seemed appropriate to the consensus-building nature of a charrette.

Seeing youth as key members of the local community, university students and faculty worked with fifth-graders at a nearby elementary school prior to the charrette, engaging them in assessing the neighbourhood and creating proposals for the museum. The university students also conducted hour-long telephone interviews with a dozen homeowners and agency representatives, which, together with the fifth graders' work, shaped the goals of the charrette. More than eighty people participated in the charrette itself, a week-long event that included youth (graduate and undergraduate students in the planning and design disciplines, and the fifth graders) and adults (team leaders from academia and practice, neighbourhood residents, and agency representatives). The charrette began with a presentation by the fifth graders and ended with a public forum attended by about twenty-five children and adults from the surrounding neighbourhood. After the charrette, the fifth graders wrote an evaluation of their experiences and about one-third of the other participants took part in open-ended interviews.

The charrette structure reflected our evolving conceptual approach to charrettes as a stage for civic engagement. As in other charrettes we have organized (see Sutton and Kemp, 2002), we attempted to construct a ritualistic 'space apart', using a time-constrained artistic process to heighten transformative thinking and provide a springboard for long-range projects. Unlike more typical contexts for youth participation (see Mathews, 2001 for a critical discussion of their limitations), we believed the charrette afforded an unconventional but productive mechanism for engaging both youth and adults. We believed that a culturally complex learning laboratory would help our students expand their capacity to integrate a diversity of perspectives. And we believed that the exploration of the turbulent historical and current conditions of the neighbourhood would facilitate human understanding and action (Calhoun, 1996) among the museum's varied constituency. As the interviews suggest, charrette participants intuitively seemed to grasp this conceptual approach.

In the next section, we present the interview data. However, before proceeding, we need to disclose the cultural characteristics of the participants, as they provide a strong subtext for the interview data. The fifth graders were almost entirely black; the design teams consisted of mostly white and a few Asian students led by primarily black architects who flew in from other urban centres to almost double the city's population of six black architects; the neighbourhood residents who participated in the pre-charrette interviews and the charrette itself were primarily white, but those attending the forum included many African Americans. In general, the neighbourhood people were less affluent than those from the academic and professional communities. This cultural stratification in relation to the contested subject matter prompted the agency to hire an armed guard for the forum, but this intervention proved quite unnecessary, perhaps due to the calming presence of youth.

Additionally, we need to provide insight into the design proposals that resulted from the charrette. The fifth graders' proposals prominently featured what the neighbourhood lacked – pedestrian pathways linking all their favourite places, including the fire station, library, and 'all kinds of stores, amusement places, churches, schools, and restaurants'. As with other children's drawings, their work also featured landscape and, in this case, elements of African-American history. Some fifth graders placed the heritage museum at the centre of the community (see Figure 15.1), while others envisioned a pea patch at its centre, the museum positioned among many special places (see Figure 15.2). Anticipating economic development, one group placed collection baskets at strategic locations, speculating that 'visitors might bring ideas and money to improve our neighbourhood and museum'. In all, the fifth graders' efforts resulted in community-directed, altruistic proposals that set the tone for the charrette, adding to other evidence that youth participants do not necessarily advocate for egocentric, youth-centred, consumer-oriented environments (Spencer, 1998).

As the interview data will reveal, the design teams greatly valued the fifth graders' ideas and stayed true to them in their own proposals. For example, one proposal positioned a large farmers' market alongside the heritage museum (see Figure 15.3) and another showed how elements of African-American history might be incorporated into the everyday landscape (see Figure 15.4). Table 15.1, which two students developed after the event, outlines four strategies that directly respond to concepts established by the fifth graders, including recommendations to: (1) use a recall of history to enhance the pedestrian experience, (2) organize a farmers' market and community pea patches, (3) promote ethnic festivals, and (4) support local entrepreneurship.

Social decision making through the eyes of charrette participants

A doctoral student in social work conducted twenty-four open-ended interviews with nine university students, four team leaders, eight neighbourhood residents, and three agency representatives who had participated in the charrette. The interviews, which occurred in-person and by telephone over a two-month period, ranged in length from ten minutes to one hour and produced 27,650 words of verbatim transcripts. After removing unclear and repetitive statements, we conducted two thematic analyses (see e.g., Boyatzis, 1998). First, we derived fifteen data-driven, descriptive themes, for example 'children's participation' and 'diversity'. At that point, we perceived some of our ideas for structuring the charrette reflected in the data. With further analysis, we derived the following six theory-driven, conceptual themes, which we could apply to 21,750 words of the transcripts:

Figure 15.1. This fifth-grade proposal weaves a centrally located museum into the fabric of the neighbourhood with a network of pathways.

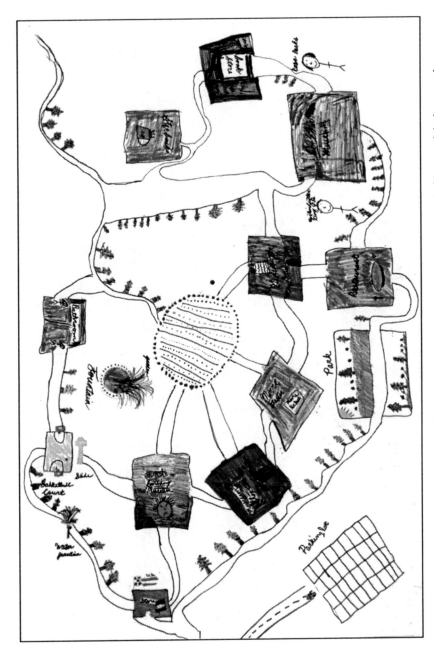

Figure 15.2. This fifth-grade proposal gives prominence to a pea patch surrounded by special places and tree-lined pathways.

Figure 15.3. This proposal by university students depicts a fabric structure billowing out from the museum to enclose a farmers' market.

Figure 15.4. This proposal by university students depicts how African-American imagery might provide a backdrop for local entrepreneurship.

Table 15.1. *Summary of community intervention strategies developed by the university students*

Strategy	Method
Use a recall of history to enhance the pedestrian experience. (See Figure 15.1) *Encourage walking and biking* Neighbourhood resident.	Reconnect the abandoned building to the neighbourhood with a streetscape that encourages pedestrian and non-vehicular traffic. Terrace the harsh embankment that was created by highway construction. Invite donors to sponsor streetscape elements. Reopen a street that was closed by highway construction as a pedestrian boulevard.
Organize a farmers' market and community pea patches. (See Figure 15.2) *Create a garden or pea patch in the existing blacktop area.* Neighbourhood resident	Host a spring-to-fall Saturday farmers' market in the old school playground. Engage local artists in designing colourful fabric structures that can be installed temporarily on special occasions. Convince developers that 'giving back' land for pea patches will pay returns in safety and an improved aesthetic and social environment.
Promote ethnic festivals (See Figure 15.3) *This should be a beacon that says African Americans were, are, and continue to be here* Neighbourhood resident.	Make the museum into a hub for existing arts organizations Paint storefronts in a consistent colour scheme and install bulletin boards and work by local artists. Install signage, banners, and public art to mark important gateways to the area. Use the old school playground to hold community festivals.
Support local entrepreneurship. (See Figure 15.4) *Create local retail space for the many existing artists and scattered small shops* Neighbourhood resident. *People can go to the museum to make donations to the homeless*	Network with local businesses, ethnic restaurants, and cultural organizations to conduct a public relations campaign. Work with the university business school to establish small businesses and create infill commercial properties for their use. Invite local artists to affiliate with the museum and establish monthly 'open studio' evenings.

1 *Situatedness*: identifying with a neighbourhood's historical and current conditions.
2 *Playacting*: inhabiting a 'space apart' to engage in rituals and have fun.
3 *Connectivity*: bridging racial, cultural, developmental, institutional, and personal differences.
4 *Openness*: welcoming the conflict that characterizes culturally complex settings.
5 *Fraternity*: embracing alternative perspectives, expert and vernacular, insider and outsider.
6 *Transformation*: envisioning what *could* be.

The interview data reveal the difficulties young people encountered in attempting to participate in the charrette's decision-making process, while also underscoring the extraordinary contributions they made to it.

    1. Situatedness The fifth graders established the importance of situatedness in their opening presentation to the design teams, reasoning that learning about 'the historical African-American people who made this country better . . . might stop race problems, and make people feel good about themselves'. They emphasized the need for learning about 'the African-American people who gave up their lives to have freedom. People need to learn about their ancestors'. Picking up on the fifth graders' perspective on history, the university students devoted considerable time to documenting changes in the area's sociospatial fabric, which impressed the neighbourhood people ('to see it in that chronological pattern and graphically was very powerful').

However, the students' own histories, most likely situated within racially segregated communities, and current isolation within an elitist university left them without the tools to address the subject matter. Referring to the challenges created by the neighbourhood's volatile political history entwined with the group's cultural distance from it, one team leader noted that 'some people were getting it, and some people weren't. Some people just didn't know what the heck was going on'. While many neighbourhood people applauded the students as above average in their responsiveness to community needs ('I think I was really surprised at more the sincerity of this group of students, and . . . that they didn't come in with a let's-show-them-how-to-do-this kind of attitude'), some recognized the students' lack of preparedness for the cultural complexity of the charrette ('I don't think [the students] were necessarily prepared for some of the passion that occurred – for the actual reactions that occurred').

The students themselves viewed their performance quite negatively, worrying that they positioned disciplinary issues above community concerns ('some of the designs wound up being more about urban planning versus landscape and nothing really about the community'); that their professional education had not prepared them for community work ('as a student and emerging design professional, we don't get a lot of experience in doing that kind of work while at that school'); and that their efforts lacked political clout ('I think mainly a lot of the community members kind of look at us as just students doing a nice little project, and they're going to go home to their places and we're going to go home to ours and is anything really going to change?').

In short, the students responded to the fifth graders' call to value the neighbourhood's history, but life-long isolation from cultural difference interfered with their ready grasp of the current sociopolitical context. While adult community members seemed more accepting of this gap in cultural understanding, the students expressed frustration at not being able to create more meaningful alternatives and, in part, blamed their education and entrenchment in disciplinary concerns.

2. Playacting   A charrette is a mini drama energized by the creativity that comes from shining a spotlight on a specific problem and then 'playing with' various solutions. In this case, the diversity of the participants heightened the sense of drama ('a charrette like this can play a very important part in providing that neutral space . . . to bring other actors, like university professors and students, who can help facilitate the middle ground between the different factions and different parts of the community'). As with situatedness, the fifth graders set the stage for playacting 'in that they provided a lot of good and also fun information for people to look over and that kind of thing'. The university students contributed their boundless energy to producing beautiful drawings ('it was very intense. My heart went out to all those who were involved in that week of incredibly, phenomenally intense design'), hampered, as in other charrettes, by an institutional failure to acknowledge their conflicting academic and personal commitments. But the team leaders – the one group that received compensation for its participation – most valued the event's intensity ('the charrette is . . . very concentrated and it's very dense and it's very intense and then it dissipates. That kind of concentration and dissipation has its own energy'). These playful, intense conventions can alter behaviour.

The design group that I sat in had a woman who had a bear vision on [the abandoned school]. . . . She was very adamant, but everybody listened and integrated her thinking and by the time it was over she mellowed quite a bit and she was much more tender in how she was articulating her concerns because she'd heard them addressed and seen them integrated into the design concepts that were set forth. . . . She was made very mellow by the process (an agency representative).

In sum, the data provide evidence that the ritualistic conventions of the charrette provided a space for thinking and acting in transformative ways, as data from other charrettes confirm. In contrast to team leaders who had a dedicated block of time for the event, regrettably students had to juggle its demands with other responsibilities. Even so, many students went well beyond the call of duty, creating a sense of energy that captured the imagination of community members.

3. Connectivity   In the case study charrette, bridging differences provided a central challenge, especially in relation to race. Notably, many neighbourhood people valued the presence of so many black architects ('I was impressed to see two, or three, or four black architects or people in the design arena. To me that was amazingly effective'). However, some students questioned the authority of the black team leaders, seeming to devalue their design expertise (as defined in school), while failing to recognize the cultural knowledge they brought to the project ('in one of our team leaders – I felt like she was there and participating perhaps even just because of her ethnic background – she was an African American. . . . I didn't see her bringing a lot of design expertise or leadership to the team'). The struggle between design excellence, narrowly defined, and the social process of bringing together people of varied backgrounds permeated the charrette.

The disconnect between the university and this particular community provided another challenge. In previous charrettes, neighbourhood residents valued coming to the university even though they lived much farther away. In this case, most interviewees (especially the students) agreed that the charrette should have taken place in the community due to the social distance between the university and this community ('it would have been nice if we had just spent the week there, and done it there and had a big sign saying come join us. It would have felt, I'm sure, a lot less intimidating to a lot of people to be able to just walk across the street').

The need to bridge such difference contrasted with the students' typical educational experiences, challenging them to learn in a new way.

To be a team is really easy when everybody on the team is generally coming from the same place and trying to get to the same place. But in the charrette this year . . . each tier – that's the students, the design professionals, and the community members were all on so many levels coming from different goals, different backgrounds . . . different ends that they wanted to achieve. . . . So that was a huge learning experience (university student).

Thus the data confirm the difficulty of bridging racial, cultural, developmental, institutional, and personal differences. Bridging proved especially difficult for students seeking to assimilate the social distancing of their chosen careers, but it also afforded them a tremendous opportunity for learning.

4. Openness The fifth graders believed the project would encourage harmony in their embattled community, explaining that the heritage museum can bring the community together. 'Don't you want to have a peaceful community? I know I do'. Despite the project's history of conflict they imagined 'the grownups would get together going on tours and having meetings to talk about the neighbourhood and how to make it better'. The charrette illustrated the difficulty of attaining the fifth graders' vision of peace ('there were a lot of sparks and conflict, and you got a peek at the politics behind a community process'), but it also underscored the value of welcoming conflict ('I mean maybe it didn't blend perfectly smoothly, but I think it's imperative to bring together a group, especially in this kind of a project'), and of embracing even your adversaries ('I think if you dodge including the naysayers, you will continue to. See it's like building a house, if you don't have your measurement done right at the foundation level, everything is gonna do weird stuff as you get further along').

Unlike the fifth graders and many of the adults, the students seemed enamoured with the tension surrounding the project, feeling that it required them to take a stand on an important issue ('gosh this project, it's sort of a political hot coal in [the city] right now. . . . I think that was a real advantage to this – that there was no room for disinterest or apathy because it was such a meaty problem, and that's seductive to students'). So while this symbol of conflict sparked the younger children's imagination as a means of bringing people together, the older youth valued its volatility because it gave them an opportunity to explore their political identities. They recognized the benefits of airing many ideas, believing that conflicts, though disruptive to the process, enlarged the knowledge base.

5. Fraternity Many interviewees recognized the benefits of embracing alternative – and typically excluded – perspectives. They saw the value of blending expert knowledge ('[design professionals] can bring a certain different perspective to something that the layman may not even think of') with local knowledge ('[experts] understand traffic patterns more than people, but then again sometimes people would say well that's not the way the community uses this'), especially that of dissenters ('In every community you have the [the activists]. They exist everywhere. The trick is how to engage them constructively, productively'). Interviewees also noted the value of creating 'a process that bridges the objectivity of the outsiders – since the facilitators and design professionals don't necessarily live or work in the community, with people who are there. . . . Not knowing the history, not having any kind of baggage . . . that's good, because the project is just fraught with – its history is one of the most difficult aspects.'

In all, the composition of the charrette reinforced the idea among the students and team leaders that 'the design team really is not us, but all of the people in the community'. Within this context, the fifth-graders' contribution shone, laying the groundwork for a 'collective that can achieve great things'.

For me, the best design team of the whole week was the children. And so this begs the question, who are the real design professionals? It's the community. They are designing – or they should design as they see fit, and we should come in to facilitate the process for them. . . . So it was really nice to see the children's work first; it really gave me a better understanding. Until that point I didn't have a clue what we were doing, until I saw the children's presentation that first morning (team leader).

6. Transformation The overarching goal of a charrette is 'expanding people's horizons. . . .That they don't go away thinking precisely the way they thought when they walked in the room before having met all these people of all these different ages. They should be changed, opinions should be changed in some way.' A number of interviewees attributed this charrette's expanded horizons to an intergenerational scaffolding of ideas ('some of the best ideas and some of the more important ideas came from the involvement of the school children, because those ideas were carried over into the charrette by the professionals and the students'). Several neighbourhood people talked about how the fifth-graders' insights began the transformative process ('having [the elementary school] students talk about the whole connection to community and the museum. That's the kind of stuff we're trying to figure out; how to tell that story more because it's the kids who had the great vision about how all these pieces and the connection between the community and this building – how [the abandoned building] fits in').

Although the fifth graders contributed a beginning vision of their community, the university students used their superior delineation skills to make that vision real ('we took a dream and showed it to them. And as we even illustrated some of the things that they had been talking about, they were able to see it in a different way, or see what they had been saying would really mean for the community'). On the other hand, having team leaders 'somewhat well-versed in community work' helped the students respond more appropriately to neighbourhood concerns. Nonetheless, several neighbourhood people stereotyped the students' proposals as impractical ('some of the things the students wanted us to do, street scenes and different things, well I just saw the dollar signs. It'd go from being a $17 million project I was thinking of to [a project with huge cost overruns] and wondering how I am going to pay for all this stuff'), failing to recognize that many proposals required more ingenuity than economic investment, as Table 15.1 demonstrates.

In addition to their design contributions, the students may have also helped transform their young protégés' perspective on university life ('for the youth in . . . that [city] neighbourhood, I think it was great for them to have this contact with university students, especially since that community probably has few of the youth planning to go on to college'), while offering them valued support, as this fifth grader notes:

At first when we got there, I was a bit scared. But when I got to know the university students, I felt better. When it was my turn to go up, I felt shaky again. But once I was up there, I felt so proud of myself. I felt proud of myself when students were stopping and watching us do the poem of Maya Angelou. I felt shy but also happy that they were listening to me instead of pretending to listen to me.

Thus the interview data reveal that participants believed the social interactions among many different people created an intergenerational scaffold that promoted visionary thinking. Generally, adults felt the youth helped open up a space for dreaming even though a few adults stereotyped the students' ideas as impractical.

A conceptual model of inclusive social decision making

The children certainly had different ideas from the adults, and the adults had different ideas than other adults. . . . I've never been to that area of [the city] before, before the charrette, and then to see students that kind of live in the area and to see elementary school kids, to see like [the activist] was there and some other more prominent figures. . . . I think that definitely it was a positive experience to have all those different kinds of people there. Because if we had only, like for example if we had only talked to children, we'd have only gotten one side of the story (university student).

The interview data suggest how social decision making can advance young people's participation within the public sphere. First, the *decision making context* should be situated, encompassing a critical understanding of the historical determinants of present realities. Situatedness helps both children and adults work within the cultural specificity of a community, while discovering possibilities for rethinking what might be taken as givens. Through an analysis of past and present conditions, they can begin to see themselves and social situations in new, emancipatory ways (Maguire, 1987). At the same time, the context should allow for the immediacy of playing around, or what we call playacting. It should provide a 'space apart' from everyday concerns that accommodates ritual and encourages participants to experiment with the conventions of social life, while helping them maintain a sense of civility (Sennett, 1978). Youth have a vital role in such playacting.

Further, the *decision making process* should facilitate the production of larger, more just, ideas. It should help children and adults bridge social boundaries, including ones that separate them along socioeconomic and cultural boundaries, according to areas of expertise, institutional affiliation, or simply due to their worldview. Communicating across these boundaries is vital to the plurality required by human life in general, by public life in particular, and therefore by democratic society (Calhoun, 1996; Sennett, 1978). The process should also evoke a sense of fraternity, which necessitates the inclusion of marginalized persons, including youth; it means balancing expert and vernacular opinion; and it means embracing outsiders and insiders. The process should welcome conflict. Participants should feel comfortable engaging in the emotional risk-taking that many people relegate to the private realm; they should forcefully express ideas to each other and view conflict as an opportunity for creative problem solving (Sennett, 1978), and for helping young people develop their political identities. Most importantly, the process should bring about transformation. Participants should strive to create bold, imaginative visions of what *could* be, which requires a sense of agency and willingness see beyond the immediacy of a particular circumstance (Calhoun, 1996) – a talent familiar to youth.

Thus, our model of inclusive social decision making includes (1) a context that has an enduring, socially critical dimension and a more transitory, aesthetic one, and (2) a process that brings people together across lines of difference, energized by conflict and engaged in bold, transformative thinking. Decision making within the public sphere should not only encourage physical, social, and cultural exchange among diverse participants, it should afford room for 'dialogue, confrontation, deliberation, and critical thinking' (Hill, 2004: 83).

Rethinking youth, social justice, and public sphere

Particularly here trying to get this broad range of ages somehow thrust together. It does humanize the process, because these charrettes, when they're only professional dominated, they can be brutal, crazed work efforts. And the final product and the quality of the final product is the sole goal because that's what we're trained to do and that's how we mostly get measured. And the way of getting there, the human process of getting there is often overlooked. But in this case, it's very important. The younger kids want to feel like they're being listened to and respected; people from the neighbourhood and the students want to feel like they've been listened to by these professionals. So, there's a whole human enterprise that's being constructed at the same time as some physical design product is being constructed (team leader).

We set out to create a conceptual model of youth participation within the public sphere by testing our emerging ideas within a community design charrette. This event generated alternatives for transforming the physical space of an inner-city neighbourhood, while bringing youth into the public domain as rightful participants in social decision making. Because boundaries among social groups continue to increase (Jenks, 2000), we wished to create a collective that would blur the distinctions between cultures, generations, skill sets, and institutions – to encourage connectivity. 'The imagery of social conversation and participation is central to the rethinking of citizenship' (Roche, 1999: 475), and such dialogue requires interdependence and the creation of egalitarian relationships (Minow, 1990). Although charrette participants struggled with tensions arising from cultural difference, the interview data provide ample evidence that young people can humanize the public sphere, contributing imaginative powers that adults may have lost.

The interview data lend credence to the premise that young people have fresher, more unfiltered perspectives. Less socialized to dominant orthodoxies, they tend to think against the grain, offering new insights and ideas. For similar, developmental reasons, they typically express greater honesty about race and class differences, tolerate and engage more productively with dissension and debate, and remain more open to participating in inclusive spaces. Since they have not learned much about the structure of mainstream society, they can readily envision many other structures. Their youthful idealism, candor, and enthusiasm – often matched by youthful selfishness, rebelliousness, and anger – seem contagious. Without young people's imagination and openness to experimentation, public discourse can become 'crazed, brutal work efforts'. We conclude that youth not only have a right to participate, their boundless capacity for transformative playacting can inspire adults to work toward inventing new roles within a socially just public sphere.

Acknowledgments

The authors gratefully acknowledge Linda Hurley Ishem, MBA, doctoral student in social work, who collected and transcribed the data for this chapter; and Tamara Myers, MED, doctoral student in education, who conducted the literature review.

References

Arizpe, L. (1992). Culture and knowledge in development. In Üner Kirdar (ed.), *Change: Threat or Opportunity for Human Progress?* (pp. 117–24). New York: United Nations.

Bojer, H. (2000). Children and theories of social justice. *Feminist Economics, 6* (2), 23–39.

Boyatzis, R. E. (1998). *Transforming Qualitative Information: Thematic Analysis and Code Development*. Thousand Oaks, CA: Sage Publications.

Calhoun, C. (1996). Social theory and the public sphere. In B. S. Turner (ed.), *The Blackwell Companion to Social Theory*. Cambridge, MA: Blackwell.

Cohen, A. (2004, January 18). The supreme struggle. *The New York Times Education Life*. Section 4A, pp. 22–5/38.

Evans, G. W. (2004, February/March). The environment of childhood poverty. *American Psychologist, 59*(2), 77–92.

Fraser, N. (2001, May). Social justice in the knowledge society: Redistribution, recognitions, and participation. www.wissensgessellscheft.org: Heinrich-Böllstiftung.

Fraser, N. and Gordon, L. (1994). A genealogy of "dependency": Tracing a keyword of the US welfare state. *Signs, 19*(2), 309–36.

Goodnow, J. J., Miller, J., and Kessel. F. (1995). Editors' preface to "Development through participation in sociocultural activity". In J. J. Goodnow, P. J. Miller and F. Kessel (eds.), *Cultural Practices as Contexts for Development* (pp. 41–4). San Francisco: Jossey Bass.

Hill, M., Davis, J., Prout, A. and Tisdall, K. (2004). Moving the participation agenda forward. *Children and Society, 18*(2), 77–96.

James, A., Jenks, C., and Prout, A. (1998). *Theorizing Childhood*. New York: Teachers' College Press.

Jenks, C. (2000). Children's places and spaces in the world. *Childhood, 7*(1), 5–9.

Maguire, P. (1987). *Participatory Action Research: a Feminist Approach*. Amhurst: University of MA Centre of International Education.

Marcuse, P. and van Kempen, R. (2000). *Globalizing Cities: a New Spatial Order?* Oxford: Blackwell.

Matthews, H. (2001). Participatory structures and the youth of today. *Ethics, Place, and Environment*, 4(2), 153–8.

Minow, M. (1990). *Making All the Difference: Inclusion, Exclusion, and American Law*. Ithaca, NY: Cornell University Press.

Roche. J. (1999). Children: rights, participation and citizenship. *Childhood*, 6 (4), 475–93.

Sanoff, H. (2000). *Community Participation Methods in Design and Planning*. New York: Wiley.

Sennett, R. (1978). *The Fall of Public Man: on the Social Psychology of Capitalism*. New York: W. W. Norton and Company.

Simpson, B. (1997). Towards the participation of children and young people in urban planning and design. *Urban Studies*, 34(5/6), 907–25.

Spencer, C. (1998). Children, cities, and participation. *Journal of Environmental Psychology*, 18, 429–33.

Sugrue, T. J. (1996). *The Origins of the Urban Crisis: Race and Inequality in Postwar Detroit*. Princeton, NJ: Princeton University Press.

Sutton, S. E. and Kemp, S. P. (2002). Children as partners in neighbourhood placemaking: lessons from intergenerational design charrettes. *Journal of Environmental Psychology*, 22, 171–89.

Tienda, M. and Wilson, W. J. (2002). *Youth in Cities: a Cross National Perspective*. Cambridge, UK: Cambridge University Press.

Valentine, G. (1996). Children should be seen and not heard: the production and transgression of adults' public space. *Urban Geography*, 17(3), 205–20.

Wyness, M. G. (1999). Childhood, agency, and education reform. *Childhood*, 6 (3), 353–68.